Breaktime and the School

Breaktime in the school is a period when pupils learn social skills they will need in the world outside. But it can also be an occasion for aggression, harassment and bullying.

The contributors to this book, who include educational psychologists, playground designers, advisers and practising teachers, give an accessible account of the burgeoning recent research into children's playground behaviour, including such issues as playful and aggressive fighting and racism and sexism in the playground. They show how an understanding of the area can inform practical action in designing an environment which encourages positive behaviour, in effective management and supervision, and in involving the children themselves in decision making and conflict resolution. The book includes case studies of ancillary staff training and guidelines to help in the creation of a whole-school policy at both primary and secondary levels. Staff in primary and secondary schools, school governors deciding on budget allocations, as well as local education authority advisers will find it essential reading.

Peter Blatchford is Senior Lecturer in the Department of Educational Psychology and Special Educational Needs at the University of London Institute of Education. He is the author of a number of books and articles on influences on educational progress, pupil perspectives and breaktime behaviour, including *Playtime in the Primary School*.

Sonia Sharp taught in mainstream and special schools before becoming an educational psychologist. From 1991 to 1993 she worked on a major research project at the University of Sheffield, investigating bullying in schools. She is currently educational psychologist for Barnsley LEA.

Breaktime and the School

Understanding and changing playground behaviour

Edited by
Peter Blatchford and Sonia Sharp

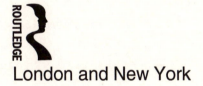

London and New York

First published 1994
by Routledge
11 New Fetter Lane, London EC4P 4EE

Simultaneously published in the USA and Canada
by Routledge
29 West 35th Street, New York, NY 10001

Typeset in Palatino by Michael Mepham, Frome, Somerset
Printed and bound in Great Britain by
T J Press (Padstow) Ltd, Padstow, Cornwall

British Library Cataloguing in Publication Data
A catalogue record for this book is available from the British Library

Library of Congress Cataloging in Publication Data
Breaktime and the school: understanding and changing playground
behaviour / [edited by Peter Blatchford and Sonia Sharp].
    p. cm.
    Includes bibliographical references and index.
    1. Recesses—Social aspects. 2. Playgrounds—Social aspects—
Great Britain. 3. Child psychology—Great Britain. 4. School
management and organization—Great Britain.
    I. Blatchford, Peter. II. Sharp, Sonia. III. Title: Playground
behaviour.
LB 3033.B74 1994
371.2'424—dc20   93–25944

ISBN 0–415–10099–2

Contents

Illustrations

FIGURES

TABLES

Contributors

Anne R. Beer is Professor and Head of the Department of Landscape, University of Sheffield.

Michael J. Boulton lectures in psychology at the University of Keele.

Fiona Cooper works for the Sheffield Advisory Service, Sheffield LEA.

Helen Cowie lectures in the School of Social Studies at Bretton Hall College, Wakefield.

Gil Fell works for Strategies for a Less Violent Society (SALVE).

Susan Humphries is headteacher at Coombes County Infant and Nursery School, Arborfield, Berkshire.

Elinor Kelly lectures in the Department of Adult and Continuing Education at the University of Glasgow.

Bill Lucas is Director of Learning Through Landscapes, Winchester.

Carol Ross is Advisory Teacher for Equal Opportunities and Behaviour Management, Islington, London.

Susan Rowe is deputy headteacher at Coombes County Infant and Nursery School, Arborfield, Berkshire.

Amanda Ryan is an environmental arts consultant.

Lyndal G. Sheat is a researcher in the Department of Landscape, University of Sheffield.

Peter K. Smith is Professor of Psychology at the University of Sheffield.

Introduction
Why understand and why change school breaktime behaviour?

Peter Blatchford and Sonia Sharp

BACKGROUND

In 1989 one of us wrote:

> playtime is largely taken for granted by everyone in schools. Staff... seem to have inherited playtime, much as they have the fabric of the building. And there is surprisingly little written material on it, either by way of policy or research. There has been a good deal of thought and debate about almost every aspect of primary education, and in many schools policies have been developed toward curriculum areas... and also equal opportunities and anti racism.... Yet playtime has received very little attention. It could lay claim to being the forgotten part of the school day.
> (Blatchford 1989).

In 1989 it was possible for one person to provide an overview of the issues and developments related to breaktime and the use of school grounds. It is a measure of the extent to which progress has been made that one person would now be greatly stretched in trying to provide a similar account.

There have been several advances in approaches to breaktime and the school grounds. There is an awareness of the value of the better understanding of behaviour in playgrounds, because of the importance of children's social relationships and of play there. There is a recognition of the exciting possibilities in the design (and redesign) of the school grounds. There is better appreciation of management and supervision issues concerning the playground. And there is more awareness of the possibilities provided by the involvement of pupils in decision making and conflict resolution.

Accordingly, this book comprises a collection of papers written by authors with different but complementary expertise. In selecting the contributors, the editors have aimed to balance those who can provide overviews stemming from a deep acquaintance with the issues and literature on a particular area with those who have a day-to-day involvement in playground improvements in particular areas.

The book had its genesis at a two-day conference at Sheffield University in November 1991, funded by the Department of Education. Many of the contributors were at the conference, where a sense developed that there was a place for a volume which would have two main aims: the better understanding of playground behaviour, and the showing of ways in which it could be enhanced.

In this introduction we want first to look at the reasons for an interest in play/breaktime and playground developments. Surveys have shown that time spent in breaks take up a sizeable part of the school day. In observations of 7-year-old pupils, who were followed continuously from when they came into school in the morning until the end of the school day, Tizard *et al.* (1988) found that 28 per cent of the school day was spent in playtime and lunch – much of this spent on the playground. This was almost exactly the same amount of time as was spent in core aspects of the curriculum – reading, writing and maths.

Physically, the playground often takes up a sizeable part of the school site. If you were able to take a crow's-eye view of the school and you could fly high overhead and look down over the school grounds, you would see that for many schools the school buildings themselves occupy a relatively small part of the plot. In many cases the surrounding grounds, including the playground, occupy a larger area. In some schools, of course, with a field or large area, the school buildings are dwarfed by the grounds.

So in both temporal and spatial terms breaktime occupies a large part of the school day and school site. Yet until recently very little thought went into how this time and this space were used. There can be little doubt that children are learning things at breaktime – perhaps a very different set of skills and attitudes from those that operate in the school and classroom. What messages are they learning? How much runs counter to the school philosophy, and how much conflicts with views that adults have about playground behaviour? We shall see in this book that there are a number of ways of improving the use of this time and space, but first it is important to have a better understanding of pupils' behaviour in the playground.

What happens in the playground is of concern to teachers, pupils, parents and governors.

TEACHERS

Teachers can have strong views about breaktime and pupils' behaviour then. There is a wide recognition that playground experiences have effects on school life more generally (Blatchford 1989). In interviews with primary teachers and headteachers in thirteen LEAs in the South-East a number of concerns were expressed. These included comments about the playground environment and supervision, but there was much interest in children's playground behaviour. These views can be summarised under five head-ings.

Aggression

There was concern about what was perceived as a large amount of need-lessly aggressive behaviour. Sometimes this was seen as a major problem because of the way in which it could set the tone for the school. As one headteacher put it, it stretches limits on what is acceptable.

Desultory behaviour

There was concern about children idling around the playground – not seeming to know what to do with themselves. Play was often described as low-level, and, for the boys, mainly tests of physical prowess.

Traditional games

These were commonly seen to be in decline. One head felt that children had lost the vocabulary of outside play. Some thought this was an inevitable consequence of social and cultural changes; some felt it appropriate to 'teach' children supposedly forgotten outside games.

Problems for certain groups

Certain groups of children, particularly girls and newcomers to school, were seen to face particular problems in the playground. Boys were per-ceived to dominate space and any available equipment. Young children – some not much beyond their fourth birthday – could be frightened by the huge space of the playground and the mass of (to their eyes) large children.

Lunchtime

There was a universal view that if problems arise they are most likely to occur during the long lunchbreak, sometimes up to one and a half hours in length. These problems have become more apparent to headteachers in the United Kingdom throughout the 1980s since teachers have been largely replaced by ancillary staff as supervisors of children during the lunchbreak. There is a certain ambivalence about this; on the one hand there is wide-spread agreement amongst heads, as well as teachers, that teachers should have a lunchbreak, but many now feel that as a result supervision at lunchtime is not always adequate. For headteachers – who could often be the only member of teaching staff on duty – it could be a difficult time. It was felt that problems that arose at lunchtime could spill over into school, and that time could be spent settling children down.

Teachers' views about playtime behaviour are clearly important. They are the main recipients of playground events, and have a keen awareness of problems that can arise. But many teachers would also be the first to admit that it is often difficult to get a rounded view about children's behaviour in the playground. If they are on duty they are often preoccupied with a group of children around them, or with an event to which their attention has been drawn. If they are not on duty, then they are, quite sensibly, drinking a well-earned cup of tea or coffee in the staffroom, or getting prepared for the next session. So teachers' perceptions can be partial.

PUPILS

If teachers are the main recipients of problems arising during playtime, children are the main participants. They are the experts on life in the playground. They have privileged knowledge, and in many cases may well be the only witnesses to what takes place there. What is more, any schemes seeking to improve playtime will need to build on their views about playtime. In the Institute of Education longitudinal study, children in thirty-three inner city schools were interviewed at two points – when they were 7 and 11 years old. When they were 7 years old they could find breaktime a distressing experience. Two-thirds of the children said they were teased and many found name calling upsetting. And two-thirds of the children said they got into fights, though most said they did not enjoy this (Tizard *et al.* 1988).

When the children were 11 years old it was possible to ask more detailed questions about breaktime (Blatchford *et al.* 1990). It was a very popular part of the school day (84 per cent said they liked it), and they liked it because of the games they could play; they could be with their friends, and it was a break from work. But some pupils had worries about the playground; for example, because of the cold, not knowing what to do or whom to play with, and disruptive behaviour. Girls were more worried by breaktime and were more likely to want the option of staying in school. As at 7 years, teasing, name calling and fighting were significant (Mooney *et al.* 1991). It is also worth reporting that the 11-year-olds had a number of impressively constructive ideas about how playtime and the playground could be improved (Blatchford *et al.* 1990).

What stands out is that, alongside the enjoyment, there is also concern, at least from some pupils, and it is this ambivalence about breaktime which no doubt gives it an extra excitement and edge. In short, it matters a good deal to pupils and they have strong views about it.

PARENTS

Parents can be especially aware of, and concerned about, breaktime behaviour and events. While it may not always be easy to get from one's children information about the day's events in the classroom, mishaps and accidents in the playground are often more easily communicated. Parents may receive information – perhaps from their own children or other parents – about problems of which school staff were not aware. One of us is a parent governor of a first school. The school is well managed and caring, with few behaviour problems. Yet even here parents are very sensitive to the difficulties their children can face in the playground, and have, through the Friends of the school, set about fund raising to provide outside play equipment.

GOVERNORS

Recent changes to the funding of schools have also heightened awareness of the school grounds. With more and more schools in charge of their own budgets, governors and staff are faced with decisions about the school grounds that hitherto were the responsibility of the Local Education Authority. The days when staff and pupils would return from the summer holidays to find changes to the playground, made by some remote force, with little connection with the views of staff or pupils, seem to be in decline. And at the same time that governors have more powers to determine how the school grounds will be used, there is much more appreciation of the potential of school grounds. So whereas the school grounds were once largely ignored and considered out of bounds, as far as decision making went, there is now much more potential for change, and local planning. With Local Management of Schools (LMS) there is the chance of a fundamental appraisal of breaktime and the school grounds.

There are a number of other reasons for an increasing awareness of the importance of school breaktimes.

MISBEHAVIOUR IN SCHOOL

Worries about behaviour in school often focus on the playground. There has probably always been concern with pupils' misbehaviour in school, but during the 1980s concern, voiced by the teaching unions and others, grew and culminated in the Elton Committee's inquiry and report (DES 1989). The Committee was mostly preoccupied with difficult behaviour within school, and it could be argued that it paid too little attention to behaviour in the playground and school grounds. But the Committee did agree with many of its witnesses that 'lunchtime is the biggest single behaviour-related problem that [staff] face' (DES 1989: 122). As we saw above, the lunchbreak can be long – sometimes up to one and a half hours – and many staff complain that most problems arise then, and they then have the task of settling pupils down, once they return to the classroom.

BULLYING

Over the past few years there has been a growing awareness of the extent of bullying in schools. Research in this area, inspired by the work of Olweus in Scandinavia, has done much to focus attention on characteristics of bullies and victims. There is a growing body of research on the incidence and types of bullying (for example, Boulton and Underwood 1992; Tattum 1993; Tattum and Lane 1989; Whitney and Smith 1993) and the development of schemes to combat bullying (Sharp and Smith 1993).

A good deal of research on bullying, again following the lead of Olweus, has developed around a concern with personality and other individual attributes of bullies (and victims). This is obviously crucial but can sometimes obscure the situational and social influences on bullying behaviour (Blatchford 1993). The vast majority of bullying incidents take place on school premises and most pupils in the playground are affected (Whitney and Smith 1993). It is therefore important to understand better the interactions and activities of pupils in school grounds in order to place specific behaviours like bullying into context.

THE PLAYGROUND AS A SETTING FOR SOCIAL AND MORAL EDUCATION

Many of the social and emotional conflicts that arise for pupils at school arise in the playground. It is at breaktime that pupils meet their friends and get the chance to interact and play with their peers in a relatively unstructured setting. Many informal lessons can be learnt by pupils, as can particular social skills that are integral to adult life. If problems arise, then their careful handling can do much to improve the school ethos. In particular, because of their privileged knowledge, the involvement of pupils in decisions about the playground – for example, supervision and behaviour there – can do much to create a moral sense. Pupils can begin to develop insights into the roots of the problems they encounter, they can learn to expand their coping strategies, understand others' perspectives and their need for space, and they can develop skills in negotiation.

The playground and school grounds can play a role in the governance of the school. A real involvement of pupils in decision making can be a major part of a whole-school approach to behaviour in school. Because of their knowledge of breaktime, and because they are in a sense those most affected by it, breaktime can be the focus around which much discussion and collaboration can take place. Observations of children's 'councils' (cf.

Blatchford 1989) and 'Quality Circles' (cf. Cowie and Sharp 1992), which seek to provide a forum for the expression of pupil views, show that much of the content of discussion revolves around events and problems at breaktime.

SCHOOL GROUNDS AS A SETTING FOR ENVIRONMENTAL AWARENESS

Reference has already been made to the increasing awareness of the use of school grounds. There is an increased understanding that the school grounds constitute a major and often under-used resource, which can be used to enhance the appearance of the school and also as a learning environment. Again, because of pupils' privileged knowledge and use of the playground, it can also be the focus for the involvement of pupils in design projects.

SCHOOL GROUNDS AND THE SCHOOL CURRICULUM

There is also growing appreciation that the school grounds can be the focus for teaching and the curriculum. Teachers – in both primary and secondary sectors – are finding it has enormous potential for use in work in maths, science, technology and other subjects. It has been calculated that a majority of National Curriculum attainment targets can be carried out by the imaginative use of school grounds.

THE PLAYGROUND AND THE COMMUNITY

The playground is often the face of the school most seen by members of the surrounding community. In a world in which schools are asked to compete with one another for recruitment, it is small wonder that some are looking to playground improvements as a way of making their school more attractive. The school grounds may also be a focus for more community involvement in the school. Parents and the wider community may not always feel able to contribute to events in the classroom, but their skills may be more easily tapped by involving them in improvements to the school grounds. Skills in building, and a willingness to give up a few hours, can be invaluable, and the finished product can be the source of pride and identification with the school. Some consider that this may also be a way of reducing vandalism.

BREAKTIME AND THE SCHOOL DAY

Breaktime in schools is deeply grained into the school day, but it is oddly arbitrary. The notion of a compulsory, fixed period for recreational break is accepted almost without question. If asked, we can easily cite some obvious functions; a chance for pupils to let off steam, and for staff to have a break. But along with other changes already cited, some people – given the problems that can arise – are also beginning to question breaktime in its present form. This can take the modest form of cutting back on time spent at break, to giving pupils more choice about going out, to more fundamental changes as in the Continental day, and doing away with the fixed period for break altogether. Others stoutly defend breaktime in its present form because of its importance to pupils and teachers. As many schools are engaging in a fundamental review of the organisation of the school day (for example, in response to the demands of the National Curriculum) breaktime is bound to come under closer scrutiny.

PRIMARY AND SECONDARY SCHOOLS

Breaktime and the use of school grounds are relevant to both primary and secondary schools. Though much of the research on pupils' playground behaviour has been done in primary schools, and though there seems to be little shared understanding and collaboration between primary and secondary schools, there are many common interests and challenges.

HOW THE BOOK IS ORGANISED

This book has been written in order to reflect, and to stimulate further, this increased awareness of the importance of school breaktimes and grounds. It aims to be a guide to the present understanding of school breaktime behaviour, and it aims to set out some difficult issues and exciting possibilities in the search for improvements.

Accordingly, the book is presented in two parts. First, *Understanding behaviour during school breaktimes*: the four chapters in Part I examine research on pupils' playground behaviour, what we can learn from play in the playground, rough-and-tumble play, and racism and sexism in the playground. In Part II, *Changing behaviour during school breaktimes*, four areas are examined: improving the school grounds, design, management and supervision in the playground; giving pupils a voice in decision making and in conflict resolution; and whole-school approaches.

The editors have deliberately encouraged two types of chapters in this book. The first are reviews of what is known in a particular area – covering the latest research and initiatives. The second are descriptions of particular schemes, written by those at the heart of the work. There is therefore a combination of review and committed case study.

In the final chapter of the book we return to points raised in this Introduction in order to identify some main themes raised by the contributors, and put forward some conclusions and pointers for the future.

A NOTE ON TERMINOLOGY

There is a problem in identifying a term which adequately describes the area 'beyond the classroom' and the time that is spent there. Common terms for the former are 'playground' or 'school grounds', but other terms are also used: for example, 'school environs', 'school yard' or just 'outside'. Terms for the time spent outside include 'breaktime', 'playtime' or – popular in North America – 'recess'. It is particularly difficult to find terms that are equally applicable to primary and secondary sectors. Given this lack of agreement, it did not seem appropriate for the editors to constrain authors to the use of terms they would not normally use. Readers should bear in mind that different terms are often interchangeable.

REFERENCES

Blatchford, P. (1989) *Playtime in the Primary School: Problems and Improvements*, Windsor: NFER-Nelson.
—— (1993) 'Bullying in the playground', in D. Tattum (ed.) *Understanding and Managing Bullying*, Oxford: Heinemann.
Blatchford, P., Creeser, R. and Mooney, A. (1990) 'Playground games and playtime: the children's view', *Educational Research*, 32 (3): 163–74.
Boulton, M. and Underwood, K. (1992) 'Bully/victim problems among middle school children', *British Journal of Educational Psychology*, 62: 73–87.
Cowie, H. and Sharp, S. (1992) 'Students themselves tackle the problem of bullying', *Pastoral Care in Education*, 10 (2) 31–7.
Department of Education and Science (DES) (Elton Report) (1989) *Discipline in Schools*, Report of the Committee of Enquiry chaired by Lord Elton, London: HMSO.
Mooney, A., Creeser, R. and Blatchford, P. (1991) 'Children's views on teasing and fighting in junior schools', *Educational Research*, 33 (2): 103–12.
Sharp, S. and Smith, P. (1993) 'Tackling bullying: the DfE Sheffield Bullying Project', in D. Tattum (ed.) *Understanding and Managing Bullying*, Oxford: Heinemann.
Tattum, D. (ed.) (1993) *Understanding and Managing Bullying*, Oxford: Heinemann.
Tattum, D. and Lane, O. A. (eds) (1989) *Bullying in Schools*, Stoke-on-Trent: Trentham.
Tizard, B., Blatchford, P., Burke, J., Farquhar, C. and Plewis, I. (1988) *Young Children at School in the Inner City*, Hove: Lawrence Erlbaum.
Whitney, I. and Smith, P. (1993) 'A survey of the nature and extent of bullying in junior/middle and secondary schools', *Educational Research*, 35 (1): 3–25.

Part I

Understanding behaviour during school breaktimes

Editors' introduction

Much can be learned about children from studying their behaviour in playground settings. Behaviour there is in a sense natural, and because of changes in leisure activities and parental fears for their children's safety, it may be for some children one of the few outside settings within which they do play and interact. The playground offers the opportunity to examine a children's 'culture', separate from adults and sometimes in opposition to the culture that operates within the classroom.

Yet there has been relatively little research on school playground behaviour, and some of this research has been anecdotal and small-scale. The aim of this first part of the book is to draw together and assess what is known from research about playground behaviour.

Peter Blatchford sets out to provide a review of what research there has been. He first of all contrasts the two different views that seem to characterise most research and comment. The first view emphasises what pupils learn and enjoy in the playground, while the second view stresses more the problems that arise. He argues that these two views have different implications for what role adults should adopt in the school playground. Following an account of pupils' descriptions of their playground activities, there is a discussion of two main themes about which there is debate: whether or not traditional games are in decline and whether or not there has been a decline in the quality of outside play. One conclusion is that it is all too easy to underestimate pupils' resourcefulness. He then looks at research on some specific and emerging areas of interest: gender differences, social relations in the playground – including teasing and name calling, fighting, friendships, rejected and isolated children, power and status and fair play – staff–pupil relations and differences between schools. The chapter ends with a look at research methods that can be used in examining playground behaviour in a systematic fashion.

Ask anyone to say what children are doing in the school playground, at least at primary level, and they will probably answer that they are 'playing'. But what do we know about this seemingly trivial behaviour? A good deal, it seems, and we are pleased that Professor Peter Smith of Sheffield University, who has devoted many years to understanding play behaviour better, has examined for us what pupils can learn from their play experiences and games in the playground, and what adults can learn from examining pupils' behaviour. He looks at age developments in outside play and types of activities, and what these tell us about child development; he examines differences and similarities between rule-governed and pretend play; and he contrasts competing explanations for gender and ethnic differences. Peter Smith finishes with a discussion of what children acquire in the playground, and what the value of breaktime might be. He concludes that the unique learning opportunities provided by play and games are in the social domain, certainly by middle childhood when rule-governed games and team games are common.

Michael Boulton's chapter is based on his growing and thorough re-search on school playground behaviour. He concentrates on two main forms of behaviour – playful and aggressive fighting – and shows how there is an ambiguity about such behaviour which makes it difficult for adults to judge accurately which is which. Another term used for playful fighting is 'rough-and-tumble' play, and Michael Boulton examines explan-ations for why children – particularly boys – engage in it. In a helpful discussion, he highlights the main differences between fighting and rough-and-tumble play, but also points out that these differences are not always straightforward; for example, in the case of the minority of children who fail to recognise the differences. Disturbingly, it seems that female adults are especially likely to perceive playful episodes as aggressive, and one consequence of this is the negative way that play fighting is viewed by many playground supervisors. This has unfortunate consequences, and Michael Boulton argues for more training and more toleration, given the possible value of play fighting and the obvious enjoyment pupils find in it. He also offers the reader the opportunity to see whether they can accurately judge two vignettes as either playful or aggressive, and, in the spirit of a detective story, leaves us to wait until the end to see whether we were right or not.

In the last chapter in Part I of the book, Elinor Kelly examines a dark side of playground interactions. She makes a number of important points. She argues that pupils' behaviour is best seen from the perspectives of pupils themselves, and draws on recent studies to illuminate how sexism and racism are embedded in interpersonal and inter-group relations. She argues that in the playground one can see pupils testing out what they know about equality and justice, and the differences between ethnic groups and boys and girls, and she shows how individuals can suffer as a consequence. She draws an important distinction between bullying – about which there has been much recent interest and research – and harassment, which is more common. The former is characterised by being intensely personal in mis-treatment of victims, whereas harassment can be impersonal, and is more acceptable because it is legitimised by attitudes and structures in the school and society. It is more connected with group dynamics: with conformity within groups and aggression towards other groups. Elinor Kelly concludes on a constructive note, by arguing that many lessons have been learnt about how schools can reinforce and structure inequalities in society, and that they can get pupils to deal with racist and sexist harassment by focusing on the playground as a site of significant social learning.

Chapter 1

Research on children's school playground behaviour in the United Kingdom
A review

Peter Blatchford

In this chapter I will review research on behaviour in school playgrounds. The chapter will aim to highlight research and views that have been influential, and identify areas for future research. It will:

1   look at two contrasting views on the nature of playground behaviour;
2   examine some specific areas of interest – behaviour in secondary school playgrounds, gender differences, social relations in the playground (teasing and name calling, fighting, friendships, rejected and isolated children, power and status, fair play) – staff–pupil interactions and differences between schools;
3   end by considering methods of researching playground behaviour.

WHAT IS KNOWN ABOUT CHILDREN'S PLAYTIME BEHAVIOUR?

There is a strong case for the view that there is too little basic research in all areas of education. But there seems an especially large gap between the major role breaktime occupies in children's school lives, on the one hand, and the dearth of research on the other. This situation no doubt owes much to the marginalised position of playtime – and to the sense that it does not really matter in the way that classroom experiences do. Yet the recent growth of research on bullying is an indication of what can happen when something is perceived as a 'problem'.

WHAT CAN RESEARCH TELL US ABOUT PLAYGROUND BEHAVIOUR?

In reviewing the research that does exist I have been struck by the contrast between two seemingly opposing views about playground behaviour. The first one might characterise as the 'romantic' view, in that emphasis is on what children learn and enjoy at playtime. The second might be called the 'problem' view, in the sense that the focus is on problems that arise. These two views have important and different implications for perspectives and policies on playtime.

The 'romantic' view

We have some splendid descriptions of children's playground activities. Iona and Peter Opie's book *Children's Games in Street and Playground*, published in 1969, has been influential. It is a marvellous documentation of the colourful and resourceful games played by children across the country. The Opies describe varieties of chasing, catching, seeking, hunting, racing, duelling, exerting, daring, guessing, acting and pretending games. It is worth quoting the Opies in order to capture something of their distinctive approach to children's games. They see the function of the game as largely social: 'Just as the shy man reveals himself by his formalities, so does the child disclose his unsureness of his place in the world by welcoming games with set procedures, in which his relationships with his fellows are clearly established' (1969: 3). Part of the appeal of the game is that it creates a situation which is under the player's control and yet is also one where the outcome is not fully known.

Games can be of great antiquity:

> The custom of turning round a blindfold player three times before allowing him to begin chasing seems already to have been standard practice in the seventeenth century.... The strategem of making players choose one of two objects, such as 'orange' or 'lemon', to decide which side they shall take in a pulling match, was almost certainly employed by the Elizabethans.
>
> (1969: 7)

One of the Opies' central themes is that control of the games has to be with children themselves; adults play no useful role and can only get in the way. There is the notion of children creating a kind of counter-culture, alien to that of adults and mysterious to them. It is particular to children of primary age. Even by their early teens children seem to have forgotten the games and lost the incentive to play.

Sluckin's book *Growing Up in the Playground* (1981) is exclusively concerned with the school playground. Like the Opies, he sees the playground as a world of rules and rituals where very little has changed over the years. Sluckin argues that there are strong incentives to acquire, in an informal way, sophisticated skills in order to play many games. He gives the example of the speed and accuracy of children's mental arithmetic – even of those struggling in maths in class – as they count ahead in dips.

For Sluckin, what the playground offers children is the opportunity for peer interaction in the context of which many lessons relevant to adult life are learnt. 'They learn how to join in a game, how to choose and avoid rules, how to deal with people who cheat or make trouble, and above all else how to manipulate situations to their own advantage' (1981: 119).

Grugeon (1988, 1991) has more recently added to the positive view. She agrees with the Opies that the oral transmission of games and rhymes is child-initiated and out of the hands of adults. She feels that games are a powerful means of transmitting cultural information, particularly about gender. She argues that its secret nature makes it difficult for adults to see and that, despite what she feels are claims to the contrary, traditional games are still common, though this seems to be true only of young girls, who use games as a means of empowerment against boys.

The 'Problem' view

This predominantly positive view of playground life stands in contrast to a more negative view of playground activity. This is a view more in line with the tone of teachers' comments (see Introduction). It stems from several disparate types of work and comment on pupils' school behaviour.

One influence was the general concern about behaviour in schools, particularly expressed by the teacher unions and the press, that gathered momentum over the 1980s and culminated in the reporting of the Elton Committee of Inquiry into Discipline in Schools (DES 1989). Problems arising during lunchtime were identified by the Elton Committee, and recommendations for management – in particular, its funding – were offered. Yet it could be that the Elton Committee underestimated difficult behaviour on the school site because it concentrated on behaviour within school, and moreover through teachers' perceptions. The effect of the playground on children's behaviour was therefore neglected.

Another influence on the negative view has been the recent growth of work on bullying. There is not space to review this research here (cf. Elliott 1991; La Fontaine 1991; Tattum 1993; Tattum and Lane 1989; Whitney and Smith 1993). There is a general recognition that bullying has been neglected and that it is more prevalent than was once thought. Bullying also tends to take place away from adults, and the majority of incidents occur in the grounds around the school (cf. Blatchford 1993).

The murder of a British Asian boy in a Manchester high school showed how violence, possibly racially motivated, could erupt in school play-grounds. It led to the Burnage Inquiry (Macdonald 1989) and a survey of name calling and teasing in schools (Kelly and Cohn 1988). Other work, to be reviewed below, has also studied teasing, fighting and name calling in school playgrounds (Mooney et al. 1991).

Another influence has been the widespread recognition that desultory and aggressive behaviour may be understandable reactions in an enclosed, bare enclosure that offers little to children. Many organisations and staff in individual schools have stressed this point, and have worked hard to show ways that school grounds can be improved and their potential realised (see Chapters 5 and 6, on playground design, in this book).

These separate strands, taken together, stress a different view of playground behaviour from those of the Opies and Sluckin. They put emphasis on behaviours occurring in the playground that are not beneficial, which can be harmful, and to which alternatives should be sought.

It is unlikely that these views – the 'romantic' and the 'problem' – are mutually exclusive. More likely, they are two sides of the same coin. As Sutton-Smith and Kelly-Byrne (1984) have argued, much outside play can also be seen as part of a struggle for domination, control and sheer terrorisation by stronger of weaker children. Interestingly, both positive and negative views indicate the existence within schools of a playground culture, different from, and in many ways in opposition to, the culture and rules that operate within the school.

But they also reflect important and different assumptions about the appropriate role of adults. The positive view, as represented by the Opies and Sluckin, carries with it the assumption that adults have no role in the pupils' playground culture.

> In the present day we assume children have lost the ability to entertain themselves, we become concerned, and are liable by our concern, to make what is not true a reality. In the long run nothing extinguishes self-organised play more effectively than does activity to promote it.
>
> (Opie and Opie 1969: 16)

The problem view, on the other hand, tends to put the focus on appropriate forms of adult intervention and supervision. One can see this in the recommendations of the Elton Committee, the schemes to combat bullying (for example, Elliott 1991; Smith and Thompson 1991), and the recent growth of training courses for lunchtime supervisors (for instance, Fell, this volume; Newcastle Education Committee 1990; OPTIS 1986).

PUPILS' DESCRIPTIONS OF THEIR PLAYGROUND ACTIVITIES

Adults face particular difficulties in understanding much of what goes on in the playground. Sometimes when in a school playground an observer can record individual behaviours, but remain unclear how they fit together – for example, what the game is and how it is played. Many staff have remarked how difficult it is sometimes to know whether children are playing or fighting. Who better, then, to act as informants than the pupils themselves?

In the Institute of Education study the children were asked to name and describe the three games they played in the playground. Full details of the methods used to classify games and the results found are given in Blatchford *et al.* (1990).

I want to concentrate here on the frequency with which different games were reported by the children. There were three clear levels of frequency. The single most common game was football, played by 60 per cent of the children. The two other most common games were the basic chasing game of 'It', 'He' or 'Had' (46 per cent) and other ball games (32 per cent) like netball, basketball, cricket and so on.

There was a second level of frequency. This comprised three types of games: seeking games (hide-and-seek, 4040 and so on – 17 per cent of children), catching games ('Runouts, 'British bulldog' and so forth – 16 per cent) and racing games (12 per cent).

Other games were played by 6 per cent or less of children. These included other chasing games (where the 'caught' joined the 'chaser', where the chased had to get back to base, where touch was attained with a ball, where the touch had a 'noxious' effect, where the chased had immunity, and where the chaser was at a disadvantage). Pretending games; daring games; guessing games using playground markings; ring, rhymes and clapping games were very rarely mentioned. No one played marbles.

These results must be interpreted with care. There are a number of factors which could affect their stability and generalisability. There are likely to be regional and seasonal differences. There are fashions in children's play, with rapid shifts in popularity. The results refer to the playground activities of 11-year-olds. Competitive team games like football tend to dominate in middle childhood (Sutton-Smith 1981) and might be expected to be peak at 11 years. Some have argued that some games tend to peak at an earlier age (Grugeon 1991; Opie 1991). The results just described therefore only represent a snapshot in time of one age group in one city. Nevertheless, we have little reason to doubt their reliability for that age group, and they do help to give a much-needed account of the comparative prevalence of different playground games.

Two general issues arise. One concerns whether or not traditional games are in decline. As we have seen, many teachers feel they are less prevalent. Some authoritive writers agree (Roberts 1980; Sutton-Smith 1981). Parry-Jones concluded that games played in Wales earlier in the century are now 'quite unknown to the present generation' (1964: 237). Yet the Opies made the salutary point that

> the belief that traditional games are dying out is itself traditional; it was received opinion even when those who now regret the passing of the games were themselves vigorously playing them.... as we have grown older our interests have changed... we no longer have eyes for the games, and not noticing them suppose them to have vanished.
>
> (1969: 14)

Grugeon took issue with the Institute of Education results, and cites examples of recently collected playground rhymes to make her point. What can we conclude? Have traditional games declined?

The debate is not as straightforward as might at first appear. At its extreme it is between those who argue that nothing has really changed and those who argue that traditional games have all but disappeared. But few would adopt either of these two positions. The Opies, for example, were in no doubt that games were constantly changing.

One needs to be clear about the evidence that is provided for claims about prevalences of traditional games. One limitation of the Opies' work and that of others is that it is not concerned with how often games occur – a point made by Roberts (1980) – but with what they can remember having played. It therefore becomes difficult to distinguish games that are rarely played from games that are common. It could be that some of the most intriguing games are actually very infrequently played (and indeed may have been rare in the past). The Institute of Education study is also imperfect, in the sense that it is based on child report and not actual frequencies. Nevertheless, a general estimate of occurrence is provided. In contrast to the work of the Opies, it is more concerned with 'performance' – with what and how often children play particular games in the school playground.

It is also important to define what one means by 'traditional games'. Webb (1984), in his introduction to a re-issue of Gomme's classic compendium of children's games, makes a helpful distinction between games of movement without singing or dialogue – he cites ball games, chasing games, marbles and conkers – and singing and dialogue games. He feels the first type of games, more associated with boys, have remained fairly steady over time, whereas the second type, more associated with girls, have declined. The Institute of Education results seem to support Webb's impression that traditional games involving movement are common, and that games involving dialogue are not. We also found games involving materials (apart from balls) to be infrequent. But we do not know if traditional games have declined over time because (to my knowledge) we do not have the necessary information on which to base such a conclusion.

There is an allied debate about the quality of outside play. As we have seen in the Introduction, there is a general view that the quality of playground play is not high, with much aggressive, low-level and desultory activity. Again, caution is required in assessing such views. It is rather easy to conflate the perceived decline of traditional games (particularly those recognisable from one's own childhood) with decline in quality of play. It may be that outside play has changed, utilising, for example, much that is attractive to children from TV, films and pop culture, but play might still be sharp-witted, complex and colourful. Many have commented on the way that children can creatively interpret contemporary events in their play – for example, in chasing games like 'Pickets and police' (around the time of the 1980s miners' strike) and 'Aids' (a chasing game within which the chased receive immunity by the cry of 'condom'). A recent informal survey of games in the Brighton area showed a number of games including 'Peggy Leggy' – a hopping game begun with the rhyme 'Peggy Leggy, lost her leggy, on the way to school. What by?'. Each child then calls out the name of the car that did the damage – Ford Sierra, Mini-Metro and so on – and the catcher then calls out one of these. The child called out and the catcher then (whilst hopping) try to push each other over. The content of this game, like many others, might be contemporary, but the basic structure might well not be. An intriguing area of research is the ongoing documentation (perhaps within one school) of changes and adaptations to playground games – how long they are played, what adaptions take place, the influence of outside events and so on.

I would like to end this section by looking at the interesting slant on historical trends in children's games that has been provided by Sutton-Smith (1981). On the basis of research on games in New Zealand and the United States, Sutton-Smith comes to different conclusions from those of the Opies. In a perspective that covers the period from the nineteenth century to the 1980s, he argues that games have changed a good deal. There has been a decline in many traditional games, such as singing games and games of skill involving materials. The ball has replaced virtually all the other play objects in the school playground. Sutton-Smith links games with the epoch within which they occur. He argues that play has become progressively domesticated, mechanised (for example, through reliance on toys), and that childhood has suffered 'zooification', by which he appears to mean it has become marginalised and under adults' control. In contrast to the Opies, he feels, 'The older view that we need only leave children alone and their spontaneity will do the rest no longer holds. Children can be spontaneous, but only in the limited, traditional ways of the world which were already given' (1981: 289).

So far this sounds like support for the negative, 'problem' view. But he remains optimistic. He argues that outside play in the nineteenth century was physical and barbaric. In a quote that might surprise some teachers, he says that the school playground 'is a less aggressive and less turbulent place in which to play. It has become DOMESTICATED. There is neither the roughness nor the fighting that there used to be.' He feels this has much to do with increased organisation of children's sports. Girls have also acquired much more freedom, hence the calming influence on outside play, but this has also led to a reduction in static singing and rhyming games. Contemporary play is less physical and social and more solitary and symbolic. If the physical play of the last century suited a rural economy, then contemporary play may help produce children capable of innovation, and of skills appropriate to a more complex social environment.

SPECIFIC ASPECTS OF PLAYGROUND BEHAVIOUR

Playground behaviour in secondary schools

Research on playground activities has been almost exclusively on children of primary-school age. This is connected no doubt with an assumption that once children move on to secondary school they do not play outside. However, recent work at the Institute of Education shows that breaktime at secondary school is very important to pupils. Fiander (1991) surveyed year 7 and year 10 children in two secondary schools. She found that much time was spent talking to friends and 'hanging around'. Games were also a feature of breaktime, with 85 per cent of year 7 and 40 per cent of year 10 pupils sometimes playing. Football was popular with year 7 boys (though the numbers playing were roughly half that found in the Institute of Education junior-school study). Small ball games and chasing games were also played. Another common activity Fiander labelled 'mucking about,' and was seen by the pupils as not purposeful but nevertheless enjoyable. She concludes that activities were overall less varied than at junior school, with an emphasis on socialising in an unstructured environment.

Given the lack of basic descriptive knowledge we have about secondary breaktime activities, this kind of study is helpful, and could be extended.

Gender differences

One of the main themes to arise from research on playground activities has been the big differences between boys and girls. These are reviewed in Blatchford (1989), Evans (1989) and Roberts (1980). Girls tend to play in smaller groups, closer to school buildings. Boys prefer open area games, with more players and more complex organisation. Girls' games tend to require more coordination and agility (such as games with elastic). Boys' games tend to be more competitive, aggressive and physical. Sex differences seem to become more exaggerated with age.

The Institute of Education research found, on the basis of pupils' reports, clear sex differences in children's playground games (Blatchford et al. 1990). Virtually all top junior boys played football (84 per cent). Slightly more than a third of the girls said they played. One could not tell from these results to what extent this was a genuine interest and to what extent girls were influenced by what happened to be the dominant game. Girls were more likely to play seeking games, pretending games and skipping games. Only girls played guessing games, daring games and ring games, rhymes and clapping games. In short, girls had a greater variety of activities than boys. Boulton (1992), in an observational study, found that boys spent more time alone, and played more football, while girls spent more time socialising, skipping and playing rounders.

It must be said that research on sex differences in outside play is often small-scale and rather anecdotal. Nevertheless, the overriding point that arises from reviewing the research is one with which many school staff would be in agreement: the playground environment tends to disadvantage girls. Barnett's (1988) results are probably typical. She looked at a small group of six fourth-year juniors. She found that the boys dominated the playgound with football. Football requires a relatively large area, and the boys were unworried by the extra space they required and the smaller space allotted to girls. Barnett found that the girls were frightened of going near the football game. Boulton (1992), on the basis of interviews with middle-school pupils, concludes that it is the boys who are responsible for single sex games – for example, because they see girls as a liability in games like football.

Barnett touches on a central dilemma of the school playground. Activities found there are an expression of children's culture or 'code', but problems arise when it becomes clear that the prevailing 'code' favours one group over another. Barnett argues that schools and LEAs need to consider the organisation of school playgrounds in terms of anti-sexist and equal opportunities policies. Blatchford (1989) discusses some of the difficulties that can be encountered. At heart is a difficulty, already met, concerning the appropriate role of adults with regard to time traditionally owned by children.

Boys and girls learn, from an early age, attitudes that underlie views about 'appropriate' gender-based activities. Dunn and Morgan (1987) found that even at nursery level boys tended to dominate equipment; more troubling, girls came to accept this. Girls then have good reason to be more discontented with playtime – as Blatchford *et al.* (1990) and Finnan (in Evans 1989) found. But they may also learn to become passive about the possibility of change. In adjusting to their limited power in the playground, to what extent are they reinforcing other maladaptive attitudes towards school work? Many have found that girls are more anxious about school work and more sensitive to negative information.

Social relations in the school playground

The playground is a valuable but under-researched setting within which to study social relations between children. We know that children are nowadays much more likely to be escorted to school and spend less time playing outside away from the home (Policy Studies Institute, *Daily Telegraph* report, 9 February 1991). The school playground is important because for some children it may be the *only* outside setting within which they can play with other children. Few settings are likely to show so naturally the ways in which children behave in one another's company. They are relatively free from adult constraints and direction.

Name calling and teasing

One aim of the Institute of Education research was to look at teasing, name calling and fighting (Mooney *et al.* 1991). The distinction between teasing and bullying may not always be clear. Teasing, though, is very common – 96 per cent of pupils at 7 and 11 years said that teasing happens, and two-thirds said that it had happened to them. These results are very similar to those of Kelly (1988) who studied Manchester secondary schools. Children who at 7 years said they teased other children more were more likely to tease others at 11 years. By far the most common form of teasing was name calling and verbal abuse, much of it individualised around physical appearance (mentioned more by girls than boys). As one said: 'They take the mickey out of their eyes, the way they speak, what colour they are and where they come from – take the mickey out of teeth, when they have gaps like me, and say you have big ears' (Mooney *et al.* 1991: 107). One needs to be careful in assumptions about teasing. Some can be enacted and mutually understood as fun, almost a sign of affection. But it was clear that it could also be unwelcome, and cause pain and frustration.

Fighting

Most of us no doubt remember fighting between children in the playground. I can remember fights – real fights – as a dramatic event that drew everyone around in a circle, as if pulled to a magnet. Rather like bullying, fighting can be looked at in isolation, perhaps as part of a concern with levels of violence in school. But Sluckin and others have shown the relevance of looking at fighting in the context of social relations between pupils. In the Institute of Education research around half (59 per cent) of the 11-year-old pupils said they were involved in fights, boys more than girls (Mooney *et al.* 1991). A similar result was found at 7 years (Tizard *et al.* 1988). Evans (1989) has reviewed research on playground fighting and makes the point that, contrary to some expectations, pupils seem reluctant to fight. One reason might be because it is so public – fighters have committed themselves to a potential loss of face, and heavy retribution from teachers.

If adults do tend to overestimate playground fights, one likely cause is the difficulties they have in distinguishing real from play fights. Humphreys and Smith (1987) and Boulton (this volume) have done much to show the often subtle differences between rough-and-tumble play and fighting.

Fighting in playgrounds – like teasing and name calling – can have complex roots in children's relationships with one another. To take an extreme case – the fight between Darren Coulbourn and Ahmed Iqbal Ullah in the playground at Burnage High School in Manchester: at one level this was a playground fight, but Troyna and Hatcher (1992) have shown the different factors that would need to be taken into account in order to understand why it led to the fatal stabbing of Ahmed. They made use of a model showing the structural, ideological, cultural, institutional, biographical, immediate contextual and interactional factors that would need to be considered.

It is common for teachers to identify individual children as the cause of most fights. But, as La Fontaine has said with regard to bullying,

> It may be more useful to consider the social context of the school within which bullying takes place. There are formal and informal groups, hierarchies of authority and of power and informal networks of friendships. Relationships between individual bullies and victims are established within these frameworks.
>
> (1991: 26)

Playground behaviours like fighting, name calling and teasing can be looked at in the same way.

Friendships

This has been the subject of attention by developmental psychologists, but recent work has highlighted the particular importance of friendships in school, which are often expressed at playtime. As most of us can remember from our school days, gaining and keeping friends is vital. Goodnow and Burns (1985) argue: 'To be at school – specially on the playground – surrounded by peers but without friends is awful.... Life brightens considerably when a friend appears.'

Friendship has many functions. Davies (1982) argues that is through friends that children build the shared meanings, sometimes not discernible to adults, that are the basis of a separate children's culture. It is only through making friends that access is gained to it, which, if true, could explain some of the anguish of rejected and isolated children, whom we look at shortly. Another feature of children's friendships is a delicate balance of sharing, obligation and reciprocity (Davies 1982; Goodnow and Burns 1985; Sluckin 1981). There is a strong sense of reciprocity; that is, behaving towards friends as they behave towards you, and, in particular, reciprocating any injury.

They also learn important social skills. Goodnow and Burns have listed these: making successful overtures, working out which children not to become friends with, maintaining an equal input into the relationship, not putting too much trust in those likely to be fickle, not being stuck with friends who no longer appeal, yet avoiding a situation where one is stranded in a friendless state.

Troyna and Hatcher (1992) have recently offered interesting insights into seemingly contradictory features of school friendships. They are particularly keen to explain how it is that children can resort to racist insults of children with whom, in calmer moments, they are good friends. Their analysis indicates the dangers, when seen in the contexts of friendships between children, of assuming that racism can be easily explained.

Children tend to have different views from those of adults about friends. They tend to like those with whom they have most to do rather than because of some likeable qualities they may have. Davies makes the interesting point that the frequent making and breaking of friendships noted, for example, by the Opies, is an adult misperception. Friendships are in fact quite stable; children use complex strategies to bargain with friends. These are not for love of a friend but because of the functions that friendships serve.

In keeping with psychological research (for example, Livesley and Bromley 1973), researchers tend to find that as they grow older children emphasise more the psychological aspects of friendships; younger children's friendships are more grounded in everyday proximity. This suggests to me an important conclusion: the playground setting is of the greatest importance in the friendships of younger children.

Rejected children

Children will not react in the same way to being in the playground. Evans (1989) has provided a review of studies which have looked at children who are rejected by others in the playground. Children who are disliked, who have few friends and who are often excluded from playing with their peers demonstrate more aggressive and aversive behaviour and are more likely to become involved in fights. At heart they do not seem to know how to relate to or play with others. There are difficulties faced by all children at times in gaining entry to games. The players may be happy with the game as it is and reluctant to allow newcomers to join and possibly spoil the game. Evans decribes how unwelcome players are told: 'The game's locked – you can't play.' I can remember when I was at secondary school playing a game of football that extended over lunchtime break for weeks and weeks. The score rose to hundreds of goals against each team, and there was a strong resistance to letting anyone join the game midway. For popular and capable children (for example, those good at football), entry may be easy. But some are rejected, and they can be devastated when they see other children later accepted into a game.

Their problems can be compounded by the strategies they use to gain entry. They may simply barge their way into a game; for example, tackling for the ball. They may resort to bribes. Sluckin observed a child offering crisps in order to get into a game. Money and other possessions might be used. Threats are another tactic, such as threatening to tell the teacher if they are not allowed to play. But all of these tactics are unlikely to be successful for long and will not solve the root problem – winning them friends. Rejected children can therefore find themselves in a progressively worsening situation; the more frantic their attempts become to join in the game, the less likely they are to be accepted.

As Evans says, the study of how friendship groups are formed in the playground is important. So too are the difficulties faced in joining playground groups. Few studies have looked at this. This is an essential feature of the alternative culture of school, and is central to children's perceptions of the school experience. Classrooms are constrained by teachers; it is on the playground that children's friendships are expressed.

A major worry is that difficulties children face in social relationships – such as rejection in the playground – can be powerful in conditioning behaviour in later life. This conclusion follows from research which indicates stability over time of social behaviour in the playground. Tamplin (1989) identified four groups of 6-year-old children who differed in terms of their degree of social participation. The groups were called 'interactive', 'social', 'self-contained' and 'uninvolved'. The difference between the self-contained and uninvolved groups was interesting. The self-contained group had few social contacts, but were involved in their activities. The uninvolved group were not involved in their activities or in other children. Tamplin found that these 'styles' related to how children behaved towards peers and how peers related toward them, and also to how they perceived themselves and their friendships. Perhaps of most interest, she found that some stable differences already present when the children were 4 years old and in nursery school. That the uninvolved children were already withdrawn at 4 years suggests long-term stability of problems.

Power and status

A point made by several authors is that games reflect power relationships in society. Sluckin points to studies of play in Mexico, which is a highly competitive society with distrust of authority. There is a corresponding distrust of cooperative games, and a prevalence of games which view authority as dangerous. This line of reasoning is intriguing. Sluckin feels that in Britain play is affected by respect for regulated competition, cooperation and the law. But one wonders what changes would be evident over time and with social and political changes. What power relationships are children learning in British playgrounds over the 1980s and 1990s?

At a more specific level, children differ in their power and status in the playground. Certain characteristics seem to be associated with power. Athletic ability and physical skill, especially in boys, can enable children to move up the social ladder. Children can acquire status from daring feats – for example, by adventures on school roofs, and engaging in illicit activities like smoking on school premises. Another factor that can be associated with status is ownership of valuable play materials. Property can confer power over who can play and what to play, though it is likely to be temporary. For staff, of course, this can be a problem because it can antogonise others. There is still much to be learnt about power and control in pupil–pupil relations.

Fair play

There are strong indications that children, when left to their own devices, are very preoccupied with fairness. Many games have built into them an integral sense of fair play. This is not to say that cheating does not take place. But, paradoxically, cheating only makes sense when in the context of a shared awareness of what is fair. There is evidence of a strong moral sense in children's informal relations in school. This is an important and under-researched topic.

We have seen how on the playground there exists a different children's culture, that can run counter to the official adult-centred school culture. Children have no difficulty in interacting in either culture – they are expertly 'bi-cultural' – but the two codes are separate and run in parallel. One way of proceeding would be to work with children in order to deal with problems and issues that arise in the playground, and in an attempt to bring the two school codes into contact with each other. This could help in the development of a moral sense in pupils that extends beyond the playground to school more generally. It could find expression in many ways. A number of schools with children's councils, for example, have found them to be an effective forum for debating moral issues such as rights and rules, in the context of real events, many of which occur in the playground. Children are likely to be more committed to rules and decisions they had a part in devising. There is scope here for work in personal and social education, and education for citizenship.

We have met several times the dilemma concerning the appropriate adult role in relation to children's informal activities, and the way positions tend to be polarised between a leave-well-alone approach and an approach emphasising effective supervision. We have arrived at a possible third alternative – one which seeks collaboration with pupils, and a willingness to allow them responsibility for actions that take place in the playground. More pupil-centred approaches are discussed in Chapters 10 and 11 in this volume.

Staff and pupils

Another neglected but important area for research concerns the interactions between staff and pupils in the playground. It is now widely recognised that the quality of supervision provided in the playground is an important factor in pupils' behaviour there (Blatchford 1989). There have been recently a number of schemes designed to improve supervision, especially that provided by lunchtime supervisors. But it is surprising, given these developments, that there is so little systematic knowledge about the interactions that take place between supervisors and pupils. This contrasts markedly with the vast literature on studies of teacher–pupil interaction in classrooms.

Evans (1990) has provided data on interactions between supervisors and pupils in three Australian primary schools. In contrast to England and Wales, where most time in the playground is supervised by lunchtime supervisors, in Australia 'yard-duty' is provided by teachers. Evans found that teachers had a poor view of this duty, regarding it as a necessary evil. He reports on the main forms of child-initiated interactions: asking a teacher to watch what they were doing, bringing something personal to the attention of the teacher, reporting an injury (real or imagined), and telling on another child or reporting a dispute. Many of the teacher-initiated interactions were directive or punitive, though it was common for teachers to chat to children and sometimes join in games. Evans feels that teachers were caught in a dilemma of wanting to be as non-interventionist as possible when on playground duty whilst at the same time having to respond with assistance to pupils. One consequence is that playground contacts tend to be officious and managerial.

School characteristics

What school factors make breaktimes in some schools aggressive, threatening or dull, whilst in others it is boisterous, pleasant and constructive? Why is it that games flourish in some schools but not others? I have been to inner city schools with small and cramped playgrounds where games were colourful and spirited. But I have also been to suburban schools with a large playground, and perhaps a field, where one's impression was of far less constructive play. Obviously, the playground environment itself will affect children's activities, but are there are other factors to do with relations and control within school, or with supervision and the provision of equipment?

There is some work on this with regard to bullying. For example, Stephenson and Smith (1989, 1991) found that bullying was reported to be much more common in some schools than in others. They found that bullying was more frequent in socially deprived areas, in larger schools with larger classes, and in schools where the head had less considered views about bullying. Whitney and Smith (1993) also found an increased incidence of bullying in disadvantaged areas. They found connections between bullying and experiences of playtime; for secondary schools there was a significant correlation between being bullied and disliking playtime very much, while for junior and middle schools more bullying occurred in schools where pupils reported being alone at playtime. Further research would be required in order to examine the causal connections involved. Is there something about playtime in some schools that facilitates bullying?

There are several school-level comparisons that would be instructive. One that could help in understanding gender differences is comparison of single sex-schools – all-boy and all-girl – and co-educational schools. Dale (1991), on the basis of retrospective accounts, found that bullying was more likely in single-sex schools, with the implication that the presence of the opposite sex had a calming influence. Girls in particular claimed that a small group could make life unpleasant for others, and that this would be unlikely to happen in schools with boys as well. But comparisons could extend beyond incidents of bullying to other aspects of playground behaviour.

Another larger-scale comparison would be regional differences such as those between rural and urban surroundings. Regional differences in playground games have been documented (for example, Opie and Opie 1969), but interest could extend to other aspects of breaktime, which, as we have said, is the time when children's culture can be revealed. Fiander, in a small-scale comparison of an urban and a rural secondary school, indicated some of the complexities. She found that the experience of breaktime was affected by the greater likelihood that children from the inner city school would go out at lunchtime ('gating'), whilst the rural children could not. There was no difference in reported bullying or fighting, but urban teachers were more likely than rural teachers to report fighting in the playground. Urban children were more likely to say they smoked; two admitted to getting 'stoned'. There were differences in games played. Family insults and cussing of the very provocative 'your mum' kind were exclusively an urban phenomenon.

These kinds of regional comparisons could help in better understanding the wider influences on playground behaviour, and ways in which it is connected to and adapts to cultural influences.

METHODS OF RESEARCHING PLAYGROUND BEHAVIOUR

Anyone who has attempted to study children at playtime will know some of the distinctive problems. Satisfying children about your role as an observer in the classroom is difficult enough, but it can be even more taxing with regard to the playground. If you are not supervising, what are you doing there? You are pounced on and relentlessly asked questions, or viewed suspiciously. As an interviewer one also faces problems. Who is this person and why is he asking these odd questions? Probably no one has asked about this part of the school day before. Even after children seem to be satisfied about your presence as an observer, there is then the difficulty of reliably recording and making sense of behaviour that is much less constrained than in the classroom. But perhaps because of the difficulties it seems to me that there is scope for imaginative approaches to methods of data collection.

The difficulties that face researchers are in principle the same as the ones faced by those wishing to study playground behaviour less formally, in the interests of a survey as part of an initiative on playground behaviour. I want to finish this review by looking briefly at methods of researching playground behaviour.

A variety of approaches have been used. These include observational approaches that make use of a previously developed check-list of behaviours and a systematic sampling procedure. Humphreys and Smith used a 'scanning' technique, noting after a time signal the activities of each child from a class in turn. Some observers (such as Evans 1990; Sluckin 1981) have spoken their commentary into a microphone, and have later analysed the tapes. Evans apparently had problems with pupils pretending to fight in order to tease him, and looking out for him while others played illicit games!

Another approach is to use children as informants and observers. This can be helpful in establishing just what game children are playing. Barnett (1988) made use of the help of two informants – not difficult to enlist, apparently. In another small-scale study of playground violence Pleydell (1990), as a teacher in the school, was worried about being known to the children as an authority figure. So in a similar vein to Barnett he enlisted the help of nine fourth-year pupils to carry out the observations. Interestingly, there were serious disagreements between pupil and lunchtime supervisor observers. What pupils saw as friendly encounters supervisors would more often see as aggressive. But overall pupil observers saw twice as many incidents of aggression.

Pupils can also be interviewed. In the Institute of Education study we interviewed children at 7 and 11 years individually in a quiet place. We found that a combination of closed questions – such as with preselected codes and rating scales – and open-ended questions seemed to work best, the open-ended answers being categorised later. But others (Goodnow and Burns 1985; Troyna and Hatcher 1992) have preferred to interview children in groups, and with a more open-ended format.

A theme of this chapter has been the separate culture of playground life. The problems faced in making sense of this culture are similar to those problems faced by anthropologists in understanding non-Western societies. Some researchers have consciously adopted ethnographic techniques in order to understand playground culture (Davies 1982; Troyna and Hatcher 1992). These techniques typically involve participant observation and unstructured interviews.

CONCLUSION

This chapter has reviewed research on children's playground behaviour. It is hoped that the reader will be persuaded that there are many areas of interest. The school playground is a unique setting within which to explore aspects such as children's playground games and features of their social relations such as friendships, teasing and fights, power and status. Social surveys have shown that because children are now spending less and less time 'playing out', the school playground becomes correspondingly more important as a social setting for outside, 'unofficial' and self-directed activities. It is a setting within which to research a children's culture that can be separate from and sometimes in opposition to the official culture of school. If it can offer insights into children's social relations, it can also act as the basis for improvement schemes within school. Further study of staff–pupil relations in playground settings should help in developing playground management schemes, and we have very little knowledge of how and why schools differ from one another in children's playground activities. Research on bullying is currently recognised as being of great importance. This chapter has set out to show that there are many other aspects of pupil behaviour that are worthy of more detailed attention.

REFERENCES

Barnett, Y. (1988) '"Miss, girls don't like playing big games; they only like playing little games": gender differences in the use of playground space', *Primary Teaching Studies*, 4(1): 42–52.

Blatchford, P. (1989) *Playtime in the Primary School: Problems and Improvements*, Windsor: NFER-Nelson.

—— (1993) 'Bullying in the playground', in D. Tattum (ed.) *Understanding and Managing Bullying*, Oxford: Heinemann.

Blatchford, P., Creeser, R. and Mooney, A. (1990) 'Playground games and playtime: the children's view', *Educational Research*, 32(3): 163–74.

Boulton, M. (1992) 'Participating in playground activities', *Educational Research*, 34(3): 167–82.

Dale, R. R. (1991) 'Mixed versus single-sex schools', in M. Elliott (ed.) *Bullying: A Practical Guide to Coping for Schools*, Harlow: Longman.

Davies, B. (1982) *Life in the Classroom and Playground: The Accounts of Primary School Children*, London: Routledge & Kegan Paul.

Department of Education and Science (DES) (Elton Report) (1989) *Discipline in Schools*, Report of the Committee of Enquiry chaired by Lord Elton, London: HMSO.

Dunn, S. and Morgan, V. (1987) 'Nursery and infant school play patterns: sex related differences', *British Educational Research Journal*, 13(3): 271–82.

Elliott, M. (ed.) (1991) *Bullying: A Practical Guide to Coping for Schools*, Harlow: Longman.

Evans, J. (1989) *Children at Play: Life in the School Playground*, Geelong, Victoria, Australia: Deaken University Press.

Evans, J. (1990) 'Teacher–child interaction during yard duty: the Australian experience', *Education 3–13* (June): 48–54.

Fiander, J. (1991) 'Our time: an urban and rural perspective of breaktime in secondary schools', MSc dissertation, Institute of Education, University of London.

Goodnow, J. and Burns, A. (1985) *Home and School: A Child's-eye View*, Sydney: Allen & Unwin.

Grugeon, E. (1988) 'Children's oral culture: a transitional experience', in M. MacLure, T. Phillips, T. and A. Wilkinson (eds) *Oracy Matters*, Milton Keynes: Open University Press.

—— (1991) 'Girls' play', *Language and Learning*, 5: 13–15.

Humphreys, A. and Smith, P. K. (1987) 'Rough and tumble, friendship and dominance in schoolchildren: evidence for continuity and change with age', *Child Development*, 58: 201–12.

Kelly, E. (1988) 'Pupils, racial groups and behaviour in schools'. in E. Kelly and T. Cohn, *Racism in Schools – New Research Evidence*, Stoke-on-Trent: Trentham.

Kelly, E. and Cohn, T. (1988) *Racism in School: New Research Evidence*, Stoke-on-Trent: Trentham.

La Fontaine, J. (1991) *Bullying: The Child's View*, London: Calouste Gulbenkian Foundation.

Livesley, W. J. and Bromley, D. B. (1973) *Person Perception in Childhood and Adolescence*, London: Wiley.

Macdonald, B. (1989) *Murder in the Playground* (Burnage Inquiry) London: Longsight Press.

Mooney, A., Creeser, R. and Blatchford, P. (1991) 'Children's views on teasing and fighting in junior schools', *Educational Research*, 33(2): 103–12.

Newcastle Education Committee (1990) Midday Supervision Training Package.

Opie, I. (1991) 'Let's play skipping-the-generation game', *Guardian*, 1 Jan.

Opie, I. and Opie, P. (1969) *Children's Games in Street and Playground*, London: Oxford University Press.

Oxford Programme for Training, Instruction and Supervision (OPTIS) (1986) 'The OPTIS guide to supervising in the lunch hour', Oxford: OPTIS.

Parry-Jones, D. (1964) *Welsh Children's Games and Pastimes*, Denbigh: Gee & Son Ltd.

Pleydell, P. J. (1990) 'Playground violence', *Education Today*, 40(3): 26–31.

Roberts, A. (1980) *Out to Play: The Middle Years of Childhood*, Aberdeen: Aberdeen University Press.

Sluckin, A. (1981) *Growing Up in the Playground*, London: Routledge & Kegan Paul.

Smith, P. K. and Thompson, D. A. (eds) (1991) *Practical Approaches to Bullying*, London: David Fulton Publishers.

Stephenson, P. and Smith, D. (1989) 'Bullying in the junior school', in D. P. Tattum, and O. A. Lane, (eds.) *Bullying in Schools*, Stoke-on-Trent: Trentham.

—— (1991) 'Why some schools don't have bullies', in M. Elliott, (ed.), *Bullying: A Practical Guide to Coping for Schools*, Harlow: Longman.

Sutton-Smith, B. (1981) *A History of Children's Play: New Zealand, 1840–1950*, Philadelphia: University of Pennsylvania Press.

Sutton-Smith, B. and Kelly-Byrne, D. (1984) 'The idealization of play', in P. K. Smith, (ed.) *Play in Animals and Humans*, Oxford: Blackwell.

Tamplin, A. M. (1989) 'Six-year-olds in the school playground', PhD thesis, Cambridge University.

Tattum, D. (ed.) (1993) *Understanding and Managing Bullying*, Oxford: Heinemann.

Tattum, D. and Lane, O. A. (1989) *Bullying in Schools*, Stoke-on-Trent: Trentham.

Tizard, B., Blatchford, P., Burke, J., Farquhar, C. and Plewis, I. (1988) *Young Children at School in the Inner City*, Hove: Lawrence Erlbaum.

Troyna, B. and Hatcher, R. (1992) *Racism in Children's Lives: A Study of Mainly-White Primary Schools*, London: Routledge.

Webb, F. D. (1984) 'Introduction' to Alice. B. Gomme, *The Traditional Games of England, Scotland and Ireland*, London: Thames & Hudson.

Whitney, I. and Smith, P. K. (1993) 'A survey of the nature and extent of bullying in junior/middle and secondary schools', *Educational Research*, 35(1): 3–25.

Chapter 2

What children learn from playtime, and what adults can learn from it

Peter K. Smith

The school playground provides a world in microcosm; a unique world, which grown-ups soon forget. At least, they mostly forget the intensity of the subjective experience which children have in the playground. We know that time in the playground is an appreciable percentage of time in school (see Chapter 1). It also can be a time of intense social interaction and marked physical activity. Playgrounds often provide generous space, and also a greater number of about-the-same-age play companions than is usually otherwise experienced. We can learn a lot about children's development from what they typically do with these opportunities. And children can learn a lot, too. What we can learn about children, and what children are learning themselves, will be the themes of this chapter.

AGE CHANGES AND WHAT THEY SHOW

There are characteristic changes with age in children's playground behaviour. These are often related not only to children's social skills, but also to their cognitive abilities; indeed, social and cognitive abilities are intimately related in the playground context.

Children tend to play in larger groups as they get older. Observations made of nursery-school children show that they most often play in pairs, less often in threes or fours, rarely in groups of five or more. Smith (1977) found this characteristic pattern in 3- and 4-year-olds in playgroups (not exactly a playground situation, but similar in terms of available space and free choice of companions). By primary-school age larger groups become more common. For example, Hertz-Lazarowitz et al. (1981), in a study of Israeli children, found that groups of five-plus children increased from 12 per cent to 16 per cent between 5 and 6 years. In a detailed study of an Oxfordshire primary school, Sluckin (1979, 1981) observed that by 7 or 8 years group sizes had increased beyond that at 5 to 6 years. This mean size of children's playgroups continues to increase up to adolescence. Eifermann (1970a), in a large-scale study of schools in Israel, found that mean group size increased further up to adolescence.

Why does this change happen? At least two processes are probably at work, which basically allow older children to play in larger groups. First, they are becoming more skilled at coordinating behaviour with several other persons. Very young children (1 to 2 years) find it difficult enough to sustain interactions for a long time with one age-mate; in toddler groups, social interactions with age-mates tend to last less than a minute. However, it is easier for toddlers to sustain longer interactions and game sequences with an adult. This is because the adult will adapt to the child's behaviour, providing a support or 'scaffolding' for the interaction – waiting to catch the child's attention, making the appropriate response, and so on. By 3 and 4 years of age, a child is sufficiently 'non-egocentric' to engage in quite long play sequences with an age-mate. However, coordinating behaviour with two or three partners is more difficult – there are additional skills about sharing time, waiting your turn, behaving differently with different partners, to be acquired.

The other, related factor is the rule structure of the game or play sequence. Just as an adult can 'scaffold' a play sequence such as Peek-a-boo with a young child, so a known rule structure can 'scaffold' interactions amongst a large number of same-age peers. But, the rule structure must be shared knowledge. If we all know how to play football, what the rules are, then it is relatively easy to coordinate a game in which some twenty children can take part. Each person has a 'role', and the expectations of someone else's behaviour are made more predictable by the shared structure of the game.

Football has 'public' rules, in the sense that there is a framework of rules (about teams, scoring goals and so on) which most people entering a game of football will already know. But understanding these frameworks of rules in itself implies some level of cognitive ability. This was first argued in detail by Piaget, in a famous study of children playing marbles in a suburb of Geneva, where he was working. At the time (the 1920s), marbles seems to have been a very popular game, with a number of variants. Piaget asked children if he could watch them and join in. When he tried to play, he deliberately made mistakes so that he would be corrected and the children would tell him what (in their opinion) the rules of the game were. (As Piaget remarked, there was a fine line to draw here between 'knowing' too much and thus learning too little, or 'knowing' too little and hence being rejected as a stupid play partner!) Piaget also questioned children directly about the rules. His findings are described in a book which he called *The Moral Judgement of the Child* (1932) because he felt the rules of children's games reflected the wider rules and morality of society. Piaget argued that at 3 or 4 years children really had no idea about rules of a game; they just tried to join in by imitating others' actions. However, even doing this, with older children, led to their getting told, for example, 'No, you do it this way', and gradually getting an idea that a game did have rules. However, by around

6 years, when a child became capable of grasping this, he or she assumed that the rules were fixed and unalterable. These are the rules! Even this over-simple idea does allow children to enter into a rule-governed game much more effectively. By doing so, they start to realise that there are socially accepted variants, which may be agreed at the start of the game. You may decide how the marbles can be rolled (or pushed, or flicked), how someone wins, whether a winner can be immediately challenged to a replay, and so forth. These experiences lead to a more mature conception of rules – by 9 or 10 years, Piaget thought – when a child recognised that rules were a social arrangement, the product of mutual consent amongst the players.

Earlier, I used the terms 'he or she'. In fact, it seems that Piaget observed only boys playing marbles. However, in a smaller-scale study he did enquire about a girl's game, 'ilt cachant', a form of Tig. He found a similar sequence of development, with the rules being understood from about 6 years onwards, though with full understanding coming a bit earlier, perhaps because this particular game had a simpler rule structure.

Although much of Piaget's work has subsequently been criticised (for example, Donaldson 1978), his study of children's games emerges relatively unscathed. Where Piaget seems often to have gone wrong is in devising tests for children which may mislead or 'trick' them into giving a wrong answer. But his 'marbles' study is not of this kind.

Piaget's work was replicated by a Spanish psychologist working first in Oxford and then in Madrid. Linaza (1981, 1984) studied both boys and girls playing marbles, hide-and-seek, rounders and football, in both England and Spain. His work resulted in an even more detailed sequence than Piaget had described; but it remained true that younger children had a poor conception of rules. It does seem as if it is not until about 6 years that most children are easily able to understand and join in rule-governed and team games such as football, without adult support. Indeed, for many teachers this marks a difference between the infant-school and the junior-school playground.

Another psychologist who has developed this tradition of research is Eifermann (1973). In her studies of Israeli children's games, she discusses how older children can use and adapt rules to maximise the 'challenge' in a game. There may be additional regulations or prohibitions introduced in a game. For example, in 'Tag' children may agree on a 'rule of permission' such as the person who is 'it' shouting 'ten for all' before setting off in pursuit. In 'wrestling', there may be a 'meta-rule' such as 'no strangling'. Rules such as these elaborate the usual game in certain ways. It can make a game more difficult; and it can provide different rules or handicaps for different participants at different age and skill levels. In this way, children can play with a number of others, with different levels of skills and of different ages, while still maintaining the challenge necessary for each player to make participation enjoyable.

AGE CHANGES IN TYPES OF ACTIVITIES

So Piaget thought that rule games were typical for children from about 6 years up; by this age, they became capable of understanding rules sufficiently to join in properly. Also, this rule structure enabled larger team games to take place. Observational studies do indeed suggest that team games are very popular in the 6- to 12-year age range. But what about younger children, and older children?

Piaget described typical play patterns of younger children in another book, *Play, Dreams and Imitation in Childhood* (1951). He thought that from 3 to 6 years children's predominant play activity was 'symbolic'. This was the time of pretend games, and sociodramatic play, in pairs or small groups. Pretend play can be quite common in infant-school playgrounds (Sluckin noted it in about 15 per cent of the time at the Oxford school he worked in), and it does seem to decrease rapidly by 9 years and older (Humphreys and Smith 1984).

Symbolic play does not have an agreed rule structure. In a pretend game, you more or less make things up as you go along. 'Let's play firemen!'; and later, 'This is a hosepipe'; and later perhaps, 'Now, let's be doctors and nurses'. The game is defined and redefined just among the participants; someone coming new to the game would not know what was happening, at first.

This could seem quite different from football, where if you know how football generally is played, you could join in any ongoing game of football very quickly indeed, because you share the common rule structure. But, the difference may not be as large as it seems. First, pretend games may have less of an idiosyncratic structure than suggested. Most sociodramatic play episodes are based on fairly familiar 'scripts' – of firefighters putting out a fire, of doctors giving medicine to a patient, of mother or father feeding baby and putting him or her to bed (Garvey 1977). Probably, shared knowledge of such a basic script is helpful if not essential if several children are to sustain a sociodramatic play episode over a period of time and through a sequence of actions. Thus, these pretend games can be seen as genuine precursors of the more obviously rule-governed games of middle childhood. Secondly, as we saw earlier, even children's team games are not set in such rigid rule structures as is often the case with adult games. Playground football is not the same as professional soccer! Rules will be adapted to the social and physical context of the playground situation at the time (so, it might not be so easy for us to join in, as we thought).

Interest in team games seems to persist up to around puberty, but not necessarily beyond. Eifermann (1971) described how older children – or young adolescents of 13 or 14 years of age – seem to revert to 'practice play'. 'Practice play' was a term used by Piaget (1951) to refer to the quite early forms of play that preceded even symbolic play – physical forms of play just done for their own sake. For infants (1 and 2 years), this practice play might involve banging objects, sucking them, hitting them and so forth. Eifermann observed some kinds of play in adolescents – mucking around, just throwing a ball but not in a game, and so on – which she felt could only be described as 'practice play': it was not symbolic, and it had no rule structure.

Eifermann explained this change in terms of challenge and role distancing. We saw how children could make rule-governed games more challenging by adapting the rules. But after a point, it may be difficult to make games more challenging in this way. Also, by early teens you may want to 'distance' yourself from games that 'children' play. So you may muck about, tossing a ball but deliberately not 'playing football' because at your age that would be beneath you! Whether we call this 'practice play' is a moot point.

It might be noted that it is difficult adequately to categorise rough-and-tumble play, which typically takes up some 10 per cent of playground time (see Boulton, Chapter 3). Rough-and-tumble play can be pretend in the sense of role playing (as in 'monsters' fighting) but need not be; and it can be rule-governed, as in games like 'Tig' or 'British bulldog'. But a lot of it is just straightforward 'play fighting'; and it can be seen in children aged 4 to 14 years.

SEX DIFFERENCES IN PLAY

Up to now, we have paid little attention to sex differences. Yet many studies show that these are pronounced in middle childhood. At one level, these can be described in terms of activity preferences. For example, boys seem to prefer team games like football, and also the more physical, play-fighting forms of rough-and-tumble (see Chapter 3). Girls often prefer games such as skipping, hopscotch, rhyming and clapping games. There is probably some biological influence or 'channelling' in some of these preferences, especially for vigorous, physically active behaviours in boys (Smith 1986). But certainly, sex differences in activity preferences can be strongly influenced by socialisation pressures. Certain activities are 'labelled' by parents, teachers and society as 'masculine', others as 'feminine'. Children imitate same-sex peers and role models, and are rewarded for showing what is considered sex-appropriate behaviour; also, by the middle- and junior-school years they are quite aware of what is considered sex-appropriate – they have acquired 'gender identity'. This results in what has been termed 'self-socialisation' by Maccoby and Jacklin (1987); children themselves are usually keen to be seen as typical 'boys' or 'girls' and do not necessarily need much outward pressure to 'conform' to expectations.

At nursery-school age, these sex differences are not so evident. Girls and boys play together quite a lot – cross-sex play partners making up about a third of the total. This may be because at 3 and 4 years gender identity is still developing, and children are not so aware of gender conventions. By 6 years, as team games become prominent, so does sex segregation in the playground. Same-sex choices of play partners increases from around two-thirds at nursery age, to around three-quarters in infant school, and up to 85–90 per cent in junior/middle school (Sluckin 1979, 1981). Most often, children prefer to play with others of the same sex at these latter ages, and also others of the same age.

According to the 'gender-intensification hypothesis' (Hill and Lynch 1982), gender roles will become more rigid with age. Especially after menarche, it is argued, girls will decline in any interest in 'masculine' activities and focus on issues of fashion and personal attractiveness. However, an alternative view (Ullian 1976) follows from the Piagetian tradition. This is that, as children get older, they get a more mature conception of gender roles as socially chosen, rather than just 'given'. Just as children's understanding of the rules of games becomes more flexible with age, so, according to this cognitive-developmental view, does their understanding of gender roles. An examination of these two hypotheses was undertaken by Archer and McDonald (1990) in a study of forty-three girls aged 10–15 years, from four different UK schools. The gender intensification hypothesis was not supported. These girls played a wide variety of sports and games, some typically 'masculine' such as soccer. They did not stop doing this in early adolescence. Furthermore, some of them clearly and explicitly adopted a flexible position on gender roles: 'perhaps, the older generation might not approve of girls playing football, but the younger generation think they can do what they want' (13-year-old); 'there are sports we don't play as much as the boys but since the football team started, girls have got the opportunity to do all the different sports that boys play now' (14-year-old) (quotations from Archer and McDonald 1990: 232, 234). These findings were interpreted as supporting the cognitive-developmental viewpoint.

If indeed girls are now participating more in football and other team games, this may have wider implications; which brings us back to what children are learning from activities such as this. Such implications were spelled out in an interesting article by Lever (1978). Lever observed and questioned children aged 10–11 years in the United States. She found that boys spent about 65 per cent of their time in formal, rule-governed games, whereas girls spent only 37 per cent of their time doing this. Furthermore, the boy's games – such a football – were team games involving direct competition. The girls' games – such as hopscotch – typically did not involve teams, and competition was indirect; not one person competing

directly against another, as in a football tackle, but one person's performance which might later be measured against another person's performance.

Lever generalised these differences to the friendship patterns found in
boys and girls. She described boys' friendship groups at this age as being
larger – more suitable for teams – and with an instrumental attitude
towards friendship such that friendship was based on behaviour, and
'playing the game'. Girls' friendship groups were smaller and more intimate, and their attitude to friendship was more expressive, based on
feelings and verbal behaviour. Lever felt that these differences had consequences for what these young adolescents were learning, or what skills they
were acquiring. Boys seemed to be practising skills of loyalty and leader-
ship in conflict situations, and of cooperating in large groups – in a way,
'political' skills. Girls seemed to be practising skills of small group intimacy
and exclusivity. These can be seen to presage what are often sex differences
in adult life – the generally greater male participation in political processes,
the generally greater female participation in intimate relationships, particularly. (Interestingly, they may also relate to tendencies to sex differences in
aggression and bullying; for boys, this is more often direct and physical –
hitting, taunting; for girls, especially older girls, quite a lot of aggression
and bullying is indirect, via social exclusion or by passing nasty stories
about someone behind her back (Bjorkqvist et al. 1992; Ahmad and Smith,
1994). These forms of aggression are more subtle and less easy to detect by
teachers, but may be especially effective in the smaller and tighter-knit
friendship groups of girls; exclusion from a tight group of three or four
peers with whom you were previously intimate is probably even more
effective and devastating than being unpopular in the larger and looser
networks of boys. The consequences for a girl in this situation is well
portrayed in the novel Cat's Eye, by Margaret Atwood (1990).

RACE AND CULTURAL DIFFERENCES IN THE PLAYGROUND

To some extent, children seem to choose play partners of the same race,
even in multi-cultural settings, in societies such as the United Kingdom and
United States. This is true even at pre-school. For example, Finkelstein and
Haskins (1983) observed thirty-eight black children and twenty-five white
children in a US kindergarten. They found that these 5-year-olds started
kindergarten with a clear own-race choice of play partners, and furthermore that this increased over the school year. Boulton and Smith (1993a)
observed playground behaviour in three UK middle schools, in which most
of the children, aged 8 to 10 years, were white or of Asian (Indian/Paki-
stani/Bangladeshi) origin. White children chose white playmates 74 per
cent of the time, and Asian children chose Asian playmates 85 per cent of
the time. Generally, this same-race preference was more marked for girls,
probably because girls were playing in smaller groups – boys spent about

two-thirds of their time in rule games, girls only about one-third. In larger team games – for example, choosing a football side – racial considerations may be less important than in a group of two or three persons. Same-race preferences have also been documented for older children in the United States (Schofield and Francis 1982).

Of course, a preference for same-race partners need not reflect any prejudice, as such. Nevertheless, the small degree of different-race interaction in schools with a fairly equal mix of racial groups may seem worrying for those who wish to promote multi-cultural attitudes. In part, same-race preferences (and their apparent increase through kindergarten to middle childhood) may reflect a consolidation of racial identity (Aboud 1988), just as gender identity becomes consolidated (slightly earlier). In part, they may reflect actual differences in preferred activities.

There has been very little research on racial differences in activity preference. One or two studies have suggested that young children of Asian origin may show less preference for pretend play activities (Child 1983), and this may follow from parental child-rearing practices. Boulton and Smith (1993a) found no difference between white and Asian children in how much time was spent in rule games, but this category could embrace quite a variety of activities.

If there were some racial differences in activity preferences, this would not be too surprising. Different racial groups in a society typically have somewhat differing cultural values and styles of child rearing. These could be expected to impact on activity preferences. The best evidence that this is so comes from studies where quite distinct cultural groups are compared.

An early example was a study by Eifermann (1970b) of games played by children in kibbutzim and moshavim in Israel. The kibbutzim – especially at the time – fostered a cooperative, egalitarian ethos; the moshavim had a more traditionally individualistic and competitive outlook. This, Eifermann claimed, was reflected in the children's games. Some games have all participants on an 'equal footing'; others have 'over-privileged' or 'under-privileged' roles, such as 'Statues' or 'Jump-rope'. The kibbutz children, compared to those from the moshavim, tended to avoid the latter games and choose those in which roles were equal. They did not avoid competition, but competed in games with a cooperative framework, such as football. This was seen as reflecting the broader cultural values into which they were growing.

Roberts and Sutton-Smith (1962) linked adult concerns in society to forms of child training and socialisation, and hence to the kinds of childhood games played. They separated the main forms of games into those of strategy, chance and physical skill. They argued that games of strategy – such as chess – trained children for obedience, typically in societies with complex social systems; whereas games of chance – such as dice games – trained children for responsibility; and games of physical skill – such as ball games – trained children for achievement. They tested this hypothesis on data from a large number of traditional societies, claiming support for it. This 'socialisation' hypothesis seems to have something going for it, but it can be overemphasised. A thorough overview of this and related work is provided by Schwartzman (1978).

A very detailed study of games in social context was carried out by Lancy (1974) amongst the Kpelle people of Liberia. He observed that children's fantasy play often mimicked adult activities such as cooking and hunting (a common observation in many societies); and that verbal games, stories and riddles presaged the kinds of verbal skills needed in debate, or (for example) appearances before the village chief during disputes. Children with more complex game skills seemed to acquire more complex work skills; though this might, of course, simply reflect general intelligence level. Overall, he felt that in games childen learned to be clever in competitive situations, but also to use caution and prudence.

WHAT DO CHILDREN ACQUIRE IN THE PLAYGROUND?

As the literature on cross-cultural studies of games suggests, what children may be learning through play and games is intimately connected with their social relationships, and the social context of home and school. Certainly, some physical and cognitive skills may be practised through games. Clearly, a child playing football is getting physical exercise and practising skills of ball-control, as well as skills of being in a team. No doubt, constructive play in younger children can help cognitive skills to do with coordinating skilled movement, understanding balance, seriating objects by length and so forth. The literature on the fantasy and sociodramatic play of 3- to 6-year-olds, too, suggests that children may be practising language and cognitive role-taking skills in these activities (Smilansky and Shefatyah 1990). For many teachers, younger children's play is vital in the learning process – as Isaacs (1929: 9) put it, 'play is indeed the child's work, and the means whereby he grows and develops'. However, what children learn through playing may not be so great in a purely cognitive sense; certainly, it has proved difficult to establish that play is any more effective than instruction or classroom learning in this regard (Smith 1988). The unique learning opportunities provided by play and games are probably more in the social domain, certainly by the middle childhood years when rule games and team play are common; while in rough-and-tumble play children may be cementing friendships and alliances as well as practising skills of fighting and dominance (Humphreys and Smith 1984: ch. 3).

Some of this social learning we have already alluded to in discussing Lever's description of sex differences in games. Another perspective comes from Sluckin's detailed study of an Oxford primary school. Sluckin emphasised the great variety of social strategies and conventions which could be used in interactions in the playground; essentially, his view saw both friendship and dominance, cooperation and competition, being maintained by skilful social behaviour. Quite often, skilful behaviour involves knowing how to 'manipulate' conventions for one's own ends. For example, in 'dips', the methods whereby the person to be 'it' is chosen, there are ways of ensuring that you are not 'it' by extending the dipping rhyme for another verse, or reversing the direction of the count and so forth.

Children also learn ways of joining new groups, and getting themselves into games. One strategy is to ask the right person: Jane – 'Can I play?' Helen – 'It's not my game, it's Tracey's.' Jane (to Tracey) – 'Can I play?' Tracey – 'Yes.' Another strategy is offering a sweet: Malcolm (to Damad) – 'You're not playing.' Damad produces a sweet. Malcolm – 'It's my game, I'll let you play. He's it.' (Points to Damad, who gives all the players sweets.) They are also learning how to make alliances: Pete – 'Once I tried to be friends with Jamie and he pushed me over into a big puddle and I got up and started chasing him and we shook on it, to make sure that we're friends.' They are learning how to present themselves in a good light to their peers. Again, this can sometimes be manipulative; a child hitting or tricking another one and then justifying it: Neill hits Graeme. Graeme – 'Why did you do that.' Neill – 'Self-defence' (quotations from Sluckin 1981).

The success of a child at these activities will influence their social status in the playground. Psychologists now distinguish several kinds of status. Popular children are often liked and few children if any dislike them. At the other extreme, rejected children are disliked by many, and few if any children like them. Both bullies, and victims of bullying, tend to be over-represented in this rejected category. Controversial children are liked by some and disliked by others; as are dominant children who are rather aggressive, perhaps 'gang' leaders. Neglected children are seldom liked or disliked strongly; they are 'in the background'. Many children, of course, fall into average or other categories (Coie *et al.* 1982; Boulton and Smith 1993b).

Rejected children, and to some extent controversial and neglected children, may show problem behaviour in the playground. This may sometimes be due to a lack of social skills – not knowing how to enter a game peacefully, not realising when a rough-and-tumble initiation is friendly, not hostile. However, not all 'problem' behaviour is plausibly attributed to lack of social skills. Some children may simply enjoy being aggressive and dominating others, and do so quite skilfully. These are differences in ends rather than means; family background circumstances and the quality of a child's attachment with parents may explain some of these differences (Smith *et al.* in press).

THE BENEFITS OF PLAYGROUND BREAKS

Life in the playground, like life generally, has its ups and downs. Certainly, steps can and should be taken to ensure that the playground is enjoyable and challenging, and reasonably safe from bullying and harassment (see Kelly, Chapter 4). Also, the purely physical benefits of playground time should not be forgotten. Playground breaks are an opportunity for fairly intense physical activity, and children are often thought of as 'letting off steam'. Leaving aside images of steam trains, one version of a serious argument is that if children sit for prolonged periods of time they accumulate 'surplus energy' which needs to be released if they are to concentrate on the more sedentary tasks of the classroom. Some relevant evidence here comes from two studies which looked at effects of temporarily 'depriving' children of exercise opportunities. The first involved 3- and 4-year-olds in a nursery class (Smith and Hagan 1980); the children stayed in the indoor classroom (fairly crowded) either forty-five or ninety minutes before going outdoors (a much larger area). Children were more active and for a longer period after the longer, compared to the shorter, confinement period; and a decrease of activity on the playground was observed as a function of time outside, as energy was expended. No gender differences were observed. Pellegrini and Huberty (in press) examined the effects of confinement on 9-year-old boys' and girls' classroom and playground behaviour. Again, children were confined for shorter and longer periods, and the duration and intensity of their playground behaviour was observed. Pellegrini and Huberty also found that confinement increased the intensity of children's playground activity. However, they did find significant gender effects: boys were more active on the playground than girls, particularly after the longer confinement period. Both these results support the idea that a need for physical exercise does increase in children – probably not so much to let off 'surplus energy', however, as to provide physical exercise, which is very beneficial at this age. Possibly, such physical activity has implications for the classroom – for example, affecting subsequent attention span in lessons; though as yet, such effects are poorly documented (Pellegrini and Huberty, in press). In general, the implications of playground time for physical exercise need much more attention (Pellegrini and Smith, in press).

However, the overall view so far suggests that the primary learning experience of the playground, for children, is a social one. Given the variety and free choice of activities available, it probably provides more in this way than the classroom, and perhaps for some children more than the home environment. Whatever the problems with playgrounds and their management, it seems to be a retrograde step to abolish them, as some schools are now doing. This is not to say that children should be made to go outside – some children prefer quiet playtimes. But the opportunity for highly social, physically active behaviours which playtime provides should not be given up lightly. The patient observer can learn a great deal about children by watching them at playtime; and, we can be sure, the children are learning a great deal about one another.

REFERENCES

Aboud, F. (1988) *Children and Prejudice*, Oxford: Basil Blackwell.

Ahmad, Y. and Smith, P. K. (1994) 'Bullying in schools and the issue of sex differences', in J. Archer (ed.) *Male Violence*, London: Routledge.

Archer, J. and McDonald, M. (1990) 'Gender roles and sports in adolescent girls', *Leisure Studies*, 9: 225–40.

Atwood, M. (1990) *Cat's Eye*, London: Virago Press.

Bjorkqvist, K., Osterman, K. and Kaukiainen, A. (1992) 'The development of direct and indirect aggressive strategies in males and females', in K. Bjorkqvist and P. Niemela (eds) *Of Mice and Women: Aspects of Female Aggression*, pp. 51–64, Orlando, FL: Academic Press.

Boulton, M. J. and Smith, P. K. (1993a) 'Ethnic and gender partner and activity preferences in mixed-race schools in the UK: playground observations', in C. H. Hart (ed.), *Children on Playgrounds: Research Perspectives and Applications*, New York: SUNY Press.

—— (1993b) 'Bully/victim problems in middle school children: stability, self-perceived competence, peer perceptions, and peer acceptance', *British Journal of Developmental Psychology*, in press.

Child, E. (1983) 'Play and culture: a study of English and Asian children', *Leisure Studies*, 2: 169–86.

Coie, J. D., Dodge, K. A. and Coppotelli, H. (1982) 'Dimensions and types of social status: a cross-age perspective', *Developmental Psychology*, 18: 557–70.

Donaldson, M. (1978) *Children's Minds*, London: Fontana.

Eifermann, R. (1970a) 'Level of children's play as expressed in group size', *British Journal of Educational Psychology*, 40: 161–70.

—— (1970b) 'Cooperativeness and egalitarianism in kibbutz children's games', *Human Relations*, 23: 579–87.

—— (1971) 'Social play in childhood', in R. E. Herron and B. Sutton-Smith (eds) *Child's Play*, pp. 270–97, New York: Wiley & Sons.

—— (1973) 'Rules in games', in A. Elithorn and D. Jones (eds), *Artificial and Human Thinking*, pp. 147–61, Amsterdam: Elsevier.

Finkelstein, N. W. and Haskins, R. (1983) 'Kindergarten children prefer same-color peers', *Child Development*, 54: 502–8.

Garvey, C. (1977) *Play*, Cambridge, MA: Harvard University Press.

Hertz-Lazarowitz, R., Feitelson, D., Zahavi, S. and Hartup, W. W. (1981) 'Social interaction and social organisation of Israeli five-to-seven-year olds', *International Journal of Behavioral Development*, 4: 143–55.

Hill, J. P. and Lynch, M. E. (1982) 'The intensification of gender-related role expectations during early adolescence', in J. Brooks-Gunn and A. C. Petersen (eds) *Girls at Puberty: Biological and Psychological Perspectives*, pp. 201–29, London: Plenum Press.

Humphreys, A. and Smith, P. K. (1984) 'Rough-and-tumble play in preschool and playground', in P. K. Smith (ed.) *Play in Animals and Humans*, pp. 241–70, Oxford: Blackwell.

Isaacs, S. (1929) *The Nursery Years*, London: Routledge & Kegan Paul.

Lancy, D. F. (1974) 'Work, play and learning in a Kpelle town', Unpublished PhD thesis, University of Pittsburgh.

Lever, J. (1978) 'Sex differences in the complexity of children's play and games', *American Sociological Review*, 43: 471–83.

Linaza, J. (1981) 'The acquisition of the rules of games by children', Unpublished DPhil thesis, University of Oxford.

—— (1984) 'Piaget's marbles: the study of children's games and their knowledge of rules', *Oxford Review of Education*, 10: 271–74.

Maccoby, E. and Jacklin, C. (1987) 'Gender segregation in childhood', in H. Reese (ed.) *Advances in Child Development and Behavior*, pp. 239–87, New York: Academic Press.

Pellegrini, A. D. and Huberty, P. (in press) 'Confinement effects on playground and classroom behaviour', *British Journal of Educational Psychology*.

Pellegrini, A. D. and Smith, P. K. (in press) 'School recess: implications for education and development', *Review of Educational Research*.

Piaget, J. (1932/1977) *The Moral Judgement of the Child*, Harmondsworth: Penguin.

—— (1951) *Play, Dreams and Imitation in Childhood*, London: Routledge & Kegan Paul.

Roberts, J. M. and Sutton-Smith, B. (1962) 'Child training and game involvement', *Ethnology*, 1: 166–85.

Schofield, J. W. and Francis, W. D. (1982) 'An observational study of peer interactions in racially mixed "accelerated" classrooms', *Journal of Educational Psychology*, 74: 722–32.

Schwartzman, H. (1978) *Transformations: The Anthropology of Children's Play*, New York: Plenum Press.

Sluckin, A. (1979) 'Experience in the playground and the development of competence', unpublished DPhil thesis, University of Oxford.

—— (1981) *Growing Up in the Playground: The Social Development of Children*, London: Routledge & Kegan Paul.

Smilansky, S. and Shefatyah, L. (1990) *Facilitating Play: A Medium for Promoting Cognitive, Socio-emotional and Academic Development in Young Children*, Gaithersburg, MD: Psychosocial and Educational Publications.

Smith, P. K. (1977) 'Social and fantasy play in children', in B. Tizard and D. Harvey (eds) *The Biology of Play*, pp. 123–45, London: SIMP/Heinemann.

—— (1986) 'Exploration, play and social development in boys and girls', in D. Hargreaves and A. Colley (eds) *The Psychology of Sex Roles*, pp. 118–41, London: Harper & Row.

—— (1988) 'Children's play and its role in early development: a re-evaluation of the "play ethos"', in A. D. Pellegrini (ed.) *Psychological Bases for Early Education*, pp. 207–26, Chichester: Wiley & Sons.

Smith, P. K. and Hagan, T. (1980) 'Effects of deprivation on exercise of nursery school children', *Animal Behaviour*, 28: 922–28.

Smith, P.K., Bowers, L., Binney, V. and Cowie, H. (in press) 'Relationships of children involved in bully/victim problems at school', in S. Duck (ed.) *Understanding Relationship Processes*, vol. 2: *Learning About Relationships*. Newbury Park, CA: Sage Publications.

Takhvar, M. and Smith, P. K. (1990) 'A review and critique of Smilansky's classification scheme and the "nested hierarchy" of play categories', *Journal of Research in Childhood Education*, 4: 112–22.

Ullian, D. Z. (1976) 'The development of conceptions of masculinity and feminity', in B. B. Lloyd and J. Archer (eds) *Exploring Sex Differences*, pp. 25–47, London: Academic Press.

Chapter 3

Playful and aggressive fighting in the middle-school playground

Michael J. Boulton

During the course of my research in middle-school playgrounds over the past seven years, I observed the following two episodes of behaviour. In the first, an 11-year-old boy chased another across the playground at full speed before he caught up with him and grabbed him round the neck. The first boy manoeuvred the second boy into a bear hug, which, with the struggling of the second boy, ended up as a head lock. The boy who was restraining the other delivered a number of punches to the face of his opponent, who broke free some thirty seconds later and made good his escape by running away at full speed. In the second episode, two other 11-year-old boys stood facing each other. The smaller of the two boys poked the other with his index finger lightly, but repeatedly for some twenty seconds. The other boy used his hand to try to deflect these pokes. While he did not appear to be unduly upset by being on the receiving end of them, he did show signs that he would have liked to move away from the other boy.

Anyone experienced in supervising children of this age in the playground will not be surprised by these two descriptions. On the basis of the admittedly slim evidence presented above, one might be tempted to infer that they were descriptions of aggression, and perhaps one might feel more confident in making this assertion for the first episode than for the second. However, in the tradition of all good detective stories, I am not going to come clean at the very beginning, and will ask the reader to wait a while before revealing whether such inferences would be justified or not. My main aim in presenting these two descriptions is to introduce the notion that children's playground behaviour may appear ambivalent to those adults who are faced with supervising them in this context. This ambivalence, or rather the way in which it is resolved, would probably have implications for the way in which supervisors respond to the behaviour of the children in their care. Perhaps this would be particularly true in the case of children's rough physical interactions, as the two scenarios described above serve to illustrate. The actions of two children chasing and hitting each other could mean different things to each of the participants, and/or to other children, and/or to adult onlookers. Perhaps the most important distinction that needs to be made by all of these people would be in terms of the playful versus the aggressive motivation of the actors. A series of studies by academics over the past couple of decades, but especially in the last five years or so, have been carried out which provided evidence to suggest that most middle or junior schoolchildren do make a distinction between playful and aggressive fighting interactions. If so, and I will present some of this evidence, then perhaps the ambivalence inherent in much of children's behaviour represents a more important 'problem' for adults than for the children themselves.

Rough-and tumble play, sometimes referred to as playful fighting, is a category of behaviour that includes such actions as hitting, kicking, poking, wrestling and chasing. Nevertheless, in most cases, the actions are not carried out with the intention to hurt or upset another child. It is a common activity in infant, junior and secondary school playgrounds. It is also the case, unfortunately, that aggressive fighting occurs with worrying frequencies in these contexts as well. To a casual adult observer, rough-and-tumble play appears similar in many ways to aggressive fighting, perhaps because they both involve the same sorts of physical actions. While most if not all responsible adults would hold generally negative attitudes towards aggressive fighting and would try to discourage children from behaving in this way, it seems that adults' attitudes towards rough-and-tumble play are more mixed. At one end of the continuum, statements such as 'I don't mind the children play fighting together as long as they are careful. It gives them the chance to blow off steam and to get some exercise which a lot of them don't get anywhere else' seem to endorse the activity. At the other extreme, rough-and-tumble play is seen as essentially the same as true aggression and 'shouldn't be allowed in this school'. In this chapter I am going to discuss recent findings on children's participation in playful and aggressive fighting, similarities and differences that exist between them, and why adults may benefit from being made aware of these findings. I will also briefly discuss the developmental implications of both types of activity for children.

INCIDENCE OF ROUGH-AND-TUMBLE PLAY AND AGGRESSION IN MIDDLE CHILDHOOD

Rough-and tumble play is a fairly common activity among middle-school pupils. As a rough estimate it has been found to take up on average about 10 per cent of their free play time (Humphreys and Smith 1987). However, this global figure obscures other important findings; namely, that there are marked individual and group differences in rates of participation. In one study, I found that whereas some children never engaged in rough-and-tumble play during a forty-minute observation period, others engaged in over 130 separate episodes (Boulton 1988). My impression is that some children habitually engage in a lot of this form of play whereas others almost always refrain from participating. The reasons why these individual differences in preferences for rough-and-tumble play (and other activities) exist are far from clear at the present time, but there is evidence that both innate tendencies and patterns of upbringing are partly responsible.

Besides individual differences there are also some important group differences. In general terms, boys have been found to engage in significantly more rough-and-tumble play than girls (Humphreys and Smith 1987). There is also evidence for a decline in participation throughout the middle-school years, so age appears to be an important factor. However, it must be stressed that such group differences reflect general tendencies, and it would be unwise to make specific predictions about any given child's probable level of participation in rough-and-tumble play from only a knowledge of their age and whether they are a boy or a girl.

Fortunately, actual aggressive fighting is much less common among middle-school children than rough-and-tumble play. Nevertheless, it still represents a major problem for schools to have to deal with despite the huge amounts of effort expended by both researchers and practitioners. For example, the Elton Committee of Enquiry (DES 1989) found that one in eight out of a sample of 1,000 primary-school teachers reported aggression among pupils to be the most or the second most pressing problem they had to deal with outside of the classroom. As with rough-and-tumble play, the playground appears to be the most common location in which aggression takes place. In a recent survey of the nature and extent of bullying among a large sample of junior/middle (and secondary) school pupils, Whitney and Smith (1993) found that 76 per cent reported that they were bullied in the playground, compared to 30 per cent in the classroom and 13 per cent in the corridors.

Aggressive activities and fighting on the playground can have some important implications for both children and teaching staff. Peter Blatchford (1989) interviewed teachers about their views on playtime and misbehaviour in the playground. He found that the problems that arose in the playground often had a knock-on effect on other aspects of the school day. Teachers were aware of the time and energy that had to be deflected away from teaching activities to sort out these problems. For children too, fighting and aggression can have deleterious effects. Those on the receiving end can experience lowered self-esteem (Boulton and Underwood 1992), and one in five of the 11-year-old pupils interviewed by Blatchford *et al.* (1990) expressed worries about bullying, being beaten up, fighting and people starting trouble in the playground. On the other hand, aggressors who are not challenged may be learning to use power-assertive methods to get what they want from fellow pupils.

While evidence is accumulating about levels of fighting and aggression in the primary-school playground, who is involved, and what the most common causes of such disputes are, there are still important gaps in our knowledge. In a recent paper (Boulton 1993b), I reported the results of an interview study involving 110 8- and 11-year-old pupils. The children were asked the question 'Have you ever had a fight in the school playground in the last year?' Overall, 51 per cent responded affirmatively, and at each age, significantly more boys than girls did so. The most common reasons why they had been involved in fighting were that they had been teased (22 per cent of responses), that they had been hit or bullied and had retaliated (17 per cent), and because of a dispute over a game (10 per cent).

The reasons why children engage in rough-and-tumble play are less clear, and this issue is addressed in the next section.

WHY CHILDREN ENGAGE IN ROUGH-AND-TUMBLE PLAY

There are a number of hypotheses that try to explain why children engage in rough-and-tumble play, but none has received overwhelming support from academic studies. At the simplest level we addressed this issue by asking a group of middle-school children the direct question 'Why do you play fight with your friends?' The most common reply was that it was enjoyable and a source of fun. One might be tempted to dismiss this type of response as trivial or not well thought-out. However, I believe it is more informative than it first appears. Many human behaviours that are essential for our individual, and hence our collective, survival are enjoyable. The pleasurable nature of essential behaviours is more likely to be the product of evolutionary processes rather than mere accident. In the same way it has been argued that at some stage in our evolutionary past, participation in rough-and-tumble play provided important benefits. Consequently, mechanisms evolved to ensure that children would engage in rough-and-tumble play, and these were essentially mechanisms that meant that individuals would derive a sense of enjoyment if they did participate.

What might these benefits have been for the young of our pre-human ancestors? Several candidates have been presented, but three hypotheses have received most attention. One is known as the practice-fighting hypothesis, and it posits that rough-and-tumble play provided practice for the development of real fighting skills that would eventually be used in serious contests to decide on mating partners, on who would have access to the best food sources, and so on. A second hypothesis suggests that participation in rough-and-tumble play provides practice for the development of hunting skills, and a third that it provides practice for the development of predator avoidance skills.

Many educators of children are not sympathetic to these sorts of evolutionary hypotheses as explanations for contemporary children's behaviour. They argue, quite rightly in one respect, that the way we live our lives today is so far removed from the conditions that we faced during the course of our evolution that it no longer is the case that humans have to compete physically for the opportunity to parent children or to get food, that we no longer have to hunt, and that animal predators have all but disappeared. Nevertheless, this view is based on an incomplete understanding of the theory of evolution. According to evolutionary theory, behaviour which in previous generations provided important benefits but which no longer does so will eventually disappear, but this will take many, many generations. An example from the world of animal behaviour may illustrate this point with more force. Many dog owners will be familiar with the tendency of their pets to circle round two or three times prior to lying down to sleep. This behaviour is thought to have been beneficial in the past because it helped to trample down foliage and make a more comfortable place for the animal to sleep. Obviously, domestic dogs that sleep inside houses or kennels do not have to perform this behaviour, and in a sense it is a waste of energy because there is no foliage to trample down. However, the fact that they still do so illustrates that some behaviours may still occur even though they are no longer beneficial.

This line of thought, partly based on evolutionary thinking, has implications for children's rough-and-tumble play and the way in which adults may realistically respond to it. It suggests that there may be an innate basis for participation in rough-and-tumble play and hence that it may be very difficult for schools and parents to try to impose a complete ban. This sort of reasoning is also supported indirectly by the fact that rough-and-tumble play has been observed in a wide variety of different cultures and countries, some very different from our own. These include Japan, the Philippines, Mexico, Africa, India, America and Australia (see Humphreys and Smith 1984). It therefore appears that rough-and-tumble play is a so-called 'human universal', and as such it is likely to have an innate basis.

Evolutionary theory is also used by some to explain the tendency for boys to engage in more rough-and-tumble play than girls. Nevertheless, it is also likely that the actual form of rough-and-tumble play engaged in by children is shaped by patterns of upbringing and exposure to certain patterns of behaviour in the media and elsewhere. For example, I have observed many children in British schools engage in rough-and-tumble play with elements of martial arts, such as karate-type kicks and chops. It would seem that these children are imitating the actions of characters they see in television programmes and feature films, a view that is endorsed by their verbal accounts in interviews. In contrast, children in some hunter-gatherer societies in Africa have been found to be more likely to incorporate the use of spears into their rough-and-tumble play, suggesting that they are imitating the actions of their elders.

EVIDENCE FOR A DISTINCTION BETWEEN ROUGH-AND-TUMBLE PLAY AND AGGRESSION IN CHILDHOOD

There is a growing body of evidence that rough-and-tumble play and aggression should be seen as distinct categories of behaviour for most children (Aldis 1975; Boulton 1991; Fry 1987; Pellegrini 1987; Smith and Boulton 1990). Some of the earliest studies were carried out with pre-school children, and sought to identify criteria upon which a distinction could be made. Many investigators focused on facial expressions, and a consistent finding was that laughter, smiling and the so-called relaxed, open-mouthed 'play face' were all features of rough-and-tumble play. In contrast, aggression was much more likely to involve such things as frowns, grimaces and bared-teeth facial expressions. Clearly, adults might benefit from using facial expressions to help them decide whether children are playing together or are actually having an aggressive fight. However, I would like to sound a note of caution about relying too heavily on facial expressions. I have observed many episodes which were clearly playful (that is, the participants themselves said so when asked) but which involved negative facial expressions such as frowns. In most of these cases, the negative facial expressions appeared to reflect fantasy themes that are often part of the rough-and-tumble encounters of young children. Similarly, during some episodes of bullying I have witnessed smiling on the part of the perpetrators, tempting me to suppose that they were receiving some sadistic pleasure from the encounter.

Several researchers have also used the outcome of bouts to make a distinction between rough-and-tumble play and aggression (McGrew 1972; Aldis 1975; Humphreys and Smith 1987). Play encounters are seen as being characterised by partners remaining together after the bout is over, whereas aggression usually involves participants moving away from one another when it ends.

Smith and Lewis (1985) extended these investigations by combining the use of these two important criteria. They observed pre-school children in free-play situations and recorded both facial expressions and the outcome of episodes. Almost half of the episodes were positive on both criteria, about a quarter were positive on one criterion and neutral on the other, and about a tenth were negative on both criteria or negative on one and neutral on the other.

Further evidence for a distinction between playful and aggressive fighting comes from questioning children who have watched both forms of behaviour on videotape. Smith and Lewis (1985) carried out individual interviews with eight nursery-school children and two adults as they were being shown discrete episodes of behaviour recorded on videotape. After viewing each episode, which either showed children engaging in rough-

and-tumble play or aggressive fighting, the participants were asked to indicate whether they thought the episode involved playful or aggressive behaviour, and also why they had arrived at their decision. The latter responses were collated into a number of categories. Both of the adults and six of the children showed significant agreement about whether the episodes were playful or aggressive. Almost half of the reasons given by the children as the basis for their discriminations were based on the physical actions of the participants. In over a third of cases they were unable to give a reason, perhaps because of poor powers of expression, or even boredom with the 'game' they were being asked to play. I used a similar technique with 8- and 11-year-old pupils, and obtained results comparable in many respects.

Although the video technique has yielded some useful data, it is limited in a number of important ways. The judgements of the children will be influenced by the nature of the episodes shown. In some episodes, for example, facial expressions may not be very clear, so that the children would be forced to pay attention to, and report using, alternative features of the episode when deciding upon the playful or aggressive nature of such episodes. A complementary technique is to interview children. In one such study (Smith and Boulton 1990) about 90 per cent of children aged 8 to 10 indicated that they could tell the difference between rough-and-tumble play and aggression, and the most frequent reasons for making this decision were the presence of laughter or crying (20 per cent), the presence or absence of a specific action (18 per cent), facial expressions (17 per cent), the force of a blow or kick (15 per cent), verbal expressions accompanying the actions (11 per cent), causing a partner pain or injury (8 per cent), outcome (4 per cent), and actions of onlookers (3 per cent). Data obtained in this way suggest that facial and vocal expressions are more widely used as a basis for judging real-life situations than it would appear from the videotape studies.

Based on the research evidence presented in this section, and the previous one, it would appear that for many children, and especially boys, participation in rough-and-tumble play is to a large extent natural, and a source of pleasure. It does not appear that rough-and-tumble play is motivated by the same desire to inflict hurt or distress that characterises serious aggression. Nevertheless, it would be wrong to conclude that there are no links between the two categories of behaviour, either in the short term or over the longer period of children's development. Hence it is necessary for those concerned with the education, development and well-being of children to consider what the implications of encouraging, tolerating or banning this type of play is for them. This issue is addressed in the next section.

LINKS BETWEEN ROUGH-AND-TUMBLE PLAY AND AGGRESSION

In some schools in the United Kingdom, and among some parents, rough-and-tumble play is discouraged or even banned because it is thought that it leads to an increased risk of accidental injury which would precipitate an aggressive retaliation and hence fighting. Certainly, rough-and-tumble play can be a vigorous activity on some occasions, but data from a number of sources seem to indicate that banning it may be an over-reaction on the part of schools and parents. In a recent study, I observed seventy-nine fights on middle-school playgrounds and categorised the causes of each one (Boulton 1993b). A small but noteworthy proportion of these aggressive interactions (14 per cent) were caused when a playful 'assault' received an aggressive retaliation. However, it is not clear what proportion of the aggressive retaliations occurred because of an accidental injury *per se*. They may have been made for another reason, such as cheating or honest mistakes about the intentions of the original actor (see below). In this study, I examined the causes of a further forty-eight playground fights. Seven of these were caused by accidental injury, but on closer scrutiny I found that in only one case did the injury occur in the context of rough-and-tumble play. Thus, the weight of evidence goes against the popular view that participation in rough-and-tumble play elevates levels of aggression as a consequence of accidental injury, although on a few occasions this link may exist.

However, some forms of rough-and-tumble play may be more of a problem in this respect than others. For example, the World Wrestling Federation programme on television appears to be very popular with children. Many of them appear to copy the moves they have seen in their own playgrounds, despite warnings by the programme makers of the risks of doing so. Jeremy Rowe of De Beauvoir School in Hackney, North London, was disturbed by the number of injuries arising in the playground out of moves such as head-locks and body slams. He said, 'No serious injuries have occurred but I am concerned about the dangers of acting out wrestling moves' (reported in the *Daily Express*, 31 October 1992). If this trend was widespread, then there would be a much stronger case for banning actions of this particular type, and perhaps this would be a more realistic response than a blanket ban on all types of rough-and-tumble play.

Another reason why rough-and-tumble play and aggression might be linked in the short term is because of deliberate cheating. Participation in rough-and-tumble play appears to require an adherence to a number of implicit rules, guiding such things as how hard one may strike an 'opponent', and the need for participants to exchange roles (Smith and Boulton 1990). As with all rule-governed behaviour, individuals might abuse the system and 'cheat' in order to benefit in some way. Smith and Boulton suggested that, 'even though most [rough-and-tumble play] bouts... are... motivationally straightforward... some bouts or invitations to bouts, involving some children some of the time, might be deliberately used to inflict hurt or maintain, improve, or display dominant status' (1990: 280). Such a view, it must be said, has yet to be systematically tested, but my own impression, based on many hours of observation of rough-and-tumble play in naturalistic settings, is that such a tactic is not common among children.

Another scenario underlying a possible link in the short term between rough-and-tumble play and aggression involves the social skills that regulate children's interactions. As we saw earlier, most children are adept at distinguishing between the two types of behaviour. However, a growing body of evidence also suggests that a minority will have problems. At the primary-school level, Sluckin argued that 'undoubtedly a certain number of children... fail to distinguish and react appropriately to rough and tumble (pretend) and real aggression' (1981: 40). I have also found that a small but noteworthy proportion of 8- and 11-year-old middle-school pupils were relatively poor at making this distinction. In the United States, Pellegrini (1989) found evidence to support the view that poor decoding skills in this domain are associated with elevated levels of aggression and low popularity with peers. Pellegrini examined the transitional probabilities of rough-and-tumble play leading into other activities. Playground encounters that involved children who were poor at making the distinction between play and aggression, and who tended to be unpopular with their peers, were more likely to turn into aggression, whereas those of children who were skilled in this area, and who tended to be popular with their peers, were more likely to turn directly into games with rules.

This sort of evidence suggests that in some individuals, the social skills which normally ensure that rough-and-tumble play bouts *remain* playful are in some way 'faulty', and this may contribute to their becoming aggressive members of their peer group. This in turn has some disturbing implications for the longer-term development of these children. Some research evidence suggests that once a child has acquired a reputation for being aggressive, this is very resistant to change even if the individual learns to regulate their behaviour in the future. Peers continue to interact with the child as if they were still aggressive, and this in turn may lead to a re-emergence of aggressive tendencies in the individual. Thus, an inability to decode playful intent correctly may, in the long run, contribute to the development of aggressive behavioural tendencies.

An important question therefore is, where do these social skills come from? Abilities in this domain could be largely independent of actual experience, suggesting that they are inborn. Alternatively, these skills may be dependent to some extent on children's experiences of rough-and-tumble play and/or aggression. Perhaps the most likely explanation is that both innate factors and social factors are important. A study that examines these issues in younger pupils is clearly warranted, not least because it could be that by banning children from engaging in rough-and-tumble play we could be taking away opportunities for them to develop social skills that allow them to differentiate between playful and serious aggression. These would be important skills both during childhood as well as during adulthood.

The weight of evidence discussed above suggests that rough-and-tumble play and aggression are not closely related during childhood for most individuals, although they may be in a minority of cases in which faulty social skills or the tendency to cheat are present. What about the possibility that by engaging in rough-and-tumble play, children are somehow 'made more aggressive', and that this tendency to be aggressive will remain with them as they progress into adulthood if it is not challenged? Gergen recently discussed this idea, and she stated that

> we might anticipate that the use of physical means of expressing one's feelings and of gaining instrumental and affiliative goals becomes a well-established 'script' for many children; later this script lends itself to actions in other circumstances, either friendly or provocative. Thus, for example, a boy who often wrestles and punches his brothers in fun may more easily use the same response in less friendly circumstances than a boy who does not do so.
>
> (1990: 383)

However, there is no direct evidence to support such a view. Moreover, the fascinating work of Doug Fry (1988) among Zapotec communities of Mexico suggests that it is the levels of aggression among *adults* that may be more likely to influence the behaviour of children, including their participation in rough-and-tumble play, rather than the other way round. Fry found that both rates of aggressive fighting and rates of playful fighting among Zapotec children were significantly higher in a community with relatively high rates of adult aggression than in a community with relatively low rates of adult aggression. He suggested that participation in rough-and-tumble play might provide practice in the fighting skills that are sometimes used in hand-to-hand fighting among adults. Fry concluded that,

> patterns of aggressive and prosocial behaviors are being passed on from one generation to the next, as the children learn to engage in different behavioral patterns that are modelled and accepted by adults in their respective community.... It would seem that the learning of aggressive and prosocial behaviors begins at an early age among the Zapotecs
>
> (1988: 1017)

This line of reasoning seems intuitively plausible to me, and it suggests that rather than making children more aggressive, some forms of rough-and-tumble play are akin to a barometer indicating the levels of aggression which characterise adult society.

ADULTS' ABILITIES TO DISTINGUISH BETWEEN ROUGH-AND-TUMBLE PLAY AND AGGRESSION: IMPLICATIONS FOR PLAYGROUND SUPERVISION

As we have already discussed, aggression represents one of the most pervasive and difficult problems for schools to overcome. One hurdle to achieving success may be, ironically, how to identify aggression when it takes place, or more specifically how adults might have problems distinguishing between playful and aggressive fighting. Some of the ways in which adults might benefit in this respect were presented in previous sections, but is there any objective evidence to show how good or, conversely, how poor adults might be at making such a distinction? Relatively little attention has been directed at formally assessing adults' skills in this domain, despite the importance of the observer in deciding what is considered aggressive behaviour.

Connor (1989) prepared an edited videotape of fourteen episodes showing 4- and 5-year-olds interacting with one of three sets of toys and in groups of three individuals. All of the episodes were selected because they satisfied the criteria for aggression used in previous studies. The videotape was shown to the three pre-school teachers of the children, and they were asked to state whether they thought each episode was playful or aggressive. All three adults perceived every episode to be aggressive. The videotape was then shown to a larger sample of introductory psychology students and students on an Early Childhood education programme, both males and females, and they too were asked to state if they thought each episode was playful or aggressive. Two striking results were obtained: females saw significantly more episodes as aggressive than did males; and those females who reported that they had played with war toys when they were children saw significantly fewer episodes as aggressive than females who reported that they had never played with war toys.

I recently carried out a similar study with a sample of forty-four British adults (Boulton 1993a). All but three of the adults made some errors when categorising nineteen ambivalent episodes, with the average being two and a half. Thus, for more than one in ten episodes, adults could be thought of as making a mistake. Given that children spend noteworthy amounts of their time in the playground in play-fighting activities and that aggressive fighting, although taking up much less time, is still a feature of the typical middle-school playground, this could be a cause for concern. Children are usually supervised in the playground by either teachers or lunch-time supervisors, and neither group is explicitly trained in how to distinguish between playful and aggressive fighting.

My research also revealed a significant interaction between the sex of the person viewing the episode and the type of error most commonly made. Adult males were more likely mistakenly to view aggressive episodes as playful than they were mistakenly to view playful episodes as aggressive, and the opposite was the case among the adult females. The robustness of this result is endorsed by the finding of Connor (1989) that adult females saw significantly more potentially ambivalent episodes involving pre-schoolers as aggressive than did adult males. Connor also provided evidence to suggest that this propensity to view ambivalent episodes as aggressive by adult females may be *increased* when the individual actually works with children on a regular basis. She imputed this tendency to 'concerns that children will get out of control or will hurt each other' (1989: 215).

Given that playground supervisors are almost always female, what are the implications of these results for the way in which children are super-vised in schools? Perhaps the tendency to err on the side of caution (that is, by having a 'readiness' to view ambivalent episodes as aggressive) is the 'least serious' type of mistake that could be made by supervisors of children in the playground. In the short term, it would be better for an adult to step in to halt an instance of playful fighting that was mistakenly construed as aggressive than to refrain from intervening in an instance of aggression because it was mistakenly perceived to be playful. Nevertheless, there may be some other, less beneficial implications of this course of action. Super-visors are often in charge of large numbers of children in the playground and the ratio may exceed one to fifty. Thus, by focusing on 'innocent' activities such as playful fighting, their attention might be diverted away from more obvious cases of aggression. Moreover, some psychologists have suggested that participation in friendly rough-and-tumble play may be beneficial for some children in a variety of ways. For example, Pellegrini (1987) proposed that playful fighting is characterised by the swapping of roles, and hence may facilitate the development of turn-taking skills. Simi-larly, I have suggested that playful fighting and associated activities may serve an affiliative function by promoting and enhancing friendships. If these and other suggestions are valid, then it would be more serious for playground supervisors, and other adults who mistakenly attribute hostile intent to cases of play fighting, to stop children from engaging in these activities. Clearly, more research is warranted on the issue of the develop-mental and educational significance of children's playful fighting and associated activities.

Why are (some) adults poor at distinguishing between playful and aggressive fighting? We might speculate that preconceived ideas could cloud some of our judgements. For example, an individual who does not accept that any 'fighting' can be playful is almost certainly going to infer that an episode of rough-and-tumble play is aggressive, whereas another individual who participated in rough-and-tumble play as a child and received pleasure from doing so may be more likely to infer that an aggressive episode was playful. Another reason for mistakes among adults is suggested by an examination of the actual process of making an inference about the aggressive versus the playful nature of an episode. For example, I have found that children are significantly more likely than adults to rely on the physical actions of the participants, but significantly less likely to use inferences about action or intent and facial expressions. Thus, adults who actually supervise children in the playground and elsewhere could be encouraged to avoid making subjective inferences about the actions or intentions of children, and instead to pay attention to more 'concrete' criteria, such as the nature of the physical actions.

CONCLUSION

In conclusion, playful and aggressive fighting occur with some regularity on the middle-school playground. For most children, the former appears to be a friendly and pleasurable activity. In the majority of cases, playful fighting is unlikely to be closely linked to aggression, but this may be the case for a minority of individuals and/or for some specific forms of rough-and-tumble play. On the whole, it appears that adults are likely to make mistakes when they try to distinguish between playful and aggressive fighting but skill in this domain could be improved with practice. Finally, the aim of this discussion is not to leave the reader with the impression that all instances of behaviour that look aggressive are in fact playfully motivated, and hence that adults should refrain from stepping in to break them up. Clearly, there are many instances in which children do intend to hurt other pupils. What I am advocating is that both children and adults may benefit from recognising the distinction between playful and aggressive fighting.

Thus, to return to the two behavioural descriptions presented at the beginning of this chapter, according to the participants themselves the former was playful but the latter was an instance of aggressive bullying. Perhaps with the benefit of the information presented here, the lunchtime supervisor on playground duty at the time might not have stepped in to halt the former and might not have simply ignored the latter. I am currently designing a programme intended to help reduce this type of mistake, and will report on its efficacy in the near future.

REFERENCES

Aldis, O. (1975) *Playfighting*, New York: Academic Press.
Blatchford, P. (1989) *Playtime in the Primary School: Problems and Improvements*, Windsor: NFER-Nelson.

Blatchford, P., Creeser, R. and Mooney, A. (1990) 'Playground games and playtime: the children's view'. *Educational Research*, 32: 163–74.

Boulton, M. J. (1988) 'A multi methodological investigation of middle school children's rough and tumble play, aggression and social relationships', Doctoral dissertation, University of Sheffield.

—— (1991) 'A comparison of structural and contextual features of middle school children's playful and aggressive fighting', *Ethology and Sociobiology*, 12: 119–45.

—— (1993a) 'A comparison of adult's and children's abilities to distinguish between aggressive and playful fighting in middle school pupils: implications for playground supervision and behaviour management', *Education Studies*, 19: 193–203.

—— (1993b) 'Approximate causes of aggressive fighting in middle school children', *British Journal of Educational Psychology*, 63: 231–44.

Boulton, M. J. and Underwood, K. (1992) 'Bully/victim problems among middle school children', *British Journal of Educational Psychology*, 62: 73–87.

Connor, K. (1989) 'Aggression: is it in the eye of the beholder?' *Play and Culture*, 2: 213–17.

Department of Education and Science (DES) (1989) *Discipline in Schools*, Report of the Committee of Enquiry chaired by Lord Elton, London: HMSO.

Fry, D. (1987) 'Differences between playfighting and serious fighting among Zapotec children', *Ethology and Sociobiology*, 8: 285–306.

—— (1988) 'Intercommunity differences in aggression among Zapotec children', *Child Development*, 59: 1008–19.

Gergen, M. (1990) 'Beyond the evil empire: horseplay and aggression', *Aggressive Behaviour*, 16: 381–98.

Humphreys, A. and Smith, P. K., (1984) 'Rough-and-tumble play in preschool and playground', in P. K. Smith (ed.) *Play in Animals and Humans*, pp. 241–66, Oxford: Blackwell.

—— (1987) 'Rough and tumble, friendship, and dominance in school children: evidence for continuity and change with age', *Child Development*, 58: 201–12.

McGrew, W. C. (1972) *An Ethological Study of Children's Behaviour*, London: Academic Press.

Pellegrini, A. D. (1987) 'Rough and tumble play: developmental and educational significance', *Educational Psychologist*, 22: 23–43.

—— (1989) 'What is a category? The case of rough and tumble play', *Ethology and Sociobiology*, 10: 331–41.

Sluckin, A. (1981) *Growing Up in the Playground: The Social Development of Children*, London: Routledge & Kegan Paul.

Smith, P. K. and Boulton, M. J. (1990) 'Rough and tumble play, aggression and dominance: perception and behaviour in children's encounters', *Human Development*, 33: 271–82.

Smith, P. K. and Lewis, K. (1985) 'Rough and tumble play, fighting and chasing in nursery school children', *Ethology and Sociobiology*, 6: 175–81.

Whitney, I. and Smith, P. K. (1993) 'A survey of the nature and extent of bullying in junior/middle and secondary schools, *Educational Research*, 35 (1): 3–25.

Chapter 4

Racism and sexism in the playground

Elinor Kelly

PLAYGROUNDS AS SITES FOR SOCIAL LEARNING

The word 'playground' is one which invites reflection. 'Play' is a complex notion. It is associated on the one hand with fun, romping, teasing and intricate rituals of behaviour which have been observed in animals and humans all over the world. On the other, it is associated also with danger – the moments when play spills beyond the confines of fun into something more challenging, the growl which becomes a bite, the cuff which lands as a punch, the songs which sharpen into screams. 'Ground' conjures up a sense of space, the equivalent of a field – open, but bounded; free, but constrained. Once we pause to reflect, we realise that we know little about the meaning of 'playground' within schools, and that we are very ignorant about the ways in which pupils use this space to explore the intricacies of the positive and negative in human relations. The word 'playground' is full of contradiction and paradox, and the behaviour of pupils must be closely observed if we are to learn what is *actually* going on, and to engage with pupils in solving the problems which arise.

It is important to connect pupil behaviour in the playground with the school itself. Most school playgrounds are bleak sites – empty spaces between buildings and perimeter walls which do not invite or encourage creative play and which lower the spirits until filled with the noise and bustle of children released from the classroom. As Blatchford (1989) has pointed out, this is precisely the basis on which playgrounds were first created – space in which pupils could be encouraged to engage in some physical exertion and to breathe some outside air. Whatever the weather, children should have some exercise, and the fact that they play was incidental to the purpose. If one were to be precise, a more accurate description of the space used in this way would be 'break-ground'.

The fascination of a playground is the potential it provides for study of the ways in which pupils use the space not just to release pent-up energy but also to interact with one another. In the course of this interaction, they are responding not only to their peers, but also to their environment, reacting, as it were, to the resources and constraints which are unique to 'school'. After all, where else do children encounter such a cross-section of society and learn so much about the ways in which hierarchies of prestige, status and authority operate? In the playground pupils develop their ethos, their responses to conflict and their hierarchies. Playgrounds are sites for social learning – of the negative as well as the positive in human relations, and the negative can overwhelm if pupils receive no guidance. For instance, if conflict is left unresolved, pupils have learnt nothing about defensive skills or about how to change or counter behaviour which is making them unhappy.

Any passer-by peering through the railings or over the wall can see that social learning in the playground is intense. Also evident, especially to the eye of the observer, wise to the complexities of culture, is the 'ecology of power' which manifests itself in the domination of space by some, while others are sidelined, and in the 'play fighting' which can also be bullying or harassment. Moreover, anyone listening to the noise of children is certain to hear the name calling which may involve joking but could also be 'cussing'. If pupils are engaged in social learning, then we can be sure that they are dealing with differences of social class, gender, race, physical and intellectual abilities; how to decide what is acceptable and unacceptable in the behaviour of others; how to deal with those who 'do not fit in'. If left to their own devices, they often order their world into hierarchical patterns of domination, subordination and marginality.

In such a context racism and sexism can thrive. Girls can be isolated and humiliated by being called 'slut'; boys picked out as 'poofters' can become pariah figures; black pupils can be called racist names. Are these occasional happenings to which schools should respond as and when incidents arise? Do they demand nothing more than crisis intervention? Should schools develop a radically different perspective on playground behaviour? If schools do focus on sexism and racism, will they kill the fun and pleasure which is an integral part of play?

Recently, some important studies have been carried out which deal with both the positive and the negative in child play and which locate the interpretation of behaviour in the vernacular of the players themselves (Cohen, forthcoming; Troyna and Hatcher 1992). These studies have been informed by what we can summarise as being 'equal opportunities' perspectives; concerned not with just racism or sexism or any other of the 'isms' but with how pupils deal with matters of justice/injustice, equality/ inequality and how they thread their ways through the complexities of interpersonal and inter-group relations. They lead us towards asking some key questions: how and when to distinguish between joking and cussing; how to clarify the difference between the impersonal abuse which becomes harassment and the personal victimising which is distinctive of much bullying. This is no easy task because it is in the interests of some pupils to

ensure that their activities are obscured by a noisy and confusing cacophony. None the less, it is also essential if schools are to become more
proficient in working with pupils to develop their social skills and their
abilities to deal with the conflicts which are as endemic in everyday life as
teasing and joking.

BULLYING AND HARASSMENT

Two fields of study have created a sense of urgency in opening playgrounds
to scrutiny and in raising questions about the 'innocence' of children's play.
One is 'bullying' – a term which is now used so openly and frequently that
it is easy to forget how recently it was brought out of the closet. For many
generations, bullying was a dark, hidden secret which brought intense fear
and pain, not least because it could not be resolved but had to be endured.
In the late 1980s bullying leapt into media headlines and onto school
agendas with great speed. In part this is because some of the most serious
cases have resulted in serious injury or even death. But the highlighting of
the issue is also the consquence of media backing for parent campaigns to
make schools safer places for their children (Kelly 1993).

One study after another has found that at least 10–30 per cent of pupils
have been affected (Besag 1989, 1992; Boulton 1992; Mooney et al. 1991;
Roland and Munthe 1989; Tattum and Lane 1989; Whitney and Smith 1993).

However, there are some assumptions in these studies which need to be
questioned. There is a tendency to look for psychological explanations of
bullying abstracted from the context of the school in which the participants
actually meet and socialise. There is also a tendency to assume that bullying
is a chance, random phenomenon which could involve anyone. Therefore
there is little discussion of the fact that certain categories of pupils actually
may be more at risk than others. A recent study which includes an ethnic
breakdown of statistics about bullying (Wolverhampton Safer Cities Project 1991) reveals that Asian and Afro-Caribbean pupils experience
considerably more comments about their skin colour than white pupils.

The distinction between harassment and bullying, as we shall see
shortly, is often blurred, not least by children who use the word 'bullying'
to describe many forms of abuse which they experience or witness among
themselves. None the less, it is important to be aware that the two forms of
behaviour are not the same, and that they have different implications when
it comes to policy and practice.

The question then becomes 'How to begin?' In discussion with pupils
and teachers, I have found that a useful starting point is to develop working
definitions which point out the differences between bullying and harassment as two forms of abusive behaviour which can appear to be the same,
but which have very different meaning for the participants and which,
consequently, demand different responses.

> Bullying causes deep pain because it comprises an intensely 'personal' mistreatment, usually of individuals by means of secret, calculated and often prolonged forms of abuse. The victims are isolated and instructed in helplessness. The bullies learn and practise distorted interpersonal skills. Bullies and victims are locked into relations of dominance and subordination, intimidation and threat. The observers collude in the submission of the victims and the gratification of the bullies.
>
> (Kelly 1993: 146)

The key elements in bullying are the references to 'personal' and 'distorted social skills'. One of the most powerful and evocative acccounts of bullying is given by Margaret Atwood in her novel *Cat's Eye* (1990). She paints a remarkable and instantly recognisable picture of the ways in which four children become locked into a relationship which is fascinating and compulsive to all parties concerned – the bully, her victim and the bully's acolytes. They all keep the secret, and the relationship is only broken after the victim has been led into a situation of real danger. The memory of the bullying endures. When her daughters approach the same age, the former victim looks anxiously for any sign that the same might be happening to them.

This interpersonal locking and particular form of fearful engagement is unique to bullying. However, harassment is essentially a different form of behaviour.

> Harassment causes deep pain because it involves 'impersonal, unreciprocated and unwelcome physical contact, comment, suggestion, joke, attention. The mistreatment is offensive to the person/s concerned and causes the victim/s to feel threatened, humiliated, patronised, embarassed; it dehumanises, makes objects of the victim/s. The harassers base their mistreatment on notions of 'normality' – a normality which is hierarchical and which legitimates mistreatment of those who are different, and therefore not equal.
>
> (Kelly 1993: 150).

In other words, harassment is distinguished by the fact that it can be legitimated by reference to an ethos which supports hierarchies of dominance, exclusion and mistreatment of those who are made into objects of mistrust, dislike, even hatred. Harassment is also tied in with group dynamics – the bonding of the in-group, the disarray of the out-group; and with the social world outside the school in which the same values thrive.

RACIST HARASSMENT

Since 1981, racist harassment has been publicly and officially acknowledged as a deeply serious issue which corrodes the quality of life for many citizens who experience everyday abuse and are at risk of random attacks. The Home Office estimates that Asian and black people are far more likely than white people to be the victims of racial attacks and that the scale of 'minor' incidents such as spitting and verbal abuse is seriously damaging the quality of life for members of ethnic minority communities.

What distinguishes racist attacks and abuse and makes them so deeply serious? In their interdepartmental report, the government states that 'racial motivation can transfer even an apparently trivial incident into something that is more than usually distressing and frightening' (Home Office 1989: para. 12). In their view, there is no easy way of defining 'racial incidents' other than by relying on the context in which the incident occurs and by giving priority to the victims' perception of motivation (para. 14). The approach they recommend has been adopted by police forces throughout Britain and by many other public services and local government departments (see, for instance, Strathclyde Regional Council 1990).

The risk of racist abuse or attack is just as high in mainly white as in multi-racial areas. In a region such as Strathclyde where 98.4 per cent of the population is white, a number of local studies have been carried out, and they underline the scale of the misery inflicted. For instance, in a 1986 survey carried out in Glasgow, 49 per cent of Pakistanis and 55 per cent of Indians reported damage to their property; over 80 per cent had experienced racial abuse; 18 per cent of Pakistanis and 22 per cent of Indians had experienced physical attacks (Scottish Ethnic Minorities Research Unit).

This has profound implications for schools. If this is what life is like for black people in Britain today, are schools doing anything either to work towards enabling black people to defend themselves better, or towards white people being less inclined to harass and torment? Even more immediately, if this is what is happening out on the streets, is anything similar going on in and around the schools themselves?

It is now known that racist name calling is common (if not endemic) in the joking, teasing and bullying vocabulary of children, but also that school action on name calling can ease the situation. Learning to deal with the differences between joking and cussing, and between 'cold' and 'hot' calling leads into greater awareness of the complex ways in which racism is knit into the cultures of children and young people (Commission for Racial Equality 1988; Troyna and Hatcher 1992).

Above all, it is in the playground that pupils learn and enact the verbal and social vocabulary of racism and anti-racism: replaying the elaborate games of domination; handling the visibility factor of skin colour; discussing or acting out television games and stories. There is a host of rituals which state and restate the social order into which pupils are inducting one another. Cohen, and Troyna and Hatcher, have carried out the most detailed studies to date and, in their different ways, emphasise the contradictory and sometimes conflicting elements which are being developed by primary-school pupils and how confused they can become if deprived of reinforcement of what is just and fair, and of explanation of what is unjust and why. Both studies established proof of the efficacy of school policies in reducing anxiety, conflict and victimisation.

SEXIST HARASSMENT

Nothing like the same political concern has been expressed about sexist harassment, although many of the same arguments apply. Few girls leave school without experience of sexist name calling by other pupils and teachers; some girls are picked out for particular forms of sexist abuse which isolate and humiliate them in ways which are excruciatingly painful. Every teacher knows what can happen to the boy who is picked out as the 'poofter' or 'wimp' who can be teased, jostled and goaded mercilessly. And yet, how many schools are giving pupils the opportunity to identify and dismantle hierarchies of sexist abuse?

Among girls the most offensive sexist terms – 'slag', 'slut', 'pro' – all imply breaches of the current sexual norms; these breaches bring them disgrace unless they can brave out the accusations with defiance. Cussing in these terms is not teasing because the girls who are targeted feel trapped and victimised. 'It's a vicious circle. If you don't go with them, then they'll call you a tight bitch. If you go with them, they'll call you a slag afterwards' (Lees 1986: 37). Girls are seen primarily in terms of their sexual reputations rather than in terms of their personalities, and they are policed not only by the dominant boys but also by other girls who use this vocabulary. The victim becomes trapped in a definition which she cannot prove or disprove and which reduces her to the status of pariah.

In male vocabulary there is nothing equivalent. Sexual prowess is to be noisily celebrated. The only occasion on which they sexualise another boy is if his masculinity can be threatened. The wimp, the poofter, is not picked out as frequently as the slags, but when he is, the effect is deadly. He is reduced to lowly pariah status; if the cussing persists he becomes vulnerable to other forms of abuse.

Much sexist harassment occurs under the cloak of 'normality'. In co-educational schools, it is so common for boys to dominate physically and verbally, and to demand and to receive more attention from teachers, that it is taken for granted. For the boys, teacher attentiveness may have contradictory effects, because they are both rewarded and punished more frequently. For girls, it often amounts to consistent neglect.

This neglect has social consequences. Away from the supervision of teachers – for instance, in the playground – the boys' behaviour can become more extreme. Girls tell of learning to avoid groups of boys because of the risk of 'sexually appraising looks, many types of threatening gestures, boys holding their noses when girls passed... and pretending to talk about them in a very obvious way' (Mahony 1985: 36). Girls who could compare a coeducational school with their previous experience of a girls' school describe their shock and consternation when they realise that such behaviour on the part of boys is not confined to the extremist few, but is 'normal'. One response is to adopt tactics of avoidance.

In the absence of positive alternative approaches what develops is a form of harassment in which girls are kept in their place by boys. Some teachers actively collude in the process, encouraging masculine domination and male group bonding. Others ignore what is going on, or, when the girls complain, they trivialise the incidents as being minor and exceptional.

GIRLS' VIEWS ABOUT THE PLAYGROUND

While drafting this chapter I discussed the playground with three young girls, each in coeducational schools in different authorities. Helen, Tess (both aged 10) and Jenny (aged 8) are observant and generous, concerned not only about their own enjoyment but also about what happens to others. I began each conversation with the question, 'If I say the word "playground" to you, what do you think about?' Their replies revealed radical differences between school policies and the impact of these school policies on their play opportunities. Helen focused immediately on the ways in which boys and football dominated her space and play. Tess spoke about how much she enjoyed playing the ball game Four Square, and Jenny told me how she and her friend Lorna 'spy on the boys'.

Helen's school does not appear to have developed a positive playground policy. The space is a bleak site, without climbing frame, swings or other play resources, supervised by the dinner ladies and, says Helen, 'if you go to the dinner lady, she says not to bother and she doesn't do anything'. The playground has lines drawn out for Four Square and for football, and people used to play netball, but now hard balls are forbidden. However, Helen has problems trying to play what she wants. Why are there problems?

> Football dominates. If we want to play a quiet game, the balls come bouncing into the middle of us. The boys are very boisterous, they get annoyed if their ball is kicked. Most of the time I play Four Square instead of football. This is a good game because it is not boisterous but even then the boys run through with their football. If the girls play football, the boys get annoyed. If the boys join in the game of Four Square, then it quickly becomes boys versus girls.

Things do not seem to be happy in her playground. She has tried to join in the football, but is only put in goal because the boys think the girls are not so good. She does not like the atmosphere of tension between the boys and girls – the boys dominate and the girls let them because the boys are stronger and the girls get frightened. The boys think they have got power. Sometimes the girls retreat to girl-only games for protection, but then the boys interfere. Helen wishes that the girls and boys could agree more but cannot see how this could be achieved. She wishes there were more apparatus and things to do in the playground, but she does not trust the teachers or the dinner ladies to do things well.

Unknown to herself, she did actually reveal something of what might be the way forward in her school when she told me that from time to time the headteacher has a ban on balls. 'When that is on, we play different games – like "Had" – which is a game where children run and catch someone who is "on" – then boys and girls play together.' In other words, banning the one game which takes up more space than any other and which is dominated by boys liberates all the children into mixed-sex running games.

In Tess's school, there is a total ban on kicking balls – hence no football. Moreover, the playground has extra facilities – a climbing frame with ropes and swings – and the teachers take turns in a roster not just to intervene when things go wrong, but also to assist the flow of play; for instance, they ring a bell when a child's turn on the swings has ended. The end result is that there is greater choice in play. Like Helen, Tess's favourite game is Four Square, and she is able to play it whenever she wants, with boys and girls, and with children from different years. 'Girls and boys play it together. It is quite popular in school for people from class four downwards. We also play handball and with basket hoops, and hopscotch.' There seems to be none of the tension of which Helen spoke. Tess referred only to one small group of boys who tease others, and most of the younger children mix together.

This association between choice in play and school playground policy is confirmed also in Jenny's school, where the emphasis has been on improving the facilities: 'I think my playground is good – it has the climbing frame, the garden, the fences, the little wall where we can sit down. It is interesting.' The 'very big juniors' play football, but there is still space for the other children to play. Indeed, Jenny and her friend Lorna enjoy 'spying on the boys' behind the shed, through the climbing frame, and saying 'boo' to the juniors so as to 'jump on them and scare them'. Interestingly, she does not know the game of Four-Square; it has not been marked out in her playground. Most of her play is focused on the climbing frame and on 'spying on Philip, a boy who everybody loves', so she does not mind the fact that football is being played, or that only one girl is ever allowed to play football with the boys.

Based on these three conversations, there seems little doubt that positive school policies can liberate children for freer play and that absence of such policy generates injustice and tension. When I questioned the three girls about who gets miserable and who gets bullied, it was no surprise to learn that Helen had the graphic examples: there is a lot of name calling in her playground; there are two boys who are cruel; there is a clever boy who wears glasses who gets picked on; there are children who are alone. In contrast, Tess and Helen were not aware of any ongoing and unresolved situations – some children were miserable when they fell over and got hurt; some children were sometimes alone; but they did not think there was anyone who was unhappy all of the time. They may be wrong; but the point is that they felt that they had full opportunity to play and they were more trusting of the ability of the school to sort out problems as they arose.

CONCLUSIONS: EQUAL OPPORTUNITIES AND BEHAVIOUR POLICIES

As a result of anti-racist and anti-sexist work, many lessons have been learnt about the ways in which schools structure relationships and reinforce the discriminations and inequalities of wider society. Schools have been challenged (by parents, by pressure groups, by politicians) to change their ways and to work more effectively towards the creation of environments where all pupils can thrive. In this chapter I have been arguing the particular need for schools to enable pupils to deal with sexist and racist harassment and to focus attention on the playground as one of the most significant sites for social learning. What are the approaches which schools have adopted in dealing with these issues?

The most common is the policy of denial. Reluctance to raise the issues of sexism and racism is widespread among teachers and ancillary staff. This is not the place to discuss the reasons for this reluctance and the means by which school staff can learn the benefits of behaviour policies. But denial of the scale of bullying and harassment leaves pupils exposed, having to improvise for themselves until an incident is so serious that the school must take action. This locks pupils and staff into a situation of *ad hoc* responses which breeds distrust and injustice.

The second most common approach is the development of punitive, incident-only policies in which 'bullies' are punished. This is inherently unsound because it deals only with the end result of complex processes in which pupils need guidance and support. The risks inherent in punitive policies were identified by the Macdonald Inquiry (Macdonald *et al.* 1989), which stated:

> In the field of education, the basic assumption behind many current anti-racist policies is that since black pupils are the victims of the immoral and prejudiced behaviour of white students, white students are to be seen as 'racist'.... Racism is thus placed in some kind of moral vacuum and is totally divorced from the more complex reality of human relations in the classroom, playground or community.
>
> (p. 402)

Most rare, but also most effective, is the approach which promotes active social learning in alliance with pupils – what Cohen has described as a 'specifically educational strategy which touches the imaginative roots of children's prejudices, in a way which actively involves (rather than alienates) children and parents, playground supervisors and teaching staff' (Cohen, forthcoming). The key elements in such an approach are principles of good professional practice which have been tried and tested in other contexts.

To start with, it is essential that any strategy is 'whole school'; that is, involving all staff and pupils, and relating to all school spaces – classrooms, corridors, playground and the routes between home and school. The clear implication of dealing with all spaces is that schools should link into inter-agency programmes, drawing on the skills and resources of youth and community workers in order to avoid conflicts spilling out of the school onto the streets.

Then there must be pupil, staff and parent involvement in the initiation, development, monitoring and revision of the policies; otherwise the neglected and alienated sections of the school will subvert any processes set in train. For instance, pupils seeking positions of dominance will seek to confuse and mislead teachers so that they do not detect which pupils are being harassed. Pupils are the best guides to what is going on among themselves, and they are far more likely to 'own up' if there is an atmosphere of trust and involvement, rather than distrust and authoritarianism.

Finally, the strategy should be guided by the principles of equal opportunities; namely, the approach which acknowledges that there are many forms of prejudice and discrimination functioning in schools and that action should be based on local circumstances and sensitive to the dynamics unique to each school. In the context of the playground, as elsewhere in the school, staff must deal with both the dynamic towards equality and harmony and the dynamic towards dominance and conflict.

> The field of social relationships among children can be thought of as a network of subject positions held together by relations of social power. The relations of power are the product of two contrary social processes. One is 'domination': the assertion of the interests of the self, or of a group, over and at the expense of others. The other is 'equality': the attempt to find the fairest balance of interests among children.
>
> (Troyna and Hatcher 1992: 48)

Surely there can be no doubt about the ways in which schools should be working if the full potential of social learning is to be unlocked in a safe and just environment. Partial, inconsistent and incoherent policies may succeed in lowering some tensions and dealing with immediate conflict, but they will not enable pupils to learn for themselves how to deal with tensions and conflict. They will not prepare pupils for life in the adult world which awaits them.

Playground work holds promise of reward if school staff work in alliance with pupils to unlearn the prejudices and discriminations which legitimate victimisation. It must never be forgotten that so long as playgrounds are neglected, there are some pupils who do not have the chance to play.

ACKNOWLEDGEMENTS

I want to thank Helen, Tess and Jenny for telling me about their playgrounds. They opened my eyes and ears in ways which I shall not forget.

REFERENCES

Atwood, M. (1990) *Cat's Eye*, London: Virago Press.
Besag, V. (1989) *Bullies and Victims in Schools: A Guide to Understanding and Management*, Milton Keynes: Open University Press.
—— (1992) 'We don't have bullies here! Resource materials for INSET and further developments – for primary and secondary schools, and colleges', London: Calouste Gulbenkian Foundation.
Blatchford, P. (1989) *Playtime in the Primary School: Problems and Improvements*, Windsor: NFER-Nelson.
Boulton, M. J. (1992) 'Participation in playground activity at middle school', *Educational Research*, 34 (3): 167–81.
Cohen, P. (forthcoming) 'Forbidden games? Race, gender and class in the regulation of children's play', in *Not Just the Same Old Story*.
Commission for Racial Equality (1988) *Learning in Terror, a Survey of Racial Harassment in Schools and Colleges in England, Scotland and Wales, 1985–1987*, London: CRE.
Home Office (1989) *The Response to Racial Attacks and Harassment. Report of the Inter-departmental Racial Attacks Group*, London: HMSO.
Kelly, E. (1993) 'Gender issues in education for citizenship', in G. K. Verma and P. Pumfrey (eds) *Cultural Diversity and the Curriculum, Vol. 2*, London: The Falmer Press.
La Fontaine, J. (1991) *Bullying: The Child's View*, London: Calouste Gulbenkian Foundation.
Lees, S. (1986) *Losing Out: Sexuality and Adolescent Girls*, London: Hutchinson Education.
Macdonald, I., Bhavnani, R., Khan, L. and John, G. (1989) *Murder in the Playground*, Report of the Macdonald Enquiry into Racism and Racial Violence in Manchester Schools, London: Longsight Press.
Mahony, P. (1985) *Schools for the Boys? Coeducation Reassessed*, London: Hutchinson Education.
Mooney, A., Creeser, R. and Blatchford, P. (1991) 'Children's views on teasing and fighting in junior schools', *Educational Research*, 33(2): 103–12.
Roland, E. and Munthe, E. (1989) *Bullying: An International Perspective*, London: David Fulton Publishers.
Scottish Council for Research in Education (1992) *Action Against Bullying*, Edinburgh: SCRE.

Scottish Ethnic Minorities Research Unit (1986) *Racial Harassment in Glasgow*, Glasgow Polytechnic (now Caledonian University of Glasgow).

Strathclyde Regional Council, Department of Education (1990) *Tackling Racist Incidents within the Education Service*, Glasgow.

Tattum, D. and Lane, D. (eds) (1989) *Bullying in Schools*, Stoke-on-Trent: Trentham Books.

Troyna, B. and Hatcher, R. (1992) *Racism in Children's Lives*, London: Routledge.

Whitney, I. and Smith, P. K. (1993) 'A survey of the nature and extent of bullying in junior/middle and secondary schools', *Educational Research*, 35 (1): 3–25.

Wolverhampton Education Department/Safer Cities Project (1991) Bullying in Schools Initiative, *Safer Schools, Safer Cities*, Wolverhampton: Education Department.

Part II

Changing behaviour during school breaktimes

Editors' introduction

This section of the book offers insights into the practical experiences of schools engaged in the process of making changes. It draws on a range of perspectives, and we have tried to balance overviews of issues and concerns with details about initiatives in particular schools. The aim is to allow the reader to gain a broader knowledge of the field, and the opportunity to relate that knowledge to specific examples.

The first three chapters explore the environmental potential of school grounds. Bill Lucas, Director of Learning Through Landscapes, argues that the neglect of school grounds – 'the first public environment of which children have sustained experience' – is a national disgrace. He describes the work and origins of Learning Through Landscapes, and the opportunities provided for school grounds by the National Curriculum and Local Management of Schools. He stresses the importance of a 'holistic' view of school grounds; that is, one that recognises the connections between the school landscape, the curriculum, the staff and the school ethos. In common with others in this book, he also stresses the need to know how children think and feel about school grounds.

Lyndal Sheat and Anne Beer, from the Department of Landscape, University of Sheffield, challenge some common assumptions about the nature of pupil participation in design projects. Teachers and designers have both tended to trivialise pupils' potential contribution to the design process. Using a ladder of participation model they identify stages in the design process, and the appropriate roles of designers and pupils in each. All too often pupils are restricted to later stages, thus reducing the value of their contribution. They then present a model of participation which provides teachers and designers with a helpful way of thinking about participatory designing of school grounds.

The Coombes County Infant and Nursery School, in the village of Arborfield, near Reading, is quite rightly one of the best-known examples of school ground improvements in the country. Susan Humphries and Susan Rowe describe their pioneering work over a period of twenty-two years, which transformed a barren, wind-swept site into a thriving and still evolving learning and play environment. The importance of this work is not only because it shows how school grounds can be improved, without huge financial donations; but it also illustrates how from the start the work was built on perceived needs in the school, and was informed by a view of education within which the barriers between classroom and school grounds have been breached. It is an inspiring chapter.

From environment we move to supervision. It is commonly recognised now that lunchtime supervision is an important job, but that it is not matched at present by the status or training accorded supervisors. Some training schemes exist but what is the national picture? Sonia Sharp provides an overview, based on a national survey of Local Education Authorities, of training offered to supervisors. She provides information on the extent and type of training and its coverage. She also identifies some common concerns. These include poor communication between teaching staff and supervisors, the lack of clarity over responsibilities, and the low status of supervisors.

These concerns are expanded by Gil Fell, who gives a lively account of her experiences in running training courses for lunchtime supervisors in Manchester. Through her chapter we hear the voices of the supervisors themselves, and gain insight into the social dynamics that operate in dining room and grounds. She points out that many supervisors have received no training of any sort since leaving school. A main aspect of her approach is the attempt to enhance the self-esteem and status of supervisors by working from their felt needs. These needs may not be fully recognised by teaching staff, who may well find this chapter illuminating, if not always comfortable, reading.

In the next section the authors reflect on ways in which pupils can be involved in resolving breaktime problems.

Sonia Sharp, Fiona Cooper and Helen Cowie argue that there is probably not a school in the country that does not want to promote harmonious and respectful relationships between pupils. Yet fundamental change will not arise through rules and policies but through a combination of policy development and pupil empowerment; for example, through training in conflict resolution. They use conflict resolution theory to show how conflicts arise, clarify some myths about conflict, and show, with examples, how conflict resolution can contribute to life in schools and in the playground.

Helen Cowie describes two initiatives: Quality Circles and peer counselling. Through Quality Circles, a system taken from industry, pupils are taught problem-solving strategies, which are then applied to the playground. This approach is an excellent example of the participatory process described earlier by Lyndal Sheat and Anne Beer. Peer counselling recognises the ability of pupils to develop skills for helping one another, in this case by being good listeners.

In the final section of the book, Carol Ross and Amanda Ryan draw on their valuable experience of working with schools which have expressed concern about their playgrounds, in order to describe a whole-school approach to playground development. They present a case study of one school to illustrate the role that consultation and monitoring can play in developing a playground policy. They stress the importance of an overall action plan, and illustrate this with one from a primary and one from a secondary school.

Chapter 5

The power of school grounds
The philosophy and practice of Learning Through Landscapes

Bill Lucas

There are more than 30,000 schools in the United Kingdom, covering an area of at least 150,000 acres. This land is, in the main, a miserable, bleak and desolate landscape. That this is also the first public environment of which children have any sustained experience is a national disgrace. It shapes children's views of place and people, in many cases in very harmful ways. It does nothing to encourage positive social interaction or the development of a sense of pride or aesthetic awareness. As I have written elsewhere: 'when torturers wish to disorientate their victims, they frequently create a featureless environment in which to place them' (Lucas 1992).

This land is, of course, the United Kingdom's school grounds, also known as playgrounds, playing fields, sports fields, sites, campuses and a variety of other terms. I prefer the phrase 'school grounds' because it carries a smaller amount of semantic baggage than the others. 'Playgrounds', in particular, is misleading on account of a number of special associations:

1   it suggests that they are solely intended for play;
2   it reinforces unhelpful educational conflicts between play and learning;
3   it is inappropriate for the secondary sector;
4   it carries associations with unsupervised public playgrounds and introduces a whole set of other 'play' words, like 'play equipment', which are not necessarily appropriate for school grounds;
5   for reasons of architectural and legislative history, playground has almost become a synonym for hard-surfaced areas.

The land around schools is the responsibility of local authorities, the Church and governing bodies. Headteachers have to ensure that it is properly supervised. It serves the needs of secondary as well as primary pupils. It provides a rich variety of formal and extra-curricular experiences as well as catering for the informal needs of young people. It is the backdrop against which teachers, supervisors, parents and other adults spend a considerable amount of time. Its signs and symbols contain a range of meanings for children which we are only just beginning to understand.

In this chapter I shall focus on the broad range of outdoor activities by exploring the concept of school grounds as a whole, by considering the overall needs of a school community in terms of outside space and by refusing to define school play in conventionally discrete terms. In particular, I will set the genesis of the organisation Learning Through Landscapes (LTL) in context, describe its philosophy and what it does, report on some of its recent research, touch on the complex subject of participative school grounds design and allow myself the luxury of a brief glimpse of both the past and the future.

LEARNING THROUGH LANDSCAPES

It was largely out of a recognition of the complex range of functions served by school grounds beyond that of 'playground' that Learning Through Landscapes Trust was set up, after an extensive research project which began in 1985. It was felt by many of those involved in this work in the 1980s, and included as a recommendation in the project report (Adams 1990), that school grounds were such an important but neglected commodity, that an independent national organisation was needed to deal with all aspects of their design, use, management and development.

So, in 1990, Learning Through Landscapes was launched as a national charity. Its stated mission was to promote widespread improvements to the quality of school grounds and to extend the range of educational activities which take place in them. This coincided with the publication of *The Outdoor Classroom* (1990) by the government. As its title suggests, this *Building Bulletin* deals mainly with the formal curriculum and, drawing on LTL's research, makes a powerful case that schools should develop their grounds to become landscapes of high quality.

Happily, the birth of LTL coincided with a growing national concern for the environment and with an emerging consensus among the teaching profession that properly structured, active learning was important – a message at first reinforced by the National Curriculum Council's writings, but more recently challenged by central government.

THE NATIONAL CURRICULUM AND LOCAL MANAGEMENT OF SCHOOLS

Two other significant national developments affected LTL's subsequent development: the introduction of the National Curriculum and of Local Management of Schools (LMS). At first sight, the more significant of these was the National Curriculum. At a stroke, what had been largely left to teachers to determine was brought under the control of central government. English, maths and science were designated core subjects. New whole-school issues, such as environmental education, health education and citizenship were introduced as compulsory elements of the curriculum.

LTL moved swiftly to ensure that guidance from the National Curriculum Council contained copious references to what was achievable in the school grounds. Curriculum Guidance 7, *Environmental Education* (1990), is illustrated with LTL photographs and provides a clear framework for environmental work outside. All of the other relevant subject guides contain reference to activities which can most easily be taught in the school grounds. More recently, the Curriculum Council for Wales in its *Advisory Paper on Environmental Education* (1993) went still further in advocating development of school grounds as an important experience for all children. It cites Jonathon Porritt: 'the creative use of school grounds reinforces positive feelings about the environment, allowing children not just to feel at home but to develop a real sense of responsibility about their environment' (1993).

In fact, it will be LMS which arguably has the greater potential to influence the quality of school grounds design, use and management. Before this initiative, the maintenance of the school estate was something carried out by the landlord, in most cases the Local Education Authority. Grass was mown, shrubs pruned and pitches or playgrounds marked, almost without headteachers knowing anything about it. LMS is gradually giving schools financial data about the cost of providing these services. Ultimately, it will free all headteachers to decide not only how much they spend, but also what they spend it on. Already some schools concerned about the long-term development of their grounds are choosing to organise the management of their landscape themselves.

LTL viewed both the National Curriculum and LMS as enabling initiatives which could work to the benefit of school grounds, provided that teachers were committed to viewing them in this light. In 1990, there was, unfortunately, no national 'play' initiative to parallel these two developments in school management. Nevertheless, LTL made it abundantly clear that it was not interested in any narrow definition of education which excluded either what Adams (1990) calls the 'informal' or the 'hidden' curriculum. These phrases assume that there are at least three elements of children's curricular experience. These are the 'formal' – all that is taught during lesson time; the 'informal' – all that happens as part of the planned school day, but outside lesson time (including breaktimes, movement between lessons, the beginnings and endings of days); and the 'hidden' – the other complex influences that operate on children in a school, and from which they learn important messages. In the sense in which the 'hidden' curriculum is used here, it refers particularly to the impact of the landscape in its widest sense on children. This includes signposting, the availability or non-availability of seating or shelter, the ethos of supervision and a range of other powerful factors.

It was clear to us that increased awareness of school grounds and new roles for school governing bodies would inevitably lead to more discussion about the management of play.

THE IMPORTANCE OF THE HOLISTIC VISION

I and all those at LTL believe in a holistic view of people and landscape. In other words, no one has exclusive rights of ownership over school grounds. Indeed, it is important that they are not dominated by the interests of any single group. Instead they are there to serve the needs of all their users, especially the children. Such a holistic view of school land sets LTL apart from every other organisation working with schools. It leads me to argue that to treat 'playtime' as a separate issue in a school is quite unhelpful.

While there has been research on pupils' experiences of breaktime, and pupils' behaviour then (see Blatchford, Smith and Boulton, this volume), no one has yet set school play in its overall context. So I hear extensive discussion about the relationship between play and gender, school play and play in general, play and bullying, but rarely school play and the overall impact of a school's landscape, curriculum, staff and ethos on these subjects. LTL seeks to set all issues relating to the use of land around educational establishments in the fullest possible context.

To separate play behaviour from the total environment, school grounds design from grounds maintenance or supervision issues from a school's ethos is artificial and unsatisfactory. While I accept that we need to know about the parts in order to be able to understand the whole, my own experience is that the parts covered in this book are rarely reassembled back into a coherent whole. This book is necessarily divided into sections, but it will, I hope, be clear that although this chapter appears in a section on playground design, it is not just about the playground, nor about design in the limited sense in which it is often used. LTL has specific views on the role of children in the design process, the nature of the design process itself, the role of professionals other than teachers and the critical importance of headteachers in managing their grounds.

LTL'S PROGRAMME OF ACTIVITIES

Learning Through Landscapes attempts to put some of these principles into practice. To do this it carries out a number of significant activities, which look increasingly unlikely to be fulfilled by either central or local government. Together, these guiding beliefs have begun to be summed up by the phrase (which is also the organisation's name) – Learning Through Landscapes. It is interesting to note that, in the three years since LTL's launch in the United Kingdom, it has been possible to persuade the Swedish government to set up a fully funded action research programme – *Skolans uterum* – modelled on LTL's work, while at home there is no such support.

From an early stage LTL saw the need for short, attractive publications to assist teachers. It recognised that it was not enough for teachers in the new educational climate simply to feel that school grounds were important. They had to be able to justify themselves. In a formal sense, this meant that any lesson needed to be linked to the National Curriculum, as in *Science in the Schoolgrounds* (Thomas 1992). When dealing with the informal curriculum, this necessitated proper understanding of LMS and the new roles of governors and parents, as indicated in *Play, Playtime and Playgrounds* (Titman 1992). In terms of the hidden curriculum this meant reference to image in the community, open enrolment and LMS. As the element about which there was also least known, LTL moved to establish further research into it.

Publications alone do not bring about change in schools. LTL recognised that, especially when dealing with the landscape, teachers need a combination of written information and local support. This is often best delivered in the form of visits from informed people on the ground.

To this end, a national network of regional support groups has been set up. Although very different in size, resources and expertise, this network is united in its determination to promote improvements to school grounds. Successful groups have a register of local good practice, run meetings and share news. Many different professions are represented. Achievements are celebrated and systems put in place which encourage members of these groups to share experiences. This network will, I am sure, grow in its effectiveness.

In some areas of the United Kingdom regional groups have the direct support of their local authority. As I write, thirty-three local authorities are members of LTL and have therefore made a financial and philosophical commitment to this kind of work. Whether local authorities continue to exist or not, it is demonstrably the case that the multiplier effect in terms of good practice is more easily visible in areas of the country where there is the support of local government.

In addition to running a membership scheme for local authorities, LTL has several thousand individual supporters, many of whom are also individual members. It has been one of the most heartening aspects of setting up LTL to see the range of people who care about school grounds in the same way that others, say in the RSPB, care about birds. All adults have a stake in the future happiness of the nation's children, and most of those with any understanding of young people realise instinctively the damaging effects of a poor school environment on their child's development. Some have direct experience of the unhappiness which can be caused and many see the obvious benefits which the development of school grounds brings.

Perhaps the most important service LTL is able to offer is impartial advice across an extraordinarily wide range of specialist areas. The Trust has expertise in senior educational management, teaching at all levels, play and child development, environmental psychology, landscape architecture, participative design, land management, grounds maintenance and, of course, in the techniques of research. With its holistic approach, it is frequently able to transcend narrow specialisation and promote a broad view of the management of school grounds. This advice is sought by government and individuals alike, and, in the main, available at no cost.

An advantage of LTL's charitable status has been that it has been able to bring in outside funding for the benefits of schools. Currently Esso, British Telecom and British Rail have all sponsored projects which, we hope, will significantly improve the quality of the educational estate.

THE EXTENT OF THE NEED

LTL's message is transmitted through all of these activities and in our dealings with schools. The extent of the problem is enormous, though, with some 30,000 schools in the United Kingdom. Recently we have established a training and conference programme which will, in the near future, provide continuing expert training in most areas of Britain.

Increasingly, it is LTL's contention that the aspect of school life which has been most neglected is neither the formal nor the informal curriculum. Rather, it is concerned with everything implied by 'the hidden curriculum'. Put simply, it has become clear that we need to know what children think and feel about their school's grounds and how this affects them. Schools can then use this information positively. We need to understand children's affective response to their environment and how this influences their development. Such information is *at least* as important as issues like understanding behaviour management, the training of supervisors or the organisation of the school day. It is, after all, the backdrop against which all of this takes place. While we know a considerable amount about where children like to play and what they like to do, we do not know much about what most school grounds actually *mean* to children.

Play companies tell schools that children need expensive fixed play equipment, arts organisations insist that children need murals and sculptures, conservation groups point to young people's interest in the environment and promote wildflower meadows and ponds. What do children think? Are they even asked? If they are asked, are they asked in such a way that what they say is their own opinion?

WHAT SCHOOL GROUNDS MEAN TO CHILDREN

LTL has been exploring the issue of what school landscape means to young people for the last two years in a piece of collaborative research with the

Worldwide Fund for Nature. Wendy Titman, who has been coordinating this research, has conducted interviews with hundreds of children using a particular technique specially designed to unlock some of the hidden semiotic messages contained in the school environment. Using specially constructed picture-boards, she has been able to identify clearly what different landscape features mean to children.

This research (Titman 1993) has been presented not for an academic audience but in a form which has been specifically geared to the needs of headteachers. New findings are set alongside clear summaries of relevant research from all over the world. LTL's intention is that headteachers should be able to translate what they read into direct management activity aimed at improving the overall quality of school grounds and therefore of all breaktimes.

The following list indicates some of the conclusions:

1   The school environment signifies a particular range of things to children. These are their readings of their school's landscape.
2   Some of these readings are very powerful and exert a negative influence on the life of the school. Schools which ignore them when designing or managing their grounds are unlikely to achieve successful results.
3   Very few school grounds or 'play areas' within them meet children's needs in terms of what they would like to be and do.
4   In the main, children see many signifiers in the school landscape of a *lack of care* towards them; 'all horrible concrete', for example, which they take very personally. It is not what they expect from their grounds.
5   Included in a longer list of positive elements are:
    'natural' colours; trees; woods; flowers; shady areas; places with different levels; places where you can climb; hide and explore.
6   Included in a longer list of negative elements are:
    Tarmac; concrete; dirt; rubbish; 'unnatural' colour; places with nowhere to sit hide or shelter.
7   In terms of two specific features often associated with school playgrounds – fixed play equipment and Tarmac – there are particular comments:
    a) Fixed play equipment rarely satisfies children, and the purchase of it may not, therefore, be good use of scarce resources.
    b) Open concrete or Tarmac is universally disliked. There would seem to be a clear need to soften such spaces and their edges, introducing more varied landscapes as a *priority*, not as an extra.
8   Simple items, whether informal seating from the edges of raised beds or old tyres, are often highly valued.
9   Children are not as enamoured of murals and playground markings as adults tend to think they are.

There is a range of other findings to which this scant summary does not do justice. Nevertheless, if I had to extract two messages for headteachers considering developing their sites, they would be:

1   look at the site as a whole, not at the playground in isolation;
2   make every effort to involve the children at every possible stage of the process of redesigning their grounds.

THE PROCESS OF MANAGING SCHOOL GROUNDS

As this chapter is part of a section dealing with playground design, it seems appropriate to dwell on this aspect of school land management in a little more detail. From the hundreds of case studies with which LTL has now been involved, a number of principles are clearly emerging. The first of these is that design of school grounds takes time. There is a tendency for schools to rush headlong from idea into action with far too little concern for the process. The headteacher reports his or her concern over playground behaviour to the governors, the PTA raises money and a single item of fixed play equipment is purchased before anyone has time to look at what was really needed. The evidence of successful work we have seen is that it almost always follows considerable planning activity carried out in the context of the whole site's development.

The first essential step is the survey. Schools need to know exactly what they have and how what they have is used. They need to work this out for themselves and not rely on the appraisal of an outsider on one particular day. In parallel to this, it is important to identify the needs of pupils and teachers. To do this with pupils is not a matter of just asking them what they would like to have in their schoolgrounds, or even of what they would like to do in their grounds – although this is a much more productive approach. Supporting any general questioning should be a range of other activities, including drama, design games, questionnaire work, structured observation, photography and mapping. Practical suggestions for teaching the formal curriculum, improving image and managing the informal parts of the school day need to be discussed with teachers.

All of this takes time, and all of it, ideally, should happen before a process of participative design begins. Without going into any specific design activities, the general principle that children can be directly involved at all stages needs to be asserted here.

Only when these preliminary stages have been undertaken can the design part of this participative process really begin. Many schools find that the assistance of a professional designer is particularly beneficial. Landscape architects and community designers certainly have skills which can be of use. The difficulty is that few have had the experience to lead to an understanding of children's landscape needs and few are used to dealing with children. What often happens, therefore, is that this activity is entirely taken over by the adults involved.

There are many tried and tested methods of helping children to realise their design ideas, from drama to observation, from visits to other landscapes to photography, from questionnaires to structured discussion, from mapping to design games. Almost all of these involve modelling as a key element. I agree entirely with David Stea's view that: 'the prime use of models is not the making of spaces in miniature, but *communication*. In fact, it ought not to matter what people come up with if it, with the aid of verbal description, communicates' (Stea 1985).

The process, in other words, is at least as important as the product; the model is a means to an end where the 'end' is effective communication. If you subscribe to this belief, it becomes very difficult to contemplate the model of playground design which has a playground expert produce a design on the basis of a walk round the site with the headteacher, with little or no sustained contact with pupils and teachers. For many children an involvement in participative design and decision making with their school-grounds can be highly significant in their development as thinking, responsible citizens.

Once the site had been surveyed and initial design ideas produced, it used to be the case that a school's involvement in the process diminished. Either the local authority or an outside contractor undertook the work and the desired changes were implemented. With LMS, things are very different now. Headteachers need to have long-term plans for their grounds as they do for other aspects of their work. Since April 1993 headteachers have been selecting and paying contractors for the routine aspects of site maintenance. There are, therefore, great opportunities for both greater and reduced priority being attached to the quality of outside spaces. There are particular challenges for secondary schools to consider radically new models of managing their grounds. These might include the creation of a new post, more like a site ranger than a teacher or member of ground staff, with multiple responsibilities. Such a person could establish a consortium of schools, linking his or her secondary with partner primaries; working to raise funds; offering support to teachers wanting to teach outside; and running extra-curricular activities for young children.

In almost all cases it will continue to be important to raise additional money for grounds development. A detailed flow chart of this management process is contained in a number of LTL publications.

CONCLUSIONS

As I write, I am aware of both opportunities and challenges bearing down on schools which are considering improvements to their grounds. In a sense nothing has changed. So when E. R. Robson, the Chief Architect of the

London School Board, said in 1873 that 'a school should appear like a school and not like a monastery, a town hall or a set of almshouses', he might just as well have been speaking today. The need for appropriately designed schools and school grounds is as true now as it was a hundred years ago.

So, too, children, notwithstanding the invention of television and the computer game, are unlikely to have changed markedly. Above all, they continue to like and need variety in the grounds, as Robin Moore puts it: 'Every child needs equal access to opportunities for asserting her or his individuality, through interaction with the environment' (Moore 1986).

The schools LTL has worked with have shown how every centimetre of their site can be designed so that it provides an infinitely varied and flexible landscape of high quality – a living resource for formal and informal child development. Such schools do not put 'play' into a little box wrapped up in breaktimes; they see it as one of a number of important needs to be satisfied by the school landscape.

I am optimistic that LTL is on the cusp of what is, at the same time, a radically original *and* also radically traditional development in educational thinking. I am confident that there is a growing ground-swell of public opinion raising voices in favour of the importance of the school environment. Certainly we inhabit a more dangerous world, and for this reason alone, school grounds should be treated more seriously as safe havens to replace the street and the park.

Let me leave the last comment to Wendy Titman: 'To children, school grounds are enormously significant. Children recognise the grounds, particularly the playgrounds of their school, as a unique place, somewhere created especially for them, apparently to do the things they enjoy and which are increasingly impossible elsewhere' (1992).

REFERENCES

Adams, E. (1990) *Report on the Design, Use, Management and Development of School Grounds*, Crediton: Learning Through Landscapes/Southgate Publishers.

Environmental Education: Curriculum Guidance 7 (1990) York: National Curriculum Council.

Lucas, W. (1992) 'School grounds can seriously damage your health!', *Education and Health*, 10 (5): 70–2.

Moore, R. (1986) *Childhood's Domain*, Dover, NH: Croom Helm.

The Outdoor Classroom (Building Bulletin No. 71 (1990), London: HMSO, and Crediton: Southgate Publishers.

Porritt, J. (1993) *Learning Through Landscapes Newsletter, Summer 1991*, quoted in *Curriculum Council for Wales Advisory Paper 17, Environmental Education*, Cardiff.

Stea, D. (1985) 'From environment cognition to environmental design', *Children's Environments Quarterly*, 2 (3).

Thomas, G. (1992) *Science in the Schoolgrounds*, Crediton: Southgate/LTL.

Titman, W. (1992) *Play, Playtime and Playgrounds*, Crediton: Southgate/LTL.

—— (1993) *Special Places for Special People*, Godalming: WWF/LTL.

Chapter 6

Giving pupils an effective voice in the design and use of their school grounds

Lyndal G. Sheat and Anne R. Beer

Of late, there has been a veritable flood of British literature on the design and use of school grounds. Two issues have been addressed: first, how to give pupils a 'voice'; and second, the kind of benefits a school or participating pupil might expect from this. Much less consideration has been given to issues related to the quality of this 'voice', the motives behind giving it in the first place, and the extent to which this voice is, or should be, heard and acted upon.

At the Department of Landscape at Sheffield University, a research project was begun in 1988 which, amongst other research goals, examined these issues (see Sheat and Beer 1989). This chapter will discuss some of the findings.

The first section of this chapter will outline some of the problems that need to be addressed when attempting to give pupils an effective voice in the design process. Following this, a model of participation will be presented as a possible solution to these problems. This provides teachers and designers alike with a means of thinking about participatory design which does not trivialise children, but at the same time provides a balance between the costs of full participation and having no participation at all. A number of techniques for involving children arising from this model will then be discussed, along with a guide for selecting techniques appropriate for each stage of the design process. Finally, as a summary to this chapter, a strategy for teachers preparing participatory design projects involving children will be suggested.

GIVING PUPILS AN EFFECTIVE VOICE: SOME PROBLEMS THAT NEED TO BE ADDRESSED

Bridging the gap between designer and educationist

One aim of the research has been one of bridging the gap between educationists and designers. Neither the elitist 'designer as the expert' approach (which has led to so many boring and predictable designs) nor the short term DIY approach (which can result in piecemeal, uncoordinated areas which make poor use of the space and resources available), offer a workable solution. The need for a combined effort has become evident recently, due, in no small measure, to the efforts of the Learning Through Landscapes project. Despite this, so far there has been little guidance offered to teachers and designers on how their respective areas of expertise might be combined within the design process. Without this combined effort there would seem little hope that the pupils, stuck in the middle, will ever be given an effective voice.

Motivations: do we trivialise children's input?

One area in which teachers and designers do seem to be united is their tendency to trivialise the child's potential contribution to the design process. Several writers (for example, Davidoff 1980; Hart 1987) have argued that this occurs mainly because adults simply cannot, or even refuse to, believe in children's basic ability to participate. Participation requires a redistribution of power and a reassessment of roles, and this can be very threatening for adults. By and large, this attitude tends to prevent any participation by children occurring at all, but when it is 'allowed' it can sometimes results in adults treating children in a very condescending manner and trivialising children's efforts (Baldassari et al. 1980: 7). In order to overcome this, designers and teachers must look to their motives for involving children. Baldassari and colleagues go on to describe ten common motivations for involving children which were first identified in Jim Johnson's paper 'A plain man's guide to participation' (1979). These are outlined in Table 6.1.

Motivation for involving pupils in the design process varies. Sometimes, this participation is little more than tokenism, in the sense of schools involving pupils because it 'sounds like a good idea' and is rewarded by public acclaim. In other schools, the participation process is used as an educational opportunity and, to a lesser extent, as a community development opportunity. In fact, of all the reasons put forward for participation of pupils within the school situation, participation as an educational opportunity has figured most prominently. However, children are seldom actively involved in the crucial initial decision-making stages when timetables for the project are set, resources allocated and so on. Likewise, there seems to be little evidence of genuine efforts to rearrange permanently (or even temporarily) the power relationships between staff and pupils through participation.

Related to motivation is the issue of estimating children's ability to participate. Even when there is a genuine desire to involve children in the design process, it can be very difficult to match it to a child's level of ability. If this ability is underestimated, then trivialisation will very likely occur.

Table 6.1   Interpretations of participation

As a design theory	Based on the view that people are perfectly capable of creating the environments they need – with the designer acting as a 'midwife' or 'enabler' only
As a means to political change	Based on the idea of 'citizen participation equals citizen power'
As a sop to public opinion	Based on designers' hopes that participation will lead to support for a design
As nostalgia	Based on a desire to return to the days when everyone did their own designing
As community development	Based on the idea of participation to rally the community into action
As education	Based on the view that through participation people will learn more about their environment and their actions and interactions within it
As aesthetic theory	Based on a reaction against modernist design – an attempt to add more complexity, contradiction and individuality
As a bandwagon	Based on the idea that participation is the 'in' thing to do – a means to legitimise all kinds of proposals
As a social conscience	Based on the 'service ethic'
As a means to a better solution	Based on the idea that the best solution will emerge by consensus once everyone understands the facts

Source: Baldassari *et al*. 1980

Equally, if it is overestimated, then frustration and disappointment will be inevitable for both the children and adults involved. A danger of this is that it may discourage all parties from any further attempts at participation.

Design requires of a child a number of skills: language and communication, spatial perception and cognition, map and plan comprehension and manipulation, creativity and divergent thinking, a sense of responsibility and care for others, and knowledge of design and associated concepts. The teacher and designer must be aware of these when drawing up the participatory design process. This will require designers and teachers working together to pool their respective areas of knowledge about the skills required for effective participation, as well as an understanding of children's cognitive and social development. It may then be decided that supplementary exercises are required to prepare the children for participation. These can in turn open up opportunities for combining the design programme with the school curriculum and National Curriculum attainment targets.

Level of involvement in decision making

The motivations for involving children in the design process also determine what level of involvement they are 'allowed' in the decision making. There are numerous typologies explaining these levels, but few, however, consider children as the main participant group. Arnstein's (1969) famous 'ladder of participation' has been often used to describe levels of child participation. (The *Childhood City Newsletter* series on children's participation (1980, 1981, 1982/83), for example, adopts it.) This ladder – as it might be related to school grounds design – can be seen in Figure 6.1.

The importance of this ladder is that it provides a guide for determining what should be regarded as an effective level of participation for children in the design process. In the ladder, each rung represents an increased degree of pupil power in the decision-making process, and it is not until the sixth rung is reached (partnership) that, according to Arnstein, the participants obtain an effective voice and real participation begins. This has severe implications for children. After reviewing some 400 cases of child participation, Hart (1987) found that participation seldom rose above the 'placation' level. Our case-study review confirms this, with the majority of cases focusing on the 'therapy' level in the form of environmental education exercises. This would indicate that currently, despite the extensive work being done in schools on school grounds improvements involving pupils, in terms of giving pupils an effective voice these efforts are missing the mark by a considerable margin.

Costs of the participation process

These problems give rise to a fourth issue that needs to be considered. In order to achieve such high levels of involvement, not only do attitudes need to change about the role children can play in the design process, but a great deal of time and effort need to be devoted to the task. Where a designer is employed, extra money often also needs to be found. These limitations are not just problems for schoolteachers and administrators, who must initiate, organise and run such projects, but for the designers too. As Oberdorfer (1988) points out, participatory design can increase a designer's workload by 20 to 40 per cent – often without proper compensation. These extra costs and lack of adequate payment were a major problem that emerged from a series of interviews, conducted by one of us, with designers involved in participatory school grounds design projects. If such designers are to continue to be involved in school design work, a reliable form of funding is essential to make up the difference between what the school itself can raise and the real costs to the designer of the participatory design process. As indicated by the interviews with designers, these costs present formidable barriers to designers and schools alike. In turn, these factors can

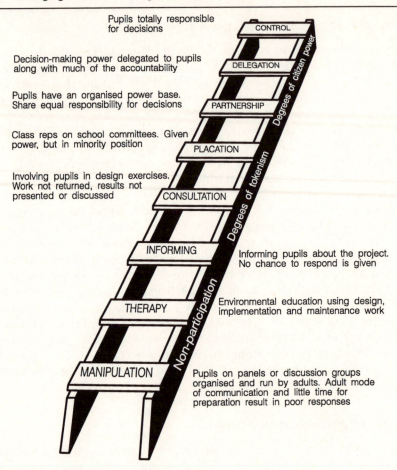

Pupils totally responsible for decisions — CONTROL

Decision-making power delegated to pupils along with much of the accountability — DELEGATION

Pupils have an organised power base. Share equal responsibility for decisions — PARTNERSHIP

Class reps on school committees. Given power, but in minority position — PLACATION

Involving pupils in design exercises. Work not returned, results not presented or discussed — CONSULTATION

INFORMING — Informing pupils about the project. No chance to respond is given

THERAPY — Environmental education using design, implementation and maintenance work

MANIPULATION — Pupils on panels or discussion groups organised and run by adults. Adult mode of communication and little time for preparation result in poor responses

Degrees of citizen power
Degrees of tokenism
Non-participation

Figure 6.1 Arnstein's ladder of participation

dissuade adults from involving children to the levels recommended by the ladder of participation.

MODEL OF PARTICIPATION

As a possible solution to these problems, we have developed a model of participation. The overall aim of the model (shown in Figure 6.2) is to provide both teachers and designers with a means of thinking about the participatory design of school grounds in a specific way. It not only aims to give pupils an effective voice in the design process, but also recognises the practical limitations of full participation.

This model stems from a belief that the DIY approach to school grounds

A Model of Participation

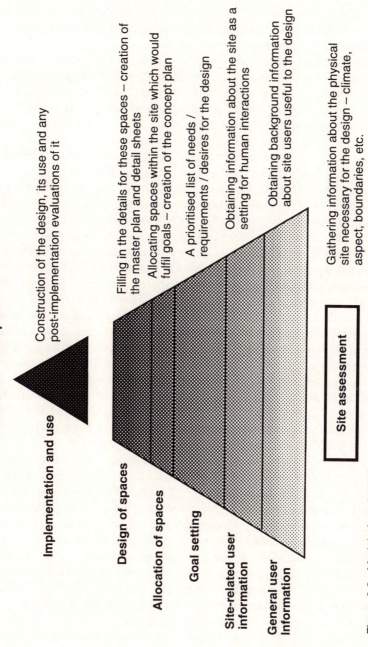

Implementation and use — Construction of the design, its use and any post-implementation evaluations of it

Design of spaces — Filling in the details for these spaces – creation of the master plan and detail sheets

Allocation of spaces — Allocating spaces within the site which would fulfil goals – creation of the concept plan

Goal setting — A prioritised list of needs / requirements / desires for the design

Site-related user information — Obtaining information about the site as a setting for human interactions

General user Information — Obtaining background information about site users useful to the design

Site assessment — Gathering information about the physical site necessary for the design – climate, aspect, boundaries, etc.

Figure 6.2   Model of participation

design, whilst tempting, is not the answer. The designer can and should be involved if possible (see Sheat and Beer 1989). It is based on the simple idea of finding a workable compromise between the extremes of full participation and no participation at all. The underlying principles of this compromise are discussed later in this section.

The model assumes that a designer will be heading the design process but, because of the time-intensive nature of full participation, will have insufficient time and resources to work directly with all the children at all stages of the design process. It therefore also assumes that teachers will act in a supporting role, organising and preparing the pupils for design sessions with the designer and preceding and following up these sessions with supplementary educational and design projects so that the participation experience can be used as an educational opportunity.

Basically, this model shows the minimum effective input into the decision making involved in the participatory design process. Each bar of the 'pyramid' represents a stage of the design process. The width of the bar represents the relative quantity of input, and the depth of the bar the relative quality of input, desirable for each of these stages. Conversely, an upturned pyramid could be drawn alongside this model to indicate the minimum designer input into the participatory design process and to show a gradual transition from pupil input to designer input.

The model begins at the 'Site assessment' stage and moves up to the 'Implementation and use' stage. This recognises the fact that a decision to make a change will almost always be taken before either the pupils or the designer (or even most of the school staff) are consulted and the participation process has begun in earnest. It is important that these initial decision makers are guided by a consideration of their motivations for involving children, as well as a respect for the children's wishes and needs, when determining the structure of the project and the role children will play within this structure.

The model should not, in any way, be viewed as a representation of an ideal participation situation. In an ideal situation, the quantity and quality of participation would be equal for all stages of the design process. Likewise, it should not be seen as a hard and fast rule to follow no matter what. If resources are available, the quantity and quality of input can be changed as required. It has been developed to show where pupils can best be involved to ensure the fullest possible educational and developmental benefits of the participation process, whilst at the same time minimising the costs of full participation (organisational demands, cost of designer time, cost of school staff time and labour input, delayed completion dates and so on).

The model allows a compromise in three fundamental ways:

The traditional versus the ideal participatory design process stages

The traditional design process follows a linear, step-wise progression through a number of stages (brief – assessment – design goals – concept plan – master plan – plan details – implementation). This is efficient, but too rigid to allow for the kind of revisions and back-tracking typical of participatory design projects. On the other hand, the ideal participatory design process often involves the cyclic movement of information from designer to user groups until a mutual decision is agreed upon (see Sheat and Beer 1989). This allows for thorough participation. The structure presented in this model is a compromise between the two. It follows a step-wise progression like traditional design, but the traditional design steps have been replaced by loose categories which follow more closely the natural progression of information in participatory design projects.

Relative amounts of input by the involved groups based on expertise

Where resources limit input by all groups at all stages of the design process, the relative amounts of desirable input can be determined by the levels of natural expertise each group can contribute towards the design. In terms of school grounds design, pupils (and other members of the school community who use the grounds regularly) can be seen as the 'experts' on the content, function and use of the grounds. Designers, on the other hand, can be seen as the 'experts' in visualising and creating school grounds as they might exist and be used. In general, the expertise held by the pupils is most useful at the earlier stages of the design, which are concerned with gathering information about the site, its users and the needs or requirements of the site; whereas the expertise of the designer is best used at the drafting stages of the process. This pattern of expertise is complementary and can be capitalised on in the participatory design process.

Quantity versus quality of input

A distinction can be drawn between quantity and quality of user input into the design process. Whereas quantity of input at each stage can be determined by balancing the relative levels of expertise the user and designer have, quality of input is determined by the perceived importance of the decision making associated with that stage in relation to the overall design. Referring back to the ladder of participation, decision making plays a central role in determining the effectiveness of participation achieved by the user group.

The depths of the bands in the model for each design stage reflect the compromise that was arrived at in our research. It was found that, in general, it was the 'Site-related user information' and 'Goal-setting' stages of the design process which required the highest quality of involvement. It is at these stages that the information gathered most affects the overall design and where most of the vital decisions are taken.

It may be surprising to see that the two design stages (Allocation and Design of spaces) are given lower priority in terms of both quantity and quality of participation. There is no doubt that they are the 'glamorous' stages of the design process and the ones that, at first, most participants (adult or child) want to be involved in. However, by these stages all the problems have been identified, goals for their solution worked out, and spaces for the site identified and described. In short, much of the fundamental decision making is complete. Design 'fixed points' have already been agreed between the designer and participants. Having participation at the design stages is undoubtedly important, but if a thorough job of involving people has been done earlier on, much time can be saved by reducing the need for back-tracking, therefore leaving the group free to focus on specific design questions.

It is important to note that two stages of the model – 'Site assessment' and 'Implementation and use' – are detached from the rest. Although 'Site assessment' is basic to good design in that it presents the designer with the facts about the physical and natural environment, it is largely a mechanical process requiring little in the way of decision making directly relevant to the end design. The gathering of site data by pupils is not therefore important to the achievement of effective participation. However, if resources are ample, pupils should have some involvement at this stage as it can provide a range of opportunities for many interesting educational projects (measuring, recording, analysing and so on), and gives pupils extra knowledge about their site which can be drawn upon in later stages of the design process.

The reasons for the separation of the 'Implementation and use' stage follows the same vein. Issues of implementation and use (including maintenance) need to be considered when project goals are drawn up. By the implementation and maintenance stages all the important design decisions have been taken – which means that pupil involvement at this stage does not contribute to effective participation in the design process. This calls into question current practice, which, as our case studies found, tended to involve children at the implementation and maintenance stages. The reasons for this were many and varied: some decision makers felt that children were unable to participate in the 'important' earlier decision – making stages; others didn't have the time, skills and/or energy to involve the children sooner; and still others held the genuine belief that this was the best time to involve the children. Examples were also found of children being used at this stage as little more than unpaid slaves or photo opportunities to publicise projects. However, this is not to say that children should be excluded from the implementation and maintenance stages as they can offer many valuable educational opportunities. In addition, even simple exercises such as planting a tree can have a great impact on a child and help develop feelings of belonging and ownership at school.

On the whole, quantity of involvement is gained at the expense of quality. Techniques such as questionnaires and general meetings mean that large numbers of people can participate, but seldom rising above Arnstein's 'Consultation' level of participation. Discussion groups and design workshops produce quality input but can only involve small numbers at any one time. Techniques focusing on quality input provide the greatest benefits and satisfactions for the individual. This general pattern can be followed when selecting appropriate techniques for each stage of the design process. In terms of selecting techniques, a range of techniques is required comprising both quantitative and qualitative methods.

METHODS OF INVOLVEMENT: PARTICIPATION TECHNIQUES

A plethora of techniques exist for involving children in the design of their school (or other) playgrounds (see, for example, Mares and Stephenson 1988; Ross and Ryan 1990; Poulton and Symons 1991; Brown 1990; Hart and Moore 1982/83). There appear to be no overall guidelines for teachers and designers to assist with effective selection.

A further aspect of the research was to investigate a range of techniques and use this to help teachers and designers to make informed decisions. This investigation took the form of a series of school design projects involving students of the University of Sheffield Landscape Department working with schoolchildren ranging from ages 5 to 18. Two secondary schools and one primary school were involved from within the Sheffield city area. Constraints of their courses meant that landscape students could not take the project further than the final design stage. However, the schools were presented with the designs to do with as they wished in the future. The techniques used in the projects were judged not only on the quality of information they produced, but also on how both the students and school pupils responded to them. The pupils and students were asked how they enjoyed using the technique, what problems they had with it, the benefits they gained from it, suggestions for its improvement and so forth.

The following is a review of a selection of techniques that were developed and tested in the study up to and including the 'Goal-setting' stage of the design process. This will hopefully provide a taste of the work done by the landscape students and school pupils in what has been identified as the most important stages of the design process.

User information techniques

This category covers techniques useful for both stage one and stage two of the model of participation. At these stages the kind of information that is required includes: the personalities and backgrounds of the pupils as related to how they use outdoor environments in general; their attitudes towards the school grounds and school life in general; evaluations of the quality and suitability of the grounds; mental images of the grounds as an indication of its memorability and importance to each individual pupil; the effects of the grounds on the behaviour of the pupil (these include both those perceived by the pupil and unconscious effects); and, finally, an account of what actually happens on site – what games are played, what interactions occur, the kinds of peer groupings that form and so on.

Site walkabouts exercise

One technique which was found to be very valuable both as a way of 'breaking the ice' between the students and pupils and providing information in a large number of the areas outlined above was our 'site walkabouts' exercise. This involved small groups of pupils (usually about six) giving two or three students a guided tour of the school. The pupils were told that no places were out of bounds and that what they said would be taken in strict confidence so that they could feel free to 'spill the beans' as much as they wanted. The technique was very popular with both groups and produced a wealth of data. It was also found to be useful for all age groups – although many of the younger ones needed coaxing to overcome their shyness and it seemed that they were intimidated by any more than two landscape students in a group.

On-site photography

Another successful technique was a photography exercise which involved school pupils taking out disposable cameras into the school grounds and compiling a series of twelve shots which they felt represented the way they viewed the school. The pupils did this exercise alone and were given half an hour before they had to report back to the landscape student in charge of the exercise. In addition to taking the photographs, the pupils filled out an information sheet describing the scene, why they took the shot, and rating on a scale how much they liked the scene. The photograph sequences and responses were then used to form picture boards. The students found the analysis of the exercise a lot of work, but, on the whole, worthwhile. The picture boards were also used later for presentations and follow-up discussions with school pupils. Although some pupils focused predominantly on negative aspects of the school, most provided a relatively balanced view of good and bad aspects.

Photo safari

This photography exercise was useful for pupils at the secondary level. Groups of pupils led one or two landscape students around their school, deciding as a group which scenes were important enough to photograph. Each child had a turn at taking photographs and the student took notes (and sometimes supplementary photographs) of points raised in the ensuing discussions. The photographs were then used to create a collage, with each scene located on a map of the school. The resultant collages provided useful information about the intimate knowledge pupils have of their school grounds as well as how the grounds are in reality.

Cognitive mapping

Several techniques were also developed for obtaining school pupils' images of their school grounds. The purpose of these was to gain an insight as to which parts of the grounds were most familiar, memorable and important to each pupil. This information can then be used to identify which spaces should then be enhanced or minimised in the final design. At the secondary-school level we first tried giving pupils a blank sheet of A3 to draw their 'cognitive maps' of the school. This was not altogether successful as, more often than not, the pupils focused on the school buildings rather than outdoor spaces. As a result, a modified mapping exercise was developed where the pupils were given a sheet of A3 paper with the boundaries of the school marked in and a cardboard template of the main school building. The pupils then had to position the template where they felt the actual building was sited, draw around it, and then fill in details of the grounds surrounding it. This proved more successful, and produced a wealth of information about how the children perceived spaces and their recall of favourite spots. This technique was not so well enjoyed by the pupils, who found the recall process hard work. The landscape students, who had to spend a great deal of time analysing the drawings, had mixed feelings about its worth.

Giant maps

A version of the mapping technique was also developed for the younger primary-school children. This was called 'Giant Maps', and it aimed to stimulate thinking about the school grounds:

- What spaces are there?
- What goes on in these spaces?
- What conflicts arise in relation to these spaces?

Using a mural-sized outline map of the school which already had the boundaries and school buildings drawn in, groups of pupils were asked to draw in as much information about their school as they could remember. This included both physical features and activities. The landscape students encouraged the children to include everything they could think of, but did not suggest elements or help by drawing in features. As the maps were being drawn, lively discussions took place which provided the students with additional information about the pupils' perceptions of their school grounds. The pupils' finished maps showed clearly which areas the pupils were most familiar with and strong associations between specific areas and activities. The exercise was enjoyed by both the landscape students and pupils, as well as providing useful information and colourful display material.

Evaluation scales

At the secondary-school level only, an evaluation method was used. This involved pupils rating a series of selected 'scenes' within the school grounds according to a set of twelve bi-polar scales. The landscape students then used these data to construct graphs for each site according to pupil age and sex. The pupils quite enjoyed participating in a 'technical' exercise, but at the same time felt that its structure limited their responses and that other supplementary methods were needed to give them a chance to express themselves more fully. The exercise did, however, provide the landscape students with a more 'solid' set of data to use.

Goal-setting techniques

'Ideal school' drawing

This stage entails not only developing lists of design goals, but also prioritising them. The most important method used in the study for obtaining the pupils' ideas for improvements in school grounds was the 'ideal school' drawing exercise. A number of forms of this exercise were tried: working alone and starting with a blank sheet of paper; working in pairs or small groups with blank sheets of paper; working individually but with free discussion about ideas within a group; individuals drawing ideas onto an outline map of the school; and individuals or pairs drawing ideas for specific parts of the school grounds. Whatever the form, the pupils were given the same instructions – that they could draw what they wanted, no matter how fantastic or unconventional. The role of the landscape students was to encourage the pupils as much as possible and provide inspiration, but not direct guidance, for those pupils stuck for ideas. This method proved to be popular with students and pupils alike and applicable to all age groups. The biggest drawback of the exercise was that the freedom produced a fair amount of unusable material. A favourite theme of young secondary-aged boys, for example, was teacher torture areas and horror movie settings! Despite this, the students felt that enough good and original ideas focusing on playgrounds, and equipment, sports facilities, seating/quiet areas and natural features, were produced.

Cue cards

A number of group discussion methods were also tried. One of these was the 'Cue cards' exercise, which involved a set of picture cards showing those landscape features that could be included in a school's grounds. The cards were then dealt out to small groups of pupils as in a game. The pupils discussed each feature, and then voted on them according to whether they wanted the feature in their school grounds. The selected cards were then priority ranked. The exercise was developed to encourage discussion within the group about needs and desires as well as to stimulate further ideas for features and suggestions for combining features as a way of organising priorities. The landscape students, whose job was chiefly to referee the discussion and take note of suggestions, were impressed by the quality of discussion achieved by the exercise. The pupils often considered the needs of other groups in the school and suggested both realistic and well-considered ideas. The pupils obviously enjoyed the exercise and were often reluctant to finish. Although as yet tested only at the primary school level, a second set of non-pictorial cards for secondary schools has been made, which includes a wider variety of features reflecting more sophisticated distinctions between types of features and the kinds of activities preferred by this age group.

School grounds design game

Another method developed for the goal-setting stage was the 'School grounds design game', to be used with secondary-school pupils. This was based on a kit of 3D landscape components, including surfacing materials, trees and shrubs, plant boxes, flower beds and so on. Each of these components had a purchase price assigned to it. The pupils were then given a template of a school yard and a budget, and asked to design the yard as they wished using whatever components they liked, as long as they did not exceed the budget. If it was exceeded, the pupils could then trade in some of their more expensive components for cheaper materials. Each purchase had to be logged on a tally sheet so that these trade-offs could be recorded – calculators are needed for this activity! This game proved to be very popular with the pupils. The designs that resulted were of high standards, with complex surface patterns and seating and planting arrangements.

TECHNIQUE SELECTION TABLE

The results of the school design projects, along with the data obtained from the interviews with the community designers and reviews of methods used in practice, were then used to develop the technique selection table (shown in Table 6.2). There are fourteen basic categories; see Sheat and Beer (1991) for a description of these categories. Table 6.2 shows their application to each stage of the participatory design process. As can be seen, the 'Site-related user information' and 'Goal-setting' stages have been broken down into information groups to clarify further how each technique category might contribute to them. It is hoped that teachers and designers alike will find this table, to be used in conjunction with the model of participation, useful for selecting appropriate techniques.

SUMMARY: A STRATEGY FOR TEACHERS

As a means of summarising this chapter, it might be useful to present a strategy for thinking about how to give children an effective voice.

First, consider your motives for involving children. Are these consistent with the ideals of participatory design as a means of transferring decision-making power to the user groups? Are these motives primarily educational? Participation solely as an environmental education exercise rates low on the ladder of participation, so it is important to consider how teaching can be used not as an end in itself, but to prepare pupils for participation. This will involve considering what skills children need for effective participation and how these might be enhanced through education. In addition, designers will often have good ideas for educational projects involving design concepts. These can be incorporated into the curriculum if the participatory project is planned well in advance.

Second, using the model of participation, work with your designer to map out a structure of the design process which will be used for your school improvements project. Where possible, involve the pupils in this also. The model should be regarded as a way of thinking about the design process, not a hard-and-fast structure which must be followed at all costs. This way of working will most likely be new, and possibly even threatening, to the designer. Shop around for a sympathetic landscape designer who will be prepared to negotiate the structure of the project with you. You can always contact the Landscape Institute for names of local designers.

Third, select participation techniques for each stage of the design process using the techniques table. A range of literature is available outlining possible techniques which you can either use directly, or as sources of inspiration for developing your own techniques 'tailor-made' for your particular design project. These may also form the basis of supplementary

Table 6.2   Techniques table

Technique categories	Stages	Site-related user information						Goal setting				
		Information about users	Attitudes towards site	Users' evaluation of site	Mental image of site	Effects of site on behaviour	Action of users in site	List of goals	Priorities for goals	Allocation of spaces	Design of spaces	Implementation and use
Survey methods, e.g. questionnaires, interviews		•	•	•			•	•	•			
Drawing, modelling or photography, e.g. to show 'ideal school grounds'				•			•	•		•	•	
Environmental evaluation methods, e.g. checklists, evaluation scales				•								
Photograph or drawing evaluation to show preferences for features		•		•				•	•	•	•	
Public meetings, presentations, assemblies, votes		•	•	•				•	•	•	•	
Creative writing methods, e.g. keeping diaries, poems, essays		•		•			•					
Group discussion methods, e.g. brainstorming		•	•	•				•	•	•	•	
Environmental knowledge methods e.g. cognitive maps				•	•	•						
Observation techniques e.g. activity maps						•	•					
Advisory groups or panels representing users			•	•				•	•	•	•	
Using secondary data to investigate themes & develop ideas		•										
Construction methods, e.g. building kits or modules												•
'Structured tests', e.g. standardised personality tests		•	•	•	•							
Games and gaming, e.g. trade-off and role-play games		•	•	•	•			•	•			

educational exercises useful for the attainment of National Curriculum targets.

REFERENCES

Arnstein, S. R. (1969) 'A ladder of citizen participation', *AIP Journal*, July: 216–24.

Baldassari, C., Hart, R. and Lockett, M. (1980) 'Participation', *Childhood City Newsletter*, 22.

Brown, F. (1990) *School Playgrounds*, London: NPFA Playground Services Ltd.

Davidoff, P. (1980) 'Respect the child: urban planning with the child in mind', in P. F. Wilkinson (ed.) *Innovation in Play Environments*, New York: St Martin's Press.

Hart, R. A. (1987) 'Children's participation in planning and design', in C. S. Weinstein and T. G. David (eds) *Spaces for Children: The Built Environment and Child Development*, New York: Plenum Press.

Hart, R. and Moore, R. (1982–83) 'Participation 3: techniques', *Childhood City Quarterly*, 9, 4 and 10, 1.

Johnson, J. (1979) 'A plain man's guide to participation', *Bulletin of Environmental Education*, November (103), 11–16.

Mares, C. and Stephenson, R. (1988) *Inside Outside*, Brighton: Tidy Britain Schools Research Project, Brighton Polytechnic.

Oberdorfer, J. (1988) 'Participatory planning and the small design office', *Landscape Architecture*, 78 (4): 64–71.

Poulton, P. and Symons, G. (1991) *Eco School*, Godalming: WWF UK Education Department.

Ross, C. and Ryan, A. (1990) *'Can I stay in today, miss?' Improving the School Playground*, Stoke-on-Trent: Trentham.

Sheat, L. G. and Beer, A. R. (1989) 'User participation – a design methodology for school grounds design and environmental learning', *Children's Environments Quarterly*, 6 (2/3): 15–30.

—— (1991) 'How to improve our school grounds', Sheffield: Department of Landscape, University of Sheffield. Part of a series of four papers on school grounds improvements which can be purchased from the Department.

Chapter 7

The biggest classroom

Susan Humphries and Susan Rowe

We welcome visitors to our school. We ask the children to become tour guides and take each visitor around the school site and through the class-rooms – two children per adult – and to give full explanations of what, and why, and how. When there is time, the visitor's child-focused tour will be followed by a second journey around the grounds and inside the school, in the company of one of the staff.

This chapter is a written guide to our school and its grounds, with details of the changes that have taken place over the years and some of the reasons for them.

The Coombes School opened in 1971 as an infant school to serve the expanding needs of the two local villages and the nearby army garrison. We are situated in a rural fringe area between Reading and Wokingham. A very large housing development 3.2 kilometres away across the M4 motor-way has altered the previously rural nature of the area, and there has been considerable building on the outskirts of Wokingham. Sixty per cent of our children are based at the local army garrison. The pupil population tends to be highly mobile as families are posted in and out of the garrison. Some postings are for three or six months; others are for two or more years. Our adjacent villages offer a more stable pupil population, although there is considerable mobility here also. Approximately 10 per cent of children travel as much as 12.8 kilometres to attend the school.

At present there are 170 children in the infant department, and we also have a twenty-six-place nursery unit offering part-time nursery education for fifty-two children. The nursery opened in September 1991.

The school is state-maintained and receives standard provision in terms of budget. There have been no extras from the Local Education Authority for the environmental work we have carried out over the years.

The school site is small; less than 0.5 of a hectare, although we do share a field area with the neighbouring junior school. Part of the field is marked with a football pitch for the junior children.

Our school stands in a part of what long ago was Windsor Great Forest. There are one or two signs of what the landscape once contained: a small area of ancient woodland – the Coombes – lies to the north of the school site, and there is a well-established hedge approximately 400 years old along our north-west boundary. The soil is very heavy clay, and Arborfield was once well-known for the quality of its bricks.

When the building contractors handed over the school in 1971, the grounds contained nothing but heavy clay and some builders' rubble. The building seemed monolithic in the exposed area it occupied, and the large square of plain Tarmac nearby added to the austerity. A peculiarity of design situated the Tarmac playground 10 metres from the school which was approached by paths across the clay ground (rock hard in a dry summer, and a quagmire in the wet). French drains criss-crossed the clay and provided temptation for would-be stone throwers or footballers. The Tarmac square was exposed to all winds: there was no shelter for the children or adults. The soil was in very poor condition, and only the ranker weeds could be found growing on the site.

The images and memories of twenty-odd years ago are stark: children leaning into the wind; children with no places to sit; bolder children chasing one another across the playground; timid children standing at the edges; children sneaking back to the cloakrooms and classrooms.

The staff were anxious to do something to soften the landscape and make it more 'people-friendly', and to reduce the aggressive behaviour of some of the children. Staff meetings were dominated by talk of possibilities: everyone had a say. The children's views were sought and we all became involved in the work that is still on-going, twenty-two years later.

It seemed to us then, and still seems now in 1993, that the view that children have of their environment is in large part determined by the way in which the adults responsible for the children view and use the same environment. If the adults who foster the children ignore the outdoor surroundings, then the potential of the environment is not realisable for either group. Children tend to take their cues from the adults with whom they have regular contact. We wanted the children to react positively and constructively with the school site, and we had to be the ones to offer the positive models. Some of this we did unconsciously and instinctively at the time: clearer views come with hindsight.

From the beginning, we viewed the outside environment as another teaching and learning space for us all. Teachers took old carpets outside for story-time; the children chalked pictures and invented games on the playground surface. We invited the army bands to give us marching concerts; regular street theatre took place in the playground, and the dinner ladies started serving the midday meal outside on sunny days. The children danced and paraded, and had maths and science lessons out of doors. Homing pigeons would be ceremonially released and observed, and we made and flew kites. The learning experiences out of doors complemented those inside the school and vice versa.

We became teacher researchers, and initiated a series of investigations into children's perceptions of their outdoor surroundings at school. During a four-year period, we collected impressions from every child in the school at the end of every term. The children were asked to draw what they remembered and liked outside at school. Each drawing was numbered in the order that it was drawn (helpful parents and other supporting adults helped the younger children to number their drawings, and labelled the drawings as necessary). We scored 6 points for the first drawing, 5 for the second, and so on down to one point for all the rest. The responses of all the children in school were assessed by the points scored by each feature of the school site drawn by the children.

Several important points emerged from these termly reviews. We noted that the key experiences introduced by the adult skewed the children's responses to and perceptions of their outside places. To take aspects of our school grounds that we describe shortly: pond dipping and studies of life in water brought ponds to a first or second position in the scoring during the term in which this had been a regular activity. Listening to music and joining in singing games on a concentric circle design marked on the playground made the concentric circles more meaningful and popular during the term when these were taught. Apple picking or sunflower harvest was a sensory experience which left strong memories which the children recalled when asked to draw what they liked about the outside at school.

Each learning experience which took place out of doors, from studies of minibeasts to kite flying, from clowns performing to tree planting, imbued the area where the experience had taken place with happy memories. The children could describe in detail why they had drawn a particular landscape feature, and could recall what had happened there even after some months. In the short term, parts of the playground became landmarks, as the tide of interest generated in the topic or event associated with that part remained dynamic and meaningful to the children.

Guidance for our planning came from the children's drawings, and from discussions with them about these. From their drawings, we see how important it is to give apparently simple things to the children, and how we as adults tend to overlook the obvious. The sight and feel of leaves being caught by the wind in a swirl, or being under a tree as it sheds its spring blossom, are circumstances which some children remember and can describe in great detail. The comments of the children have influenced much of what we have done in the school grounds. We have used the children's responses to our investigations to guide our work outside, and it seemed to us that as we embarked on work out of doors we should canvass the children, listen to them, and interpret regularly and with care what they said.

When we started to improve our school's surroundings, we were acting to meet obvious and immediate needs. We believe that it is possible for any school to enrich its outdoor area by using it in new and exciting ways. Those playgrounds set in deprived, inner city locations can be imbued with feelings of exhilaration and expectation on the part of the children. By constructive and imaginative approaches to the National Curriculum and the teaching taking place out of doors, the school community can begin to see its setting in a new light, without planting one tree or digging out a single pond.

The knowledge of the grounds which comes from their regular use puts into bold relief some of the changes which will need to be made to improve things like seating quality, shelter, assembly points, play equipment and planting. The way we had been using the grounds as a teaching space led us into environmental change and improvements, based on our awareness of our school's landscape and our formal use of it as the largest classroom.

THE DEVELOPMENT OF THE SCHOOL GROUNDS

In 1971, we began our environmental work. The area requiring immediate action was that between the school building and the Tarmac playground. We covered two-thirds of this ground with paving slabs, and we enclosed the remaining one-third of land with a low brick wall, to make a 'minibeast garden'. The wall is 0.6 metres thick and crenellated, and because the ground on which it is situated slopes, the height varies from 50 cm to 1 metre. The results were that the children had more play space, and no longer had to negotiate the narrow pathways across clay. The long, low surface provided by the wall gave informal seating for thirty or more children, and the children were able to climb and balance on the wall, and sit and talk within the niches.

The ground within the wall was designated as a minibeast sanctuary, and favourable conditions were set up so that the area would be inhabited by plant life, insects and small creatures. The soil was heavy clay, and we were advised to break this down by planting potatoes. We did this for two years, with moderate success. We added compost (leaves, vegetable matter, decaying logs), and the natural effects of weathering eventually gave us the right soil conditions to begin a planting programme. A herb layer was encouraged by planting vetch, nettle, clover, thistle, ivy, naturalised bulbs and grasses. A shrub layer was formed by planting holly, hazel and hawthorn, and a tree layer was started with silver birch, apple and crab apple. A programme of coppicing and pollarding was begun to ensure sturdy and variable growth. We wanted the trees we planted to resemble those in natural woodland, rather than the standard specimens found in public parks.

The brick walls of the minibeast sanctuary provided a setting for an assortment of wildlife, as well as offering informal seating. The colonisation of the wall by plants, algae, mosses and lichens was a slow but fascinating process, and was accompanied by growing numbers of snails, spiders, beetles, ladybirds and other animals and minibeasts. The children were able to sit on the wall and reach into the garden for the creatures and plants they wanted to study (both in teaching sessions with a teacher, and also during free playtimes). A rule was set that no human feet would enter the garden, and that all living specimens would be returned unharmed to their habitat.

The success of this small, partly walled garden informed our planning for further areas of the grounds. We were able to recognise certain principles and put them into action on a larger scale. It also helped us to clarify our vision of the school landscape in the future. We wanted the school to be set in a wild garden; to be truly a 'kindergarten'. We wanted trees and smaller plants, animals, insects and birds to be part of the children's daily outdoor experiences. We wanted the playground to be in the centre of an environment which changed and responded to the annual cycles of plant growth and decay. Above all, we wanted to create a purposeful setting for children to play and work in: a setting which would both enable the whole range of the curriculum to be taught more effectively, and would also provide an aesthetically pleasing and ecologically valuable backdrop to everyday school life.

Beyond the newly created paved area and the small garden, the Tarmac playground looked bleak and uninviting, and so it was to the playground itself that we next directed our attention. We sought the children's opinions and they asked for colours; we responded to their requests by painting vividly coloured patterns on the Tarmac. We marked out concentric circles, a number snake, a square divided into hundreds, a logic track, hopscotch, and a variety of diagrams for traditional maths games. We used rubberised marking paint when we could afford it, and also sent out appeals for cans of brightly coloured gloss paint. We mixed together cans of similar colours so that we would have a good quantity of one shade to paint a design. The teachers took the children outside to work formally on the designs, teaching mathematics skills and strategy games. It was interesting to note that during their free playtimes, the children continued to use the designs and play the games they had been taught. Even more interesting, we noted how the children themselves negotiated new rules or invented new games to play on the designs. The dinner ladies noted that the children's play became more inventive and less aggressive when the designs were marked out. Over the years, we have been careful to change the markings, or to renew them at regular intervals, in response to our and the children's needs.

People have since suggested that the children themselves should design and mark out the patterns they want on the playground. It has been our experience that the very young children who attend our school cannot easily do this and produce a result of high quality which will appeal to the whole pupil group. However, we do regularly give the children chalk, and ask them to mark out designs of their own choice in the playground. These designs are ephemeral and they disappear with the first shower of rain, but we always take note of what the children have drawn; we take photographs and colour slides; and we act upon some of the children's chalked suggestions.

We had observed how the children congregated on the walls of the new minibeast garden and we reflected upon our own preferences when working outside. We felt that there was a great need for informal seating: not just to give the children the chance to sit down and talk and play, but also to have areas of the playground where classes of children could be drawn together in comfort for teaching purposes. Playground seating became our next priority, but we could also see a multiplicity of uses to which that seating could contribute. The grass verges of the playground were rapidly deteriorating as the children overran them in the course of their play. We felt that, by enclosing the playground with low walls, we would prevent further deterioration of the soft landscape, and we would provide seating areas and create a more intimate overall atmosphere. As and when we could afford the materials, we began to build low brick walls, between 50 cm and 1 metre high, and about 25 cm in width on three edges of the playground. The work was done gradually, as we could afford it, or when a generous donation of building materials was given by a parent or friend. We became used to saying 'yes' to any offer of materials, because we knew that we should eventually find a purposeful use for them.

As each small section of wall was completed, it was put into immediate use by the children and adults. At one point, a group of children asked if it would be possible to have a castle to play in. We invited the children to design a suitable castle in their formal maths sessions, and they came up with a scheme to build a hexagonal castle in the planned west wall of the playground. They wanted to be able to climb up into the castle, so the final design accommodated this request. The children helped the bricklayer (at that time, our caretaker, George Prior) to carry the bricks and breeze blocks and to mark out the hexagonal design. The completed raised castle was an instant success in the playground and it also provided a secluded, enclosed and intimate teaching area.

The castle was followed by a 'look-out tower' in the north-west corner of the playground. We wanted the children to have places where they could be taller than other children, where there would be an overview of the whole playground, and where groups of children could meet out of the way of the hurly-burly routines and games. The walls, castle and tower served these purposes.

On the northern edge of the playground we built a wall which included a seating area and a tunnel. With safety in mind, we offset the tunnel from the playground edge: the entrance is behind a steep step. In order to get into the tunnel from the playground, it is necessary to stop and climb. We felt that there would be an inherent danger if children were able to run directly into the tunnel opening. The tunnel (a large-diameter concrete sewerage pipe) leads the children from the main part of the playground to a garden area. In some public play areas, we had seen large concrete pipes placed apparently at random. We felt that these had very limited use for small children, and could be the cause of some nasty collision accidents; they also appeared to lack purpose. A tunnel is so much more intriguing if it does lead somewhere. Ours takes the children from a large open space to a small pathway enclosed by trees. By using the tunnel, the children have an escape route, or a short-cut, to a notably different play area.

Over the years we have added a variety of equipment to the playground. Our experience has shown us that, by offering areas of interest and challenge, the time that the children spend outside (quite substantial in terms of the total number of hours spent at school) could be given additional quality. In so many playgrounds there is nothing for children to do except wander aimlessly, stand on the edges, or engage in games that entail running, often with a ball. We have discouraged ball games, except in the summer when the children may play on the grass field, and we have filled the playground with different play options. We brought in huge logs and set these to one side of the playground: these logs are used by the children for climbing, hiding and seating and as a general meeting spot. We bought large concrete structures – a saddle, hollow cubes and stepping stones – and grouped these at different points in the playground. We have bolted together groups of old car, lorry and tractor tyres and set these in one corner. Some tyres we stacked together and filled with concrete to make super-safe, soft-edged stepping stones. As well as being used in children's free playtime, the staff now have a variety of outdoor resources which are used for explicit teaching. For instance, in a maths lesson the children may be asked to hide inside a cylinder, to stand on top of a cuboid, to put a finger on a circle, or pentagon, or triangle, to meet in the largest square or the smallest hexagon.

The opportunities for teaching in the playground are endless, and the imaginative teacher is never short of a curriculum resource outside. We have found that what the children do formally in lesson times outside tends to be adapted into their free play and augments it. If the outside areas are planned and set so that they contain challenging regions which can be used for formal and informal teaching, there can be a more thorough use of the environment. The areas can be used for taking children out in groups for the specific teaching of maths, language, science, singing, drama, history, geography and so on, in the knowledge that many of the children will reflect on and expand these activities during their free play times. Somehow the playground becomes a more social place because it has so many purposes: it also becomes a place of intellectual challenge and adventure.

At the same time we were developing the hard spaces outside, we were also putting into action our plans for the soft landscape. The new brick walls surrounding the playground meant that it was possible to plant immediately behind the walls: young plants would be given some protection from the children's explorations. We brought in some topsoil for these new gardens, but most areas of garden were created by the dumping of tons of road sweepings and autumn leaves. The local District Council were tipping these valuable sources of compost on public tips: we asked them to dump them at school instead. The leaves and sweepings (from residential areas rather than traffic-heavy main roads) were dumped wherever we needed new garden or had planting plans, and were left to decay naturally. The process of decay is quick: within six months to a year we resource ourselves with fertile humus where we want it. We do not advise planting directly into new areas of compost because of the massive amount of heat generated by decay in the first weeks. The compost heaps provide a free tree nursery as seedlings germinate in them; however, the loss of new plants from the heat of decay means that most 'free' tree seedlings do not survive.

The idea of schools being responsible for the planned planting of trees and the tending of pockets of land was one which appealed very strongly to us. We set a tradition that each child would have the opportunity to plant trees during his or her time at the school. Our planting around the playground edge was multi-purpose: the trees would eventually shelter the playground and offer shade on hot days; they would soften the harsh edges and give a more intimate feel; they would put children into nose, hand and eye contact with them, and they would bring a host of creatures, particularly birds, to the area. Additional bonuses came in the crops that the children would be able to harvest: apples, pears, cherries, plums, chestnuts, conkers, walnuts, hazel nuts, acorns, ash keys and so on. The gathering of harvests is one of the most enjoyable aspects of gardening, especially for young children. Long-term planning is very important and means that edible fruits can be gathered each year. The crops will not all be collected by the same children who helped with the planting, but some crops must be guaranteed to all the children every year. Because the children are directly involved in the planting programme, they develop a sense of ownership of their landscape, and a pride in it. Children often return to the school site and remark on the tree(s) which they personally planted years ago. We have a steady stream of 'old pupils' who come back to check out what is happening both indoors and in the school landscape.

The area of our planting activities was not confined to the playground edges: the children with their teachers have been actively developing the whole school site, and we now have pockets of maturing woodland around the school. Growing a future wood is a most rewarding experience. Some of our trees have been raised from seeds, pips or stones, but most have been bought as whips so are large enough to be owned by the child planter. The 'grow-your-own-forest' idea has been foremost in involving all the children, past and present, in doing something practical about the conditions in one small part of planet Earth. There are also other gains: from time to time, the front drive gate is locked and the car park at the front of the school emptied, in order that the children can have a different play venue where trees dominate the landscape. There are great benefits to be drawn from this change of play area, not least that the children's sense of ownership of the whole school site is enhanced, and their sense of place and location is heightened. It is interesting to consider that every £5 invested in a tree will accrue interest for the future. Man-made educational resources depreciate in value; our stock of trees, bushes and plants increases in educational, aesthetic, ecological and social value each year.

The planting programme includes spring-flowering bulbs, and a wide variety of annual crops as well as trees. The children grow sunflowers, pumpkins, marrows, potatoes, tomatoes, beans, herbs and flowers. They harvest the fruits of their work, and use these in school to support the curriculum, and they take any surplus home. The growing of food, the preparation, cooking and eating together of it, have tremendous significance for young children. It concentrates on basic life skills, and demonstrates how children themselves can sow, reap and eat from the soil. The planting, nurturing and harvesting of food crops is central to human life on Earth.

In order to protect the soft landscape, and to keep humans off the planted areas and the delicate creatures which inhabit them, we built all-weather concrete pathways (nature trails) which encircle the school grounds. A teacher can lead a group of children around the grounds at any time of year, without damage to the landscape or to shoes, and it is possible to have outdoor walks for learning, teaching and pleasure. Each section of pathway was completed as we could afford it (some sections were done metre by metre), and to mark each section, we buried a time-capsule (a sealed biscuit tin containing a piece of work from each person at the school and other items of interest – coins, newspapers, the National Curriculum documents!) for future archaeologists.

We believe that it is vital that the children are active collaborators in each improvement we undertake and that they are involved at the planning stages right through to the fruition of every project. It may be tempting to see the work completed quickly, which could mean that it is often done with outside help, out of school hours, and without the children being directly involved in it. We argue that developments should take place over time, that each improvement should lead into the next, that each stage is evaluated and that the work is perceived as an organic whole, with the children as focal points throughout. The development of school grounds is not a project which can be said to have an end: the process should be ongoing and should involve the whole school community each year.

We aim to provide as many different types of natural habitat as possible within the school grounds. There are now four pond areas, flights of steps, a heather garden, a turf bank, a ditch complete with a bridge, wild-flower meadow areas, a willow bank and a turf maze. There are obvious environmental and ecological benefits which accrue from these developments, as well as social gains for the whole school community.

Visitors are often surprised at the degree of 'freedom' we give the children to explore and use some of these different areas at playtimes. Obviously, there are no-go areas (the ponds, the ditch and so on), but equally the children do not have to stay within the confines of the Tarmac playground. There are places directly off it which they can visit, where the adult supervision will be less intense and where there is an element of trust. It has been our intention to give the young children in our care some personal responsibilities and some choice. The children learn to respect the few rules we impose and see the sense of them, and we notice how they care for and watch out for one another when they are outside. Children need to be able to disappear (from an argument, a bully, a chase) and reappear when they choose, when the problem has been solved or when a mood has changed. We feel that most playgrounds are too simple and do not satisfy the need we all have for complex situations. We all need to have quiet areas, hiding places, places for cooling off, as well as open spaces and public places. By examining our needs and preferences as adults, we influence our planning for children outside at school and cater for the children's needs, which are not so very different from our own.

We believe that children at work and play in a lively, changing and diverse landscape will react imaginatively, and build up high expectations and happy recollections of school life. As a group of teachers, we agreed to develop the grounds as a living unit to be enjoyed for aesthetic reasons as well as for curricular gains. We knew that the care and imagination which we gave to the indoor classrooms needed also to be given to the outdoor setting of the school. We wanted every window to offer a different and changing daily picture of the natural world. The gains may well be more than curricular or aesthetic: it is possible to add features and events to the landscape which will nurture the social, emotional and spiritual development of every human being in it. The grounds add value to the children's learning in all its spheres; they help to modify both expectations and behaviours; they influence children and adults profoundly. They provide opportunities for us all to live in a community rich in wildlife and in which people, plants and animals may coexist with mutual benefit.

We try to use the grounds imaginatively, and throughout the year we plan for a whole range of events and experiences which take place out of doors. In the last three months, the children have welcomed a camel to the playground arena (part of a block of work on the Nativity); acted out an Epiphany journey (making shelters, erecting tents and so on); replayed the old village tradition of beating the bounds on the perimeters of the school

land; planted and harvested mistletoe; made Chinese dragons and celebrated the Chinese New Year with outdoor parades and dancing; picked
bunches of daffodils to take home as a celebration of spring; made hurdles
from home-grown willow; helped to groom a visiting horse; talked to and
observed a falconer with his hand-reared buzzard; watched foresters at
work coppicing and pollarding some of the trees. Each term has a cycle of
events taking place out of doors, which are rewarding in themselves, which
enable us to meet the requirements of the National Curriculum, and which
bring excitement, anticipation and expectation to the children.

The work in which we have been involved for more than twenty years
has been for our community a worthwhile and necessary enterprise, which
has affected all those people who have taken part in it. We are constantly
engaged in the effort to create, maintain and improve an outdoor environment at school which we hope will positively influence learning and which
will enhance every aspect of the lives of the individuals in it.

Chapter 8

Training schemes for lunchtime supervisors in the United Kingdom
An overview

Sonia Sharp

This chapter describes the outcomes of a study of the nature and extent of provision for training of lunchtime supervisors throughout the United Kingdom. The study involved writing to all Local Education Authorities asking them to describe provision available within their area. There are, of course, drawbacks to this kind of investigation: as a researcher you rely on your letter arriving with the right person, and on that person being willing and able to reply. Nevertheless, the overall response rate was 52 per cent, thus allowing a fairly substantial but still incomplete picture of supervisor training in the United Kingdom to be established.

It was obvious that, as a result of decentralisation of school budgets, much training is now organised by schools themselves. This makes it harder for the LEAs to keep accurate records of the nature and extent of training for supervisors. It seems likely that more training is taking place than is recorded here. However, there were enough similarities to enable me to draw some broad generalisations about the nature and extent of training courses on offer in the United Kingdom. These will be described in the latter part of this chapter and it is hoped will offer some guidance to prospective course planners. The study also highlighted some concerns with regard to lunchtime supervision. Obviously, every school is distinct and is likely to face unique difficulties in improving the quality and effectiveness of supervision, but there are some aspects of lunchtime supervision which seem to give cause for concern in many schools. These will be addressed in the first part of the chapter.

First, though, it may be worthwhile reflecting briefly on the effect of recent educational changes on supervision and on training.

FINANCIAL AND POLITICAL CONTEXT

The changes in conditions of service for teachers, introduced in the 1960s, began a gradual move away from teacher involvement in lunchtime supervision in schools. This change was precipitated by the withdrawal of goodwill during the teachers' action in the mid-1980s when most teachers stopped participating in lunchtime provision for pupils. During that period, not only did schools have to establish alternative methods to teacher supervision but there was also recognition of the benefits for teacher performance that taking a lunchbreak can bring. Since then, the role of the lunchtime supervisor in the management and organisation of the school dinnerbreak has become more central. As they have been pushed towards assuming more responsibility for this midday break, so it has become more apparent how ill-equipped and poorly resourced they sometimes are for this demanding job.

The Elton Report (DES 1989) recognised that lunchtime is a vital and often neglected feature of school life in the way in which it can affect behaviour in the school. The Report urged an increase in teacher involvement over this period, and recommended that supervisors be trained in skills in behaviour management. Since the Report was published there has been an upsurge of interest and action in relation to training lunchtime supervisors and implementation of lunchtime behaviour policies. Of course, some innovative schools or LEAs did provide training for their supervisors prior to the Elton Report, but these were few and far between.

Local Management of Schools (LMS) has resulted in funding for education being managed by individual schools rather than being held centrally by LEAs. This has had a two-fold effect on the training offered for lunchtime supervisors.

The first effect has been to free schools to spend money on training for supervisors. Prior to LMS, some LEAs had interpreted the guidelines for how the central training budget could be spent as excluding ancillary staff such as supervisors and care assistants. This meant that any initiatives for training had to be run without a budget or be funded by individual school's personal funds. There were some Authorities, however, who did not feel constrained by these guidelines and did run training schemes for supervisors paid for from central funding. These increased in number in 1990 when money provided from central government under the GEST scheme encouraged midday supervisor training. The cost of such training schemes is usually shared between the school and the Authority. Sometimes this kind of training arises through negotiation with educational psychologists or other support services. The future of such initiatives is uncertain as budgets are increasingly delegated to schools.

The second effect of LMS is that training for all staff is now on a priority basis. Training for supervisors vies with training needs of other staff, the environmental repair of buildings, the need for curriculum resources, the cost of the day-to-day running of the school.

Some problems faced by schools relating to supervision involve management and organisation of the lunchtime system and the way supervisors are perceived within the school. The next section explores some of these 'common concerns'.

COMMON CONCERNS

The main concerns were:

- confusion and lack of clarity about authority and responsibility;
- poor communication between teaching staff and supervisors;
- health and safety matters;
- lack of status.

These issues are not discrete – they all interweave, sometimes strengths in one area compensating for problems in another. Any school wishing to enhance the quality of its lunchtime provision may find it helpful to consider its own practice in relation to these areas. We will consider each of these areas in turn.

Authority and responsibility

The clear definition of roles for both supervisors and teaching staff during the lunchtime period is an essential step in streamlining supervision. There are times when a teacher is present in the yard or at the dinner table during the lunch hour. This may be because the school has a system for supporting supervisors, or it may be because the teacher enjoys eating lunch with the pupils. Whatever the reason, supervisors report feeling unsure about who is in charge in these situations. They more often than not assume that the teacher is 'in charge' and therefore restrain themselves from asserting their own authority. Naturally, the teacher may be unaware that this is the case, and expects the supervisor to take control of the situation. This can lead to inconsistency in behaviour management and organisation as well as re-inforcement to pupils that the teacher is more important than the supervisor.

This message is reinforced further in the unfortunate situation which arises when a teacher directly contradicts a supervisor, as in one case where a supervisor indicated to a group of pupils that they might clear up their table, and a teacher almost immediately told them to sit down and allowed another group to go. This kind of situation can also help to reinforce gender stereotyping, as supervisors are almost always female, and staff who are around at lunchtime are very often senior management who are still (although becoming less so) predominantly male.

An example of indirect contradiction was offered to me at a recent training course. A supervisor had been told by the headteacher that a certain grassy slope was out of bounds. A number of parents had complained about their children's muddy clothing resulting from falls when running up or down the slope. A group of pupils had persistently been ignoring the supervisor's attempts at implementing this rule. After a week of repeated intervention, the pupils finally took heed and were just leaving the slope to walk round the path when someone else appeared running down the slope: the headteacher!

Allowing children in at lunchtime also can cause problems. Permission slip systems (that is, where pupils receive a signed paper giving them permission to enter a usually restricted area) do not always work and can be inconsistently applied by members of the teaching staff. Supervisors may also be confused about who is responsible for pupils who remain inside at lunchtime: is it the supervisors or is it the teacher who has given them permission to stay inside? If there was a fire, who would have a record of which pupils were in or out?

Sometimes, the tasks assigned to the supervisors are unmanageable and therefore lead to inconsistency in practice and can undermine supervisors' authority. For example, in one school, supervisors were not only expected to control the large lunchtime queue but also simultaneously to manage the pupils who were in lunchtime detention and who occupied armchairs along the opposite side of the corridor outside the headteacher's office.

In situations where supervisors do assert their authority, they can meet with abusive retorts. These include challenges such as: 'My mum/dad says you're only a dinner lady so you can't tell me what to do!'; or more recently, 'My parents pay the poll tax, so you can clean that up – I'm not going to.'

They also may meet with derisive comments about their appearance, education and social class. Supervisors from one secondary school, situated in a leafy suburb and boasting a high level of examination passes, were frequently subjected to quips such as: 'How many GCSEs does it take to be a dinner lady?' as well as constant verbal sexual and racial harassment. If they wish to follow an incident up, they are more often than not given blatantly false names or simply sworn at and then ignored. In another school, a primary, the supervisors were concerned about the behaviour of a particular group of boys who dominated the limited playground space with a game of football, upsetting other pupils with their aggressive be-haviour towards anyone who wanted to do anything else, and being selective about who could play at all. After discussion with the headteacher, a rota system was introduced. A week later, the boys were playing on a 'no football' day. One of the supervisors challenged them, to be told that they had seen the headteacher and he had changed his mind – they could play football every day and use the whole yard. A discussion with the headteacher revealed that, indeed, the boys had gone to the headteacher and he had agreed to revert to the old situation. The supervisors felt belittled on two counts: first, the headteacher had changed back to the old system without consulting or even informing them; second, they felt that their authority had been undermined.

There are many schools, of course, which have begun to address the issue of authority and responsibility. Teaching staff and supervisors have spent time discussing their roles, in particular where confusion about authority can arise. Their roles and responsibilities are then communicated to parents and pupils, who are expected to respect the supervisors as managers of lunchtimes.

Supervisors have also been linked to classes or year groups in a bid to encourage better and more personal relationships between pupils, teachers and themselves. They are invited to attend year assemblies or special events. In some cases, mostly in primary schools, lunchtime has been cut by five or ten minutes to allow supervisors time to spend with 'their' class. Schools have even introduced a mentor system, as an extension to training schemes, which enable supervisors to discuss matters of discipline with a member of the teaching staff with a view to enhancing their behaviour management skills.

Communication between teaching staff and supervisors

Supervisors can feel left out and frustrated by lack of information either about rule changes or about specific children. Similarly, they can notice that a child is behaving in a way which is out of character or likely to cause concern but have no mechanism for making that information known to the appropriate teacher.

They may have good ideas about the ways in which lunchtime, in particular the dinner queue, can be made more effective. Too often they have no voice in school matters. The combination of no communication system and lack of status can bring about a devaluing cycle which leads to supervisors not even bothering to mention their suggestions.

Sometimes, causes of great stress to supervisors can be simply remedied, but without effective communication they can cause the whole lunchtime system to descend into chaos. In one large secondary school the majority of pupils stayed for school dinner. All of the pupils arrived simultaneously for lunch and then had to go up to the counter three times – once for the main course, once for the second course and once to clear their plates. This meant that there was an immense queue of hungry pupils jostling to get their place. Once in the dining room, pupils were constantly being rushed by supervisors to eat and clear. In a bid to ease this crush, the school had invested in a vending machine. Unfortunately, they had placed it in the same corridor as the lunchtime queue. The lunchtime supervisors felt that the situation would be eased by moving the vending machine to a less crowded position and staggering entrance to the dinner hall by five- or ten-minute intervals per year group. Additionally, if cost allowed, they felt that trays or 'flyers' which allow pupils to collect all courses at the same time would speed up service and reduce movement in the dinner hall. They discussed this frequently amongst themselves but had not dared to approach the headteacher with their suggestion, mainly because there was no set forum to do so.

More serious consequences of poor communications relate to children's emotional or physical state of health. One child had a specific medical condition which required careful monitoring. On one occasion the child came to the supervisor at lunchtime complaining of sickness. The supervisor told her to stay quiet and if she still felt ill in fifteen minutes, to come back. The child collapsed and was taken to hospital. Teaching staff knew that they should contact the doctor immediately if the child complained of sickness. Nobody had told the supervisor.

In trying to improve communications, schools can implement a number of strategies. The most popular and most efficient include bulletins or notice boards for supervisors which post details of pupils who are to go to lunch early, changes in school routine for that day, and so on. Also, in the same way as notebooks are often used to allow parents and teachers to exchange comments on the child's progress, therefore facilitating communication between parents and teachers, so lunchtime books can allow messages between supervisory and teaching staff about specific children or special arrangements.

Establishing a regular pattern of meetings for supervisors can be very helpful, although there is a danger of these remaining on a superficial level if not managed correctly. Supervisors need to be encouraged to contribute their ideas in a meaningful way. There is a danger in perceiving such meetings simply as a forum for 'clearing the air'. Outcomes of such meetings need to be clearly agreed and followed up.

Involvement of supervisors in any training or policy development which concerns behaviour management, discipline, equal opportunities, special educational needs and so on not only serves to provide educational opportunities for the supervisors but also helps to break down the prejudicial and stereotyped barriers about supervisors. Helpful training topics can include dealing with children with special needs and multi-cultural issues. Shared training also makes a statement about the status of supervisors in the school community. The discussion which takes place within it can help to establish a more consistent and cohesive set of attitudes and values about children and education amongst all staff. This in turn enables teachers and supervisors to share common goals, which will shape the way they interact with children and will reinforce messages about standards of behaviour and the importance of lunchtime in the school day.

Health and safety matters

Supervisors may receive no training in first aid, yet be expected to cope if a child has an accident during the lunchtime. Although there will always be a member of the teaching staff on hand, they may not be immediately obtainable and crucial decisions may have to be made by the supervisor at that time. Supervisors have requested basic first-aid training and also information on how to deal with conditions which require a specific response, such as epilepsy. As part of their supervisor training scheme, Avon LEA issue a pocket-size easy-reference card which not only provides general information about duty times, names of teaching staff available for support and disciplinary procedures, but also describes action to be taken in case of different injuries. In Gloucestershire, supervisors are advised to wear small pouches containing essential first-aid equipment. They can then respond to minor accidents without having to enter the school buildings. The pouch includes plastic gloves: supervisors often have to 'mop up' after accidents. Supervisors need to be aware about risks connected with HIV, not only for themselves but also for other pupils.

Supervisors also feel strongly that they should know about individual children's medical conditions and that they can be trusted to keep such information confidential. In addition to children who are medically vulnerable, there are also other children about whom they feel they do not have enough information. Supervisors do not need to know exactly what is troubling a child who is unhappy, but it can help in their management of them if they know that there is a problem of some kind.

Supervisors also need to know about child protection procedures, signs of drug abuse or bullying and procedures for dealing with adults who enter the playground or campus. They also should be able to execute the fire drill, as it is possible that a fire could break out during the lunchtime period. A fire practice should be held during lunchtime in the same way as it is held during lesson time.

Another quandary supervisors face is what to do with a sick child. They can send them in, but to whom? Who remains responsible? Organisers of training courses also commented on myths which have arisen around health and safety matters. One group of supervisors believed that they should never touch a child. Their interpretation of this restriction had been extended to include not comforting a crying child and not tending an injured child. Without the opportunity for discussion or clarification, regulations can be distorted and misunderstood.

Difficulties also arise when a supervisor is not able to come to work, potentially over-stretching the rest of the team. Some schools have begun to address this by having a cover system operated by teaching staff.

Lack of status

Underlying all of these difficulties, however, is the pervasive problem of lack of status for the supervisors as perceived by themselves, other staff, pupils and parents. Supervisors are sometimes viewed as 'non-people' – nobody knows their names except for perhaps the headteacher, and they are not always sure of the teachers' names. They are often openly contradicted and ignored. They may be completely left out of any behaviour management scheme the teachers operate, therefore suggesting to pupils and parents that they are not credible managers of behaviour. Subtle messages about their status are sent via language and behaviour of teaching staff and pupils. 'Staff' meetings are not usually for all staff, but only for teaching staff. In some schools, supervisors are not allowed to use 'staff' toilets or the 'staff' room. These exclusions suggest that they are not real staff, and therefore do not merit the respect given to teaching staff.

Some schools who have sought to address the matter of status have begun to look at how they describe meetings or places. 'Teaching staff' meetings are for teachers; 'staff' meetings are for everyone. Supervisors have been encouraged to attend some staff meetings and also have been given time to have meetings of their own, perhaps with a senior teacher so that they can communicate their ideas and views; they have been included in working groups which tackle policy development concerning behaviour and discipline; they are expected to operate the same behaviour management system as teaching staff (both rewards and sanctions); they are addressed by pupils and parents in the same way as teaching staff; they are invited to make changes to the organisation of lunchtime which they feel will make the system more effective; and they are encouraged to view themselves as managers of lunchtime and are backed up by teachers when necessary.

TRAINING

In this section of the chapter I will describe some of the main features of the courses currently on offer in the United Kingdom.

Organisation and funding

The responses from the LEAs fell into four categories. First, *no provision*: 25 per cent of the Authorities who responded did not provide any training for supervisors and knew of no schools within their region which did so either. Second, *school-initiated responses*: in 12 per cent of cases training was organised by some schools in the area, either individually or on a cluster basis. Although the LEA had not been involved directly, the training was often assisted by local advisory staff or educational psychologists.

Third, *joint venture between LEA and schools*: this category was the most common. Fifty per cent of respondents reported a dual system, usually initiated by the LEA, whereby the LEA provided a pack or training course and headteachers enabled the supervisors to use the materials or to attend a course either by offering payment, time off in lieu, or encouraging voluntary attendance. In a few cases special arrangements were made, such as teachers covering lunchtime whilst supervisors attended. Payment of supervisors to attend was not necessarily common practice. Most schools seemed to prefer to use the hours built up by way of teacher training days when supervisors are actually paid but do not work. This adds up to five hours per year.

Where a pack was provided, it was most often the OPTIS materials developed by Oxfordshire. Newcastle and Birmingham LEAs have also developed commercially available packs which have been used by some other Authorities (see pages 131–2 for contact addresses). Some LEAs had developed their own courses. Most of the Authorities who responded to my request for information about training for lunchtime supervisors also had materials and resources developed by their staff. Some Authorities wished to remain anonymous, but others are acknowledged at the end of this chapter. Schools which are interested in providing training courses for supervisors may wish to contact course organisers who are geographically near to them.

Training courses were mostly being run by centrally funded staff such as behaviour support teams, educational psychologists or other advisory staff. Some respondents expressed considerable doubts about whether existing, centrally funded training would continue under LMS, and some provided examples of abandoned schemes.

Fourth, *LEA supplies all*: 13 per cent of LEAs were able to run courses and pay for lunchtime supervisors to attend. This was possible because of specific funding allocation, either via GEST money made available after the publishing of the Elton Report or because of local prioritisation. All of these initiatives were only temporary in duration, the length of time for which the training was on offer depending on the extent of the funding.

COURSES ON OFFER

Courses for supervisors vary in length, ranging from one morning or afternoon to up to two days. The most popular structure is a series of four or five hourly sessions with a week or fortnight between each meeting. This hour can precede or follow on from the lunch hour or, where teachers are releasing the supervisors from their duties, can replace their normal working time. The weekly gap between sessions enables supervisors to try out suggestions immediately and then discuss how well the strategy or activity has worked in practice.

The choice of location depends on the feelings of organisers and school staff or on convenience and numbers. Individual site-based training offers an opportunity to focus on specific issues relating to the school. It poses no difficulties to supervisors in terms of transport and facilitates negotiation of change arising from the training with headteacher and other staff. In very crowded schools, however, there is not always a suitable space for the training to take place. Centrally based training enables supervisors to discuss their school with supervisors from other schools. This has been commented upon as a positive feature during evaluation. It can also encourage supervisors to talk more freely about the problems they face in their own schools. It is more cost-effective in terms of organisers' time, but can incur expenses for travel and room hire.

Some courses are for supervisors only. Other courses involve the headteacher at some stage in the training process. This will either be in the form of a final meeting or joint discussion during the course. One centrally run course expects headteachers to attend two of the three morning sessions. For part of the time the supervisors and headteachers work in separate groups and for the remainder the heads and supervisors are equally involved in the sessions. In particular, the headteachers are encouraged to share management strategies for situations about which the supervisors have voiced concern.

In describing their courses, organisers have emphasised the advantages of preliminary meetings and follow-up meetings which include senior management. In the preliminary meetings, aims and expectations are established; in the follow-up meetings, outcomes are agreed and evaluated. For example, Jane Wilkinson and Val Gardiner, from Gloucestershire LEA, precede their training course with a visit which enables them to spend lunchtime with the supervisors on duty. During this time they also consider environmental improvements which might be introduced. Marjorie Sunderland from Bury LEA not only meets the headteacher and the supervisors but also insists on discussing the training at a full teaching-staff meeting prior to the beginning of the course. She feels that this is an important stage which encourages more active results from the training than initial meetings with the headteacher only. Her course provides 'building blocks': she can introduce the supervisors to helpful strategies, she can work with them to highlight specific difficulties in the lunchtime system, but it is up to the headteacher and staff together to institute lasting change. In Lincolnshire, the Behavioural Support Service offer 'Food for Thought: a Course for Lunchtime Supervisors'. They have extended their package beyond just a prior meeting and a follow-up with the headteacher by introducing a 'booster' session for supervisors so as to encourage and maintain long-term change.

COURSE CONTENT

The content of the various courses encompasses a range of issues. All of them include aspects of behaviour management and consideration of the role of the supervisor. The management skills which teachers employ to direct children, to resolve conflict and to command respect sometimes involve subtle shifts in tone or facial expression or are communicated through body language. Quite basic organisational techniques help teachers to maintain an orderly classroom. A number of the courses on offer aim to highlight these to the supervisors so that they may begin to incorporate them into their own practice. Other issues introduced are:

assertiveness skills
bullying
child abuse
Children Act
communication skills
confidentiality
conflict resolution
consistency of approach
cooperative games
dinners
drug abuse
encouraging positive behaviour
equal opportunities
first aid
HIV/Aids
indoor play activities
interpreting children's body language: play or aggression?
movement and positioning in the playground
non-verbal communication
personal effectiveness
play organisation
playground games
protecting children from abuse
recruitment
relationships with children/staff/parents
reporting systems and structures
talking with children
team building/team skills
sanctions and rewards
school rules
stress management
wet lunchtimes

With only a few exceptions, supervisors had no choice over which course they attended. If the course catered for individual schools, there was obviously more flexibility about content. The uptake of the course by schools was based on the decision of the headteacher or senior management. Only two Authorities wrote directly to the supervisors and aimed their course information at them. Ealing Education Service was notable in publishing a glossy brochure detailing a range of ten different job-related courses specifically for supervisors and other ancillary staff as well as the option of school-based training. They also encourage schools to run shared training days on pertinent issues such as the development of whole-school behaviour policy.

Similarly, of the range of training packs available commercially, only two are addressed directly to the supervisors themselves (materials prepared by OPTIS and Gil Fell). Most are designed with course organisers and headteachers in mind. It is also apparent that, although primary schools are well catered for in this area, secondary schools have only a limited selection of resources available.

OUTCOMES OF TRAINING COURSES

Evaluation which has followed the courses has indicated that training lunchtime supervisors is felt to be worthwhile by headteachers and by supervisors themselves. It must be noted, however, that most evidence available seems to arise from self-report evaluations completed by teaching staff and supervisors. A future development could be to introduce additional, more objective measures for monitoring changes in pupil or staff behaviour resulting from such training and intervention. Pupil perspectives on the effects of playground changes could also be sought.

Nevertheless, teachers and supervisors report:

- improved communications between teaching staff and supervisors;
- greater self confidence amongst supervisors;
- reduced referral of problems to headteacher/teacher;
- more respect for supervisors from teachers, pupils and parents;
- more constructive handling of difficult situations;
- de-escalation of conflict;
- more orderly lunchtimes, more positive atmosphere;
- happier children.

Limitations

The plight of the supervisor is far more complex than can be resolved by training focused on the supervisors alone. The supervisors are part of an interacting system which reflects the collective attitudes and values of the school, the community and the wider social and political context. The effectiveness of supervision is an issue for primary and secondary schools alike. For secondary schools, in particular, improving supervision is an obvious step in addressing problems arising around the school grounds or corridors at lunchtimes or at breaktimes. Although the focus for this chapter has been on providing training for lunchtime supervisors, it is worth noting that supervision provided by some teaching staff at breaktime has potential for improvement as well.

A few hours of training is not going to resolve all problems. In one follow-up session, a trainer found the supervisors terribly disappointed. They had gone away from the training session full of hopes and encouraged that things would improve, not least because some of the improvements they had identified with the headteacher required only minor organisational changes. Unfortunately, once the course was over these seemed to be forgotten. The lunchtime supervisors felt let down and were quite demotivated by the experience. Headteachers and other staff must be committed to the concept of supervisor training.

Schools should also consider their recruitment and induction procedures for supervisors. Governors and headteachers need to be sure that the person appointed has the right kind of qualities to care for children. Once appointed, a clear job description and effective induction can help iron out problems caused by lack of clarity about role and responsibilities. There are also wider political issues relating to pay and conditions of service. Schools can have some effect on these matters now they are responsible for their own budgets.

The school, having invested in the supervisors, should strive to maintain change and continually seek for improvement. In some cases, the supervisors do feel empowered enough to make changes regardless of teacher support. However, the most satisfactory and long-lasting change is going to be achieved through working together to make lunchtime better.

CONCLUSIONS

The current trend indicates that training for lunchtime supervisors is being recognised as a valuable and worthwhile investment which can enhance the quality of life for all concerned with lunchtime in schools. Supervisors are being recognised as capable and responsible members of the school management system who are responsive to changing demands and have an entitlement to professional development.

The social and educational value of the lunchtime break should not and must not be underestimated. During this time, pupils learn skills for citizenship which will reach far beyond their school years. The playground *can* be a better environment, and ensuring that supervisors are properly trained is a key feature in achieving this.

Even if schools do not feel able to invest in training for their supervisors, there are many aspects of the lunchtime period which can be modified and amended in order to provide effective supervision. The principal areas to focus on are:

1 improving the status of supervisors;
2 clarifying roles and responsibilities of supervisors and teachers during lunchtime;

3   establishing effective two-way communication systems between teaching staff and supervisors;
4   sharing behaviour management strategies, first-aid skills and other helpful information with supervisors;
5   making the lunchtime system efficient and effective.

Without conscious effort, schools do communicate messages about how different sections of the school community are valued, and these messages affect how these groups are treated by others in the system. Headteachers, teachers and supervisors themselves can do much to boost the status of supervisors: by giving them a voice, by including them meaningfully in decision-making processes, by recognising them as valued members of staff.

ACKNOWLEDGEMENTS

Many thanks to all the LEAs who responded to my survey, including those who wished to remain anonymous.

RESOURCES

Commercially available packs and materials

Cross phase:

Jeanette Karklins and Phil Kirby (1993) 'Midday supervisors' in-service programme: open learning pack', Inspection Service and Training Services. Norfolk County Council, Norfolk Educational Press, County In-service Centre, Witard Road, Norwich, NR7 9XD. Tel.: 0603 33276.

OPTIS, 'Lunchtime supervision' (1986) Oxfordshire Programme for Training. ISBN: 0-948396-21-0.

For primary schools:

The video '395 to lunch' developed by 'The project on the management of children's behaviour and emotional needs' is part of a pack called 'Practice to share: the management of children's behavioural needs' (1990) Birmingham City Council/National Primary Centre, and is available from National Primary Centre, Westminster College, Oxford OX2 9AT. Tel.: 0865 245242.

The 'Primary lunch time resource pack', developed by Myra Robinson and Nick Weston and published by Newcastle upon Tyne Education Committee (1990), is available from the Education Support Service, Silverhill Centre, Stocksfield Avenue, Newcastle upon Tyne. Tel.: 091 274 5490.

Gil Fell (1992) 'She's only a dinner lady', training video and pack, SALVE, can be contacted via Gil Fell, Project Coordinator, 11 Alexandra Road, South, Whalley Range, Manchester M16 8GE.

Jane Wilkinson (1992) 'Cooperative play' and 'Wet playtimes', and Val Gardiner 'Midday supervisors' course' (trainers' and supervisors' pack), available via Gloucestershire LEA, Shire Hall, Westgate Street, Gloucester.

For secondary schools:

Sue Trotter (1993) 'The secondary lunchtime supervisors' course', Bolton Metro, PO Box 53, Paderborn House, Civic Centre, Bolton BL1 1JW.

Consultancy

Play Factors, children's play and leisure consultants, can be contacted via Christine Andrews, 1 Littleworth Lane, Esher, Surrey KT10 9PF. Tel.: 0372 464284.

Gloucestershire Elton Associates, 127 Slad Road, Stroud, Gloucestershire GL5 1QZ. Tel.: 0453 757329.

Strategies for a Less Violent Environment can be contacted via Gil Fell, Project Coordinator, 11 Alexandra Road, South, Whalley Range, Manchester M16 8GE.

Marjorie Sunderland, primary consultant, 14 Houghton Avenue, Bacup, Lancashire OL13 9RD.

Local initiatives

The following LEAs have been involved in training lunchtime supervisors, either through running centrally organised courses, by making materials available for schools or by other means of support. In most instances the training officer for the LEA has information about schools which have initiated training or personnel who might offer training. This is not a complete list, as some LEAs preferred to remain anonymous:

Avon, Birmingham, Bolton Metro, Devon, Ealing, Edinburgh, Fife, Hammersmith and Fulham, Hampshire, Harrow, Havering, Hillingdon, Gloucestershire, Lambeth, Lincolnshire, Merton, Newcastle upon Tyne, Newham, Norfolk, Nottinghamshire, Oxfordshire, Shropshire, South Tyneside, Sunderland, Warwickshire.

REFERENCE

Department of Education and Science (DES) (Elton Report) (1989) *Discipline in Schools*, Report of the Committee of Enquiry chaired by Lord Elton, London: HMSO.

Chapter 9

You're only a dinner lady!
A case study of the 'SALVE' lunchtime organiser project

Gil Fell

ORIGINS OF THE PROJECT

SALVE – Strategies for a Less Violent Environment – was originally my response to classroom teachers telling me that they often spent much of the afternoon's teaching time sorting out difficulties that had arisen over lunchtime. This need to improve the overall lunchtime environment co-incided with the time when the role of the 'dinner lady' changed to that of lunchtime organiser/supervisor as a result of the teachers' strikes of the late 1980s. It became apparent that suddenly there was an enormous army of untrained, low paid women (without exception all lunchtime organisers I have met have been female, although I know that some male lunchtime organisers do exist) responsible for children for between a fifth and a quarter of the school day. The main aim in developing training for primary school lunchtime organisers was to enable them to do their job more effectively, to raise their status, and thus to contribute towards reducing the overall level of violence in the school. For the purpose of this project, violence was defined in its broadest sense to include anything from excessive noise, whistle blowing and shouting to overt physical violence and bullying.

I have worked directly in more than twenty primary schools in the Manchester area and indirectly, through a series of courses, with the senior lunchtime organisers of at least thirty more. These courses were organised by Manchester LEA during 1991 and 1992. Each participating school sent the headteacher or deputy, a teacher, the senior lunchtime organiser and a parent governor. Over four weeks, they began the task of developing a whole-school approach to the times and spaces outside the classroom.

I am aware that the bulk of this work has been carried out in an inner city with its own peculiar problems of poverty and deprivation. Lunchtime organisers in Manchester may also be unusual in being entitled to some paid training time, and therefore were paid for the time they spent on the course. Nevertheless, I believe that the core problems are those that will strike a chord with lunchtime organisers everywhere. The development phase of the work culminated in the production of a training video and accompanying manual called 'You're only a dinner lady' which has served to spread the work of the project nation-wide.

THE APPROACH

The core philosophy from which I sought to develop the training was that a lack of self-esteem is a root cause of aggression and violence in adults and children alike. The better we feel about ourselves, the less likely we are to respond aggressively to the imagined slight or accidental push and the more able we are to deal assertively with perceived threats or criticism. Thus the underlying theme of the whole project was to make lunchtime organisers feel better about themselves and to do all that was possible to increase their status and their visibility as valued members of the whole school staff.

Lunchtime need not be just a gap between two blocks of important teaching or learning time which has to be filled with a minimum of trauma and bloodshed. Rather, it can be a positive and creative period of the day which, given the right approach, can provide a wealth of opportunities for non-curricular learning. These include the social skills of talking and eating together, as well as learning to play together and to cooperate and develop skills for successfully dealing with the conflicts that will inevitably arise from time to time. Lunchtime organisers are, on the whole, an under-used and undervalued resource: an untapped reservoir of talents and experience. Altogether, I have worked with lunchtime organisers with an accumulated total of experience in excess of 1,500 years: what riches to draw upon!

The approach I have developed evolved through my experiences of working with conflict over almost a decade. It is by no means the only approach but it starts from the needs of the participants themselves. There is no simple package of training that can be delivered to any lunchtime organisers in any school with a guarantee of instant change; neither is there a magic formula which, if correctly applied, will remedy all lunchtime ills.

For very many of the women I have worked with this has been the first training they have had since leaving school. Consequently, it was very important to make the course both accessible and acceptable to them. The key to achieving this was listening; lots of it. This was followed by the development of a tailor-made package to meet as many of their expressed needs as possible. From the beginning we dealt with the problems as perceived by the lunchtime organisers themselves rather than as seen by the headteacher or school in general. The priorities of the two groups were often very different.

The pattern of sessions which emerged was an initial one-hour 'diagnostic' session during which their problems were listed and prioritised, followed by two two-hour sessions. These were directly based on the prioritised needs from session one. The headteacher was usually invited to take part in the final session to give the lunchtime organisers a chance to talk over the needs and solutions identified during the course. From the start, it was firmly established that this time was theirs. In almost every case, it was the first time the lunchtime organisers had ever had the opportunity to sit down all together to think about their work and how it might be improved.

Emphasis was also placed on valuing their experiences, their intentions and their ideas, and finding ways to acknowledge and celebrate the wealth of experience they possessed. Clashes of values were not uncommon. For example, lunchtime organisers often had very different expectations from those of the teachers about what behaviour is acceptable from the children. It was over such issues that the work began to develop on two levels.

In schools where there was a firm commitment to the development of a whole-school approach, these differences in values and expectations were taken on board and lunchtime organisers were, and felt they were, included in the process of change. In others, training for the lunchtime organisers was almost separate from the general functioning of the school. In these cases the impact was more limited. Sometimes it felt very much like a cosmetic exercise, but the very act of providing training at all did help to raise their status and visibility. At one school, where I ran two courses, nothing on a practical level had changed between the first and second sessions, but there was a marked change in the lunchtime organisers' attitudes towards themselves and their work. The second time they were much more confident and clear about their needs and full of ideas about what they might do.

My conclusion was that the impact of the work depended on its being part of a concerted, whole-school approach towards the development of a positive management strategy for dinner-time. However, at a minimal level, the very process of the course itself raised the status of the women in the school.

THE PROBLEMS AND SOME EXAMPLES OF GOOD PRACTICE IN ACTION

Sometimes the list of problems felt endless. There were the tirades born of frustration and a feeling of invisibility; problems with the inevitable 'half-dozen' children; difficulties with other members of staff. We had lists that were short, and those which ran into scores of items. However, out of the seemingly disparate sheets of paper it was quickly possible to group the needs into commonly occurring categories.

To combat the problems came a welter of ideas. One of the joys of the project was to work with lunchtime organisers and watch the ideas start to flow and the enthusiasm start to grow. Schools where the ideas were translated into action and positive changes resulted were reward indeed.

Lack of respect

This was a crucial issue everywhere and was named as a priority by the lunchtime organisers in every school. 'You're only a dinner lady,' 'My mum says I don't have to take any notice of what the dinner ladies say' were daily taunts in many schools. The lack of respect did not come only from the children and their parents. Tales of having worked in a school for years and the headteacher still being unaware of your name were not uncommon, nor were tales of teachers walking past in the corridor without even saying 'hello' or 'good morning'. Sometimes there was deliberate undermining of the lunchtime organisers' authority by countermanding a decision in front of the children; for example, about whether or not it was wet play, or whether coats had to be worn.

Lack of respect is a cyclical problem. The lunchtime organisers want respect from the children and from other staff members, but respect has to be earned. Treating others with respect only comes through having self-respect, so the starting point was always to find ways of enhancing the lunchtime organisers' own self-image.

It is generally agreed that a major change in attitude takes time. Some quite simple steps are available to begin the process. For example, most schools issue a booklet about the school to parents and prospective parents. These can refer specifically to the responsibilities of lunchtime organisers as part of the school staff, and can also describe what behaviour is expected of pupils at dinnertime. This would immediately inform parents of the role of lunchtime organisers and also simultaneously confirm their status.

Other ideas include a letter home on a regular basis explaining the school's approach to lunchtime, making time to introduce the lunchtime organisers to the children, inviting them to school events; or thanking them for their contribution to the school. In one school, the lunchtime organisers feel themselves to be a full part of the school staff and so they organise and run all the trips and Christmas parties as well as regular staff socials and outings.

Some schools have made the supervisors' role the theme of projects. The pupils have interviewed the lunchtime organisers, which makes them more real to the children. In other schools, the children have drawn round them and coloured in the figures before putting up life-size silhouettes in the hall.

Whatever is done, the more anyone's work is appreciated the more willing they become to put in extra effort and time to make it even more rewarding. In the end it is the children who benefit.

Relationships with other staff

Problems in respect to relationships with teaching staff have already been mentioned. Another area which was common enough to be of concern was difficulties in relation to the kitchen staff. Sometimes this was historical. Until recently, the dinner ladies often served under the jurisdiction of the head cook. Following re-organisation, the dinner ladies were managed by a senior lunchtime organiser, separate from the kitchen staff. This loss of 'kitchen power' has caused enormous resentment in some places where memories of how it used to be linger on. It can lead to friction, and create an atmosphere where the lunchtime organisers find it too uncomfortable to claim the free lunch which forms part of their pay. In some schools, there were stories of having no place to sit or eat, the food being given to the children or thrown away. In one school, where the training had to take place in the dining room, the head cook sabotaged much of our time together by pushing round a very noisy trolley to lay tables and repeatedly lifting a heavy and extremely noisy metal hatch up and down. The world of lunchtime organisation is rich in anecdote and saga. Difficulties in working relationships provided one of the richest veins of all!

In some schools the lunchtime organisers enjoyed a more positive relationship with the kitchen staff. In those where there were difficulties, a first step was made by inviting at least the head of the kitchen to the last session and involving them in any ideas for change. Instigation of a regular, if brief, weekly meeting between the headteacher, senior lunchtime organiser and head cook was helpful in creating clear communication channels.

Lunchtime organisers' own needs

In addition to respect and good working relations with other departments, lunchtime organisers reported needs of a much more practical and mundane nature, such as lockers where bags and coats can be stored safely. In one school the lunchtime organisers were granted access to the bottom of the head cook's cupboard to store both bags and coats, and that was shared with ill grace. Somewhere specific to hang your coat shows that you belong to an establishment; that you are part of the staff and entitled to take your coat off to do your job.

Many of the women rely on public transport and juggle complicated timetables to fit all the facets of their lives together. This is made even harder if they are not allowed to bring shopping, done on the way to school, with them because it cannot be stored safely. It is also demeaning if purses and bags have to be taken to the secretary to be locked away. Schools where the lunchtime organisers had a space, with or without lockers, that they could call their own were rare indeed.

One school I have just worked in had already developed a whole-school approach to behaviour and play. They have created a staffroom for their lunchtime organisers out of an old cloakroom. It has storage space, tea-making facilities and comfortable chairs. The lunchtime has been reduced at this school to preserve the lunchtime organisers' working hours and so they have instituted a regular weekly staff meeting/training session.

There was also a great need for lunchtime organisers to have equipment of their own that the children could use either outdoors or inside in wet playtimes. This will be considered in detail in the sections on the playground and wet playtime.

Lack of communication

Poor communication is at the root of many misunderstandings and conflicts, and is a key area of concern for lunchtime organisers in any school. For example, there often seems to be lack of clarity about just who is in charge at dinnertime – who decides if it is wet play, for instance, or whether or not the children are to wear coats? Sometimes the lunchtime organisers, although nominally in charge, do not feel in control because some teachers will appear in the dining room or playground and undermine their authority.

Communication difficulties are almost bound to arise in a situation where the working times of two groups of people do not overlap unless special efforts are made to prevent them. If teachers are dealing with a child in a certain way and fail to communicate this to the lunchtime staff, then there is a likelihood of two different approaches clashing with each another, the children spotting the loophole and exploiting it. This is unfair to everyone.

Confrontation over who has permission to stay in at lunchtime is a common feature of a poor communications system. Children can be very adept at saying 'Miss X said I could', and running off to get retrospective permission from the staffroom before the lunchtime organiser has time to question them.

Of concern to many lunchtime organisers is the lack of basic information about the children in their care. This can vary from not being told about special dietary requirements to basic health problems such as asthma or epilepsy, or social, personal or behavioural difficulties. The former could have serious repercussions if a child became ill after eating 'forbidden' food when the lunchtime organisers are responsible for the children's welfare. There are always the issues of confidentiality to be considered, but enough can usually be said to prevent the child coming to physical harm or for lunchtime organisers to handle children coping with emotional problems in a sensitive and appropriate way.

A basic security element is involved in the handling of some information. For example, if a child is to be collected during the lunchtime by a parent, the lunchtime organisers should be informed and the child told to tell them before they go. With an increasing number of custody disputes this can be important. In one school, a child's parent turned up, the lunchtime organiser quite rightly took the child and parent to the headteacher to check the visit out, but whilst she led the way the child was whisked away by its father. Fortunately, on this occasion everything worked out all right.

Problems of communication were amongst the first to be tackled in many schools. Positive results can be simple, swift and straightforward and cost nothing other than a little thought. A clear system of passing on information from each class teacher to the senior lunchtime organiser about which children have permission to stay in over lunchtime saves a lot of unnecessary misunderstanding and helps children understand supervisory roles.

Regular staff meetings for the lunchtime organisers with the headteacher make a lot of difference, both to the smooth running of lunchtimes and to the self-esteem and status of the lunchtime organisers themselves. It is through open and frank sharing of viewpoints that real teamwork can begin.

Following the training sessions, the lunchtime organisers in several schools decided that they enjoyed meeting together specifically to talk about work, so they set up regular half-termly meetings for themselves, giving up their own time to do so.

Problems in the playground

Another main source of playground problems revolves around the fact that large numbers of children are in a confined space with nothing to do. Boredom often spills over into aggression and fighting.

A major strand of the project's work has been to help lunchtime organisers remember the games they used to play and to hand these on to pupils as well as to introduce them to new and cooperative games. No single game will occupy all of the children for all of the time, but games can keep some of them amused for a while and spark off new ideas that the children will develop for themselves.

The domination of the available play space by a group of year 6 boys playing football whilst the girls huddle in knots round the edges is also a common problem which many schools struggle to address. The banning of football results in its being played with rolled-up sweaters, stones or drink cans. It seems more creative to limit the space available to several five-a-side games. Other ideas are to provide cones around which the children can practise their dribbling and to find as many ways as possible for them to develop their ball-handling skills. Carpet tiles provide inexpensive and movable seating for pupils who do not wish to race about.

It was suggested, at one point, that lunchtime is the children's free time and should not therefore be filled with yet more organised activity. It was never part of the project's intention to do this, the aim being to provide suggestions that lunchtime organisers might use with children in search of an idea for amusing themselves creatively. This is often a particular problem for children coming up into reception from a nursery with a fully equipped and secure environment to somewhere where they have to amuse themselves for maybe half an hour, in a vast and empty space. Linked to this issue is the matter of wet playtime.

Wet play

Wet play can be described as 150 children divided between five classrooms and three lunchtime organisers, with a few broken crayons, some scrap paper and six tatty comics.

Difficulties are often compounded by the children being confined to their own classroom without being allowed to enjoy any of the equipment they use freely during the rest of day.

One school decided to revolutionise its wet play regime. First, it made a careful analysis of the space available and then set about using it to the best advantage. The key move was to take the children out of the classroom where they spent all day and to give them a choice of activity. This released the classroom to the class teacher and prevented work and equipment being inappropriately used. The pupils were able to choose between stories, songs and rhymes in the library; organised games, including using an indoor-size parachute in the hall; or playing with games and puzzles along the corridors. The senior lunchtime organiser was given some money for equipment by the school, and she sent a letter out to parents appealing for games and puzzles they were ready to discard. She received enough to provide plenty of varied occupations for the children on wet days. At this particular school, which has also provided simple outdoor play equipment, the number of incidents reported to the senior lunchtime organiser has dropped from about ten to an average of one a day.

In schools where the children are required to go to their classrooms, it is possible for the lunchtime organisers to create boxes of suitable games, puzzles and toys for the children to play with. Simple games tend to work best, and there are plenty of paper-and-pencil games which will amuse clusters of children.

In Manchester I have run three courses on developing cooperative group work through circle dances, games and the use of stories, puppets and masks. These have been popular amongst lunchtime organisers, and it is now possible to go into schools and find pockets of children learning to dance in circles, making masks out of junk materials, or wrapping themselves in pieces of material to act out bits from favourite stories!

Lining up

Lining up is frequently a major task for lunchtime organisers, which takes up a large amount of time, ingenuity and energy. Having visited a school where lining up has been abolished as a waste of the children's time, and having seen how the children just melted away into school at the end of dinnertime, I personally question whether it is necessary at all. Various schools have tried differing approaches. One which seems effective is to tackle it year group by year group. The children quickly learn that the first whistle is for the year 4s, the second for the 5s, and so on. Each year group then goes in as soon as its line is complete. This cuts the lining-up time by well over half and leaves everyone feeling much less fraught.

The dining room

Most school dining rooms would win design awards as echo chambers. A combination of high ceilings, bare walls and uncovered floors, often coupled with a serving hatch with kitchen behind, makes a cacophony of high-pitched voices, rattling cutlery and washing-up noise. This noise is one of the commonest lunchtime problems and its reduction is one of the most sought-after solutions.

One strategy frequently adopted to reduce the problems of dinnertime has been to make it shorter. In many schools this involves pressure to get children fed as quickly as possible. Consequently, many infants, in particular, have to be constantly hurried, and this often leads to children abandoning their food rather than struggling on.

In each school I have asked the staff to think about the kind of atmosphere they would like to create, bearing in mind that there will always be noise and that eating together is an important social occasion. As a solution, one school collected dried and silk flowers that parents were ready to discard and made small table decorations for each table which are still there over a year later; respected and appreciated by the children. In the same school, service was not working well, with juniors coming over to serve the infants, so they experimented with the infants serving themselves. This has worked very successfully. The children have clear guidelines and grow in competence and self-esteem, taking responsibility with a minimum of fuss and bother.

Queuing is a great time-waster and cause of noise and strife in dining rooms. Sometimes it cannot be avoided but it is worth searching for ways of reducing it as much as possible. Letting the children into the dining room straight from washing their hands rather than making them line up again to go into the dining room can stagger the queue a little. An even more radical approach in one school was to put lunchtime onto a split shift, with half the school breaking from 12.15 to 1.15 and the rest 12.30 to 1.30 p.m.

Children who eat their packed lunches in the dining hall rather than in a classroom can reduce the number of knives and forks clattering at any one time. Another, more costly idea is to use mobile screens to break the dining room into smaller units, with a lunchtime organiser in charge of each. The screens are low enough for adults to see over but high enough to stop children shouting from table to table. This could be extended so that the lunchtime organiser eats with the the children herself, giving more of a family atmosphere and building up a positive relationship with the children.

Examples of schools with innovative approaches to dinnertime abound. A serious and critical look at the facilities available and a clear sense of direction form the basis for change. Throughout the project I have emphasised the importance of experimenting with ideas and trying them out. They might not work and will most certainly need fine tuning, but they will have been tried. Traditional approaches are not always the best.

WHOLE-SCHOOL APPROACH

This is not the place for going into details of how to develop a whole-school approach, but a few personal observations on what I have seen during the project may be pertinent.

In many schools dinnertime and playtimes are major problem areas which can be dealt with negatively, by eliminating playtimes, reducing the lunch period and shortening the school day. Positive responses involve taking the problems on board and seeking creative ways of tackling them. The project has sought to encourage the latter and find ways of developing and encouraging positive management strategies, particularly at dinnertimes.

Power is an issue which arises when major changes are being contemplated. Lack of respect is a power issue which has already been mentioned. Those who feel the most powerless can exert a form of negative power in the form of subtle sabotage – like the cook with the noisy trolley. Teachers, although overtly welcoming the possibility of smoothly running dinnertimes, can also feel threatened by the advent of trained lunchtime organisers offering a professional service. They too can sabotage attempts at change by preventing lunchtime organisers from trying new ways of doing things. For example, in one school where they wanted to move furniture to make space to play games at wet playtime, the deputy head refused to allow it because 'we'd have to spend all afternoon putting back the chairs and tables'. Senior managers and teachers need to be proactive in promoting the status of organisers. It is up to the teacher to say 'Good morning' to the lunchtime organiser rather than expecting the person who perceives herself to be less powerful constantly to make the first move.

A commitment to a concrete, whole-school approach develops into a real force for change within the school. Making change is a challenge. The threat it can pose should be acknowledged and respected. Real change takes time and patience, and usually involves making mistakes from time to time.

A recipe for change involves taking an infinite measure of careful listening and an equal amount of imagination, followed by wide and free consultation. Break down the aims and objectives into bite-sized pieces. Make clear the time scale involved, and devise careful structures for who does what. Whilst mixing the above, ensure that the communication continues to flow freely. From time to time, evaluate each stage and adjust the ingredients accordingly. Season the above liberally with vision, faith, humour, patience and boundless enthusiasm, and allow to bake until ready!

I have watched this recipe in action, and have felt privileged to have contributed in some small part to the overall picture of change. Seeing the lunchtime organisers grow in confidence and enthusiasm has been rewarding but there is still more that could be achieved.

WHERE NEXT?

My personal conviction is that, for the work with lunchtime organisers to take root and effect real changes in the lives of the women and the children, the only starting point is with their needs and feelings. This conviction has grown stronger throughout the project. Education is predominantly a middle-class occupation with middle-class values. I was struck one day when I visited a school in the midst of a bleak and desolate housing estate: walking into the school was like entering a magical island. All the windows and doors were covered in wonderful things, completely shutting out their world. What message did that give to the children whose everyday world was out there? Somewhere, for me, there needs to be a congruence between the two, a meeting place where the children's world can be valued too.

Having dealt largely with immediate, practical problems, the second phase of training seems logically to involve introducing ways of coping with problems of behaviour and control. Again the starting point is the same, but using basic assertiveness skills and work on body language coupled with exploring ways of coping with conflict. This will be the subject of a future paper. However, it is worth emphasising the value of using one's own life experiences to help explore the experience of childhood. Putting an adult into children's shoes helps to develop empathy. Thinking about what would have helped at the time is a good source of meaningful and creative ways forward.

The key to training for me is accessibility. It must be seen to be relevant and of practical use in the everyday world of work, rather than being a package someone from 'out there' comes in and delivers before waltzing out again. For lunchtime organisers, training is not, on the whole, an everyday part of their lives, and must be seen to have a point. I believe that lunchtime organisers are a source of great wealth in our schools and a resource which should be developed to the full.

Chapter 10

Making peace in the playground

Sonia Sharp, Fiona Cooper and Helen Cowie

'I was playing here first.'

'Well, I'm here first now!'

'Well, just get out of the way, you!'

'So make me, stupid!'

'I'll push your face in!'

'Get off me pig face!'

'Miss, Miss, she hit me!'

'No I didn't, Miss, she hit me first!'

There is probably no school in the country which does not have aims or policies designed to promote respectful and harmonious relationships amongst pupils. Yet, how many times a week do similar dialogues, accompanied by all manner of put-downs, pokings, pushings and pullings ring out in our playgrounds? How many times do adults move in to 'sort it out', to request, to cajole, beg or command pupils to resolve their problems cooperatively? Nevertheless, simply telling children not to argue or fight does not necessarily make an impact. Unless we provide children with alternative ways of managing their own disputes constructively and teach them the necessary skills, they are likely to continue in well-learnt patterns of fight or flight.

The Education Reform Act (1988) required schools to provide a broad and balanced education which promotes the spiritual, moral, cultural, mental and physical development of pupils within society. The National Curriculum Council (1993) goes further, and states that these 'dimensions underpin the curriculum and the ethos of the school. Their importance is reinforced by their place in the new inspectorate framework for schools which derives its authority from the Education Act, 1992.' From now on, social and moral issues will be firmly placed back on school agendas. In this chapter we will explore one way in which a positive working environment can be achieved.

A recurrent theme in this book has been the involvement of children in enhancing the playground environment. We will continue to examine this theme from the perspective of conflict resolution. Conflict often occurs either overtly or covertly all around the school. Nevertheless, in most schools it particularly manifests itself in the playground. Unlike other interventions described in previous chapters, conflict resolution must be taught initially in the classroom rather than being directly introduced to the playground. Rules and policies about lunchtime or breaktime may superficially improve behaviour by imposition of adult 'legislation', but we propose that meaningful behaviour change will result from the *combination* of policy development and pupil empowerment through skills teaching. The benefits of teaching conflict resolution will be experienced not only at lunchtimes and breaktimes, but also throughout the school.

The Elton Report (DES 1989) identifies the importance of involving those people directly associated with disagreement and conflict situations in the resolution process. Who could be more central to peer conflict than the pupils themselves? In examining ways in which schools can use conflict resolution theory and practice to improve the social environment of play-time, this chapter addresses four key areas:

1   Understanding conflict.
2   Attitudes towards conflict.
3   The process of creative conflict resolution.
4   Teaching creative conflict resolution in schools.

UNDERSTANDING CONFLICT

The first step towards encouraging pupils to sort out their problems more creatively is to help them to increase their understanding of conflict and to explore their own attitudes towards it. A conflict is essentially a disagreement, an argument, a struggle, a battle, and can range in intensity from a minor squabble to an international war.

A conflict occurs when the actions of one person attempting to meet their needs appears to threaten, prevent, hinder or in some way seem incompatible with another person's efforts to meet their needs. Conflicts can be divided into different categories. For example, they can be considered in terms of the participants: from intrapersonal – the internal struggle which an individual might experience when faced with a moral dilemma or difficult decision; through interpersonal, inter-group and international conflicts which involve tens of thousands of people. They can also be explored in terms of intensity and complexity: noisy conflicts and quiet conflicts; trivial disagreements and bloody wars.

Conflict can also be defined in terms of its causes. Kreidler (1984) identifies three major sources of conflict:

(a) *Conflict over resources*: when two or more people want something that seems in short supply, such as the space for football; the attention of a special friend or adult; a place at the head of the dinner queue; a particular role in a game.

(b) *Conflict over values*: values are the basis of our personal belief system and are often expressed in terms of 'good/bad', 'right/wrong', and words like 'honest', 'fair' or 'equal' are used. When values appear to be in conflict, disputants tend to perceive one another's actions as a personal attack. They may personalise the conflict because they feel threatened. When threatened, people are likely to become defensive and cling more tenaciously to their own position.

(c) *Conflict over needs*: people have many needs; for instance, for friendship, belonging, power, self-esteem, acceptance, independence, achievement, fun. Any of these can appear to conflict with the needs of others, either overtly or subtly. Clashes over needs are often played out over material things; for example, the child who is upset about losing a particular seat at the dinner table feels the need to sit in a group of peers whose acceptance is important to him or her.

William Glasser (1984) argues that, whereas limited resources and different values may appear to be the cause of conflict, it is unmet needs which are truly at the root. Although people often believe that conflicts are caused by external factors – 'He made me do it, Miss!' – Glasser suggests that all conflicts originate within. Although most people share similar needs, each individual pictures differently the things she or he believes will satisfy those needs. In order to understand and resolve conflict creatively it is essential that pupils grow in awareness of human commonalities and differences. Conflict will not be resolved effectively as long as one pupil believes that his or her interests are being threatened by another. Unmet needs must therefore be expressed, and any solution must be seen as meeting those needs if the conflict is not to recur. Expressing needs requires self-awareness, an adequate language of emotions and, of prime importance, a safe climate.

ATTITUDES TOWARDS CONFLICT

Creative conflict resolution involves clearly defining the problems that arise in conflict situations and identifying and implementing solutions that are non-violent, that meet the needs of the persons involved and ideally improve the relationships of those persons. For children to be able to engage in this process they need to be aware of what conflict and conflict resolution mean, share their own experiences of these and gain insight into their own attitudes towards them. Additionally, they need to be willing to try out new approaches, and, of course, they need to learn the skills which will enable them to do this.

In trying to understand the meaning of conflict, it is helpful to consider some of the myths which exist about it.

The myths of conflict

Conflict is bad

When asked to brainstorm words and images associated with conflict, many children and adults use negative terms such as 'violence', 'hate', 'get even', 'war', 'anger'. These negative attitudes which say that conflict is bad, causes pain, fear and anger, and spoils relationships and so forth are the results of messages about conflict assimilated from parents, peers, teachers, the media and personal experiences. If we are to work constructively with conflict, then we need to help pupils examine their own experiences, attitudes and fears. We need them to recognise that:

- Conflict is a normal and inevitable part of daily life. No one is 'bad' because they experience conflict.
- Conflict can be positive. Through conflict we can learn more about ourselves and others, build better relationships, learn new and better ways of sorting out problems.
- It is the way in which people respond in a conflict situation which makes it either helpful or harmful.
- We cannot eliminate conflicts but we can learn to resolve them better.

Conflict is a contest

We often assume that the outcome of a conflict will be for one person to 'win' and one person to 'lose', or at best for both people to give something up in order to reach a grudging compromise. We can, however, reframe conflict from a contest to be won or lost into *a problem to be solved*, so that all people get what they need. The key idea which underpins all creative conflict work is *looking for a 'win–win'*. Looking for such a solution is no guarantee of finding it. However, approaching a conflict as if all participants could win shifts attention away from the participants and onto the problem itself and how to tackle it creatively.

There is a right way to handle conflict

Many people tend to become stuck in one or two 'conflict styles', even when they are not appropriate. Given the prevailing attitude that conflict is negative and usually produces winners and losers, it is hardly surprising that many people have learnt to respond in variations of two basic ways: fight or flight.

If someone is determined to win, they are likely to respond aggressively, either verbally or physically or in some other way to 'beat' their opponent. In other words, they apply 'fight' strategies to the situation. This might involve blaming the other, attacking or refusing to listen to their viewpoint, calling them names, or adamantly stating a personal position.

Alternatively, when someone is afraid that they might lose or believes that conflict is wrong, then they may well ignore or avoid a situation even to the extent of breaking off a relationship. They take 'flight' from the conflict. In such instances, however, negative feelings often leak out elsewhere, maybe in gossip with others, resulting in a 'fester fight' which slowly and insidiously poisons a number of relationships.

In any given situation, a 'fight or flight' response may be the appropriate one. A supervisor or teacher who sees a child about to push another off the climbing frame would wisely use all her or his power to stop the child rather than attempt negotiation! However, far too often these aggressive or passive approaches do not effectively resolve the conflict even though they may appear to halt it in the short term. They also tend to produce a lot of emotional or physical pain and leave people feeling trapped or powerless, reinforcing the notion that 'either they win or we win and there is nothing we can do about it'.

Sometimes, as educators and as adults, we can assume that children automatically know how to avoid and resolve the minor and major disagreements which arise in everyday life around school, just as they do in the community and at home. We forget that conflict management skills are learnt and can be improved with practice. Toch (1972) researched violent behaviour in male prisoners, and demonstrated that their aggressive approach to difficult situations often arose because they had not learnt non-violent strategies. Johnson and Johnson (1991) report that children from the most privileged backgrounds were often unable to manage conflict in a positive and constructive manner: children do not automatically have the necessary skills. Their research identified that much conflict was dealt with by employing bullying behaviour: put downs, teasing and insults, or by calling on someone with more authority and power to 'sort the other person out'. Research in the United Kingdom (Whitney and Smith 1993) shows us that a quarter of children in primary schools and one-fifth of pupils in secondary schools are bullied more than once or twice in any school term. Most of this bullying behaviour occurs outside the classroom. How much of this bullying behaviour could be avoided by teaching children how to resolve their conflicts peaceably and constructively?

THE PROCESS OF CREATIVE CONFLICT RESOLUTION

Conflict resolution is identifying and implementing solutions to the problems in conflict situations. It is not about eliminating conflict but about using it productively. To be able to find effective solutions children need to be able to express their feelings and their needs and to be able to listen well to other people.

Problem-solving approaches try to find a satisfactory solution which will meet the needs of all involved in the best way possible. Collaboration involves negotiation and agreement about mutually satisfactory alternative solutions. Collaboration leads to a win–win outcome. Although collaboration may take time, it is perhaps the most positive way to resolve a conflict situation.

Without being taught how to do so, children rarely utilise the full range of responses available; often they favour one or two particular styles depending on their experiences, their status within the relationship and their motivations. They may be driven by either a desire to meet their goals, in which case they may pay little regard to the feelings of the other person; or they may value their relationship with the other person more than their own objectives. Often, it may be the very nature of their relationship with the other person which can lead them into conflict. A first step in learning how to resolve conflict is an awareness about which styles of conflict they tend to use most and an understanding that there are in fact a number of options open to them which may be more or less appropriate in a given situation. There is no one right way to resolve conflict.

A key issue in resolving conflict is to distinguish between what people want and why they want it. In conflict situations, people often express their wishes (their position) rather than their needs or interests, although it is their unmet needs which underlie the conflict. For example, in the playground, two children are fighting over a bag. The supervisor asks them, 'What do you want?' They simultaneously reply, 'I want the bag.' The supervisor then asks, 'What do you need the bag for?' One child wants something to carry their PE kit in, the other wants a book that is in the bag. Both can gain in this situation as long as they clearly express their needs.

Schools do not always give children opportunities to resolve their own conflicts. Kreidler (1990) places different methods of conflict resolution on a continuum which has two dimensions:

1   the emphasis placed upon direct communication between the disputants;
2   the extent to which the disputants remain responsible for finding their own solution as opposed to turning to a third party.

The continuum moves from collaborative conflict resolution on one end through to legislation at the other. The further away from collaboration one moves along the spectrum, the more the conflict escalates and the less likely it is that a win–win solution will be determined. The disputants are left powerless and possibly without their fundamental needs in the situation being recognised or met.

The six different methods of conflict resolution on the continuum are:

Communication
Negotiation
Mediation
Arbitration
Litigation
Legislation.

Communication and negotiation involve the children concerned directly with the dispute or disagreement only. At the communicating level they are simply talking with one another. When negotiating, they follow a structured process to find a solution. A neutral third person may be called in to mediate. The mediator helps the children to find a solution but does not prescribe what they should do. She or he assists the individuals to recognise what they need and facilitates communication about this. The starting point of mediation is that the mediator is not engulfed in the emotions which get in the way of a resolution to the conflict. Teachers and pupils can be trained as mediators (Kingston Friends 1987; McCaffrey and Lyons 1993). They can learn to go through a series of stages which enable each participant to reach a form of agreement, based on each of their needs in the situation (see Table 10.1).

When communicating, negotiating or mediating situations, the responsibility for finding a solution rests with the children directly involved in the conflict. With arbitration, responsibility for finding a solution is passed to a third party. The disputants often spend more time talking directly to the arbitrator than to one another. Often the decision of the arbitrator is binding

Table 10.1   The mediation process

Defining the problem
Identifying feelings
Listening to each person
Visualising an ideal solution
Expression of needs and interests by both parties
Review of possible options
Mutual evaluation of potential outcomes of options
Negotiation of a plan of action and agreement
Signing of agreement
Agreement to meet again and evaluate the result.

Source: Leimdorfer 1992

and has to be followed by the disputants. The conflict can also be resolved by an authority figure (a legislator). This completely distances the individuals involved from the negotiation and decision-making process. Each person tries to convince the legislator that they are right and the other person is wrong. The legislator makes a decision based on the rules of the system and their understanding of the conflict. When litigation occurs, a new rule or law is introduced to try to eliminate that kind of conflict arising again.

Some of these responses to conflict can be seen in action within schools. Ideally, intervention by adults in a conflict situation in the playground begins at the *mediation level*: trying to help the pupils to find their own solution. Unfortunately, more often it starts with arbitration or legislation: deciding what will happen for the children. A common outcome of continued arbitration by adults in the playground is a perceived need for 'litigation': the development of a behaviour policy or code of conduct – a large hammer to crack a potentially small nut! We would argue that teaching children how to resolve conflict should be an integral part of a whole-school policy in behaviour management. All the more so because they are bound to encounter conflict as they go through their lives, whether in family quarrels, disputes over property or rights, disagreements in the workplace or acts of aggression.

TEACHING CONFLICT-RESOLUTION SKILLS IN SCHOOLS

As mentioned earlier in this chapter, to be able to encourage children to resolve conflict constructively, they need three things: awareness, willingness and skills.

Awareness

Children need to know what conflict is and how they feel about it. More often than not, conflict will be viewed negatively by the majority. Teachers can refocus this by asking, 'Is there anything good about conflict? How might there be a positive outcome from a conflict situation?'

In helping children to understand how conflict arises and what it entails for them, it is helpful to offer visual images and catch phrases which they can quickly refer to. Slogans such as 'Look for a win–win' or 'Hands are not for hurting' can be adopted by the children and the adults within the school. The Grace Contrino Abrams Peace Foundation in Miami, United States, have 'Rules for fighting fair'. These are:

1 Identify the problem.
2 Focus on the problem.
3 Attack the problem not the person.

4   Listen with an open mind.
5   Treat a person's feelings with respect.
6   Take responsibility for your actions.

They also discuss a series of 'fouls'. Fouls are *not* fighting fair. They include name calling, blaming, sneering, not listening, getting even, bringing up the past, threats, pushing, hitting, put-downs, bossing, making excuses, not taking responsibility. In a conflict situation which is escalating, children can be reminded by peers and adults, 'Is this fighting fair or is it a foul?'

Time spent on defining conflict, introducing the concept of how conflicts quickly escalate and how they can be de-escalated, understanding the different outcomes of conflict – in particular, the benefits of win–win solutions – is essential groundwork for motivating children to try out new skills.

Willingness

Children who understand why something is worth doing are more likely to put it into practice. By demonstrating the win–win solution, children understand that everyone gains – no one has to be a loser. An example of an activity which introduces the notion of win–win is described in Table 10.2.

Skills

There are two key skill areas for conflict resolution. The first is to be able to express feelings and needs in a clear, direct and honest way. The second is to be able to listen carefully to someone else.

Active listening skills and assertiveness techniques can form the basis of communication enhancement training. The active listener attends very carefully not only to the words which people use but also the underlying messages and emotions. She or he is attentive, and does not detract from the other person's statements by interrupting, offering advice or relating their own similar experiences. More sophisticated active listening skills include paraphrasing, clarifying, reflecting and summarising.

Assertive statements are based on a structured sentence, often known as the I-message. Lange and Jakubowski (1976) identified five kinds of assertive statement, each a progressively more elaborated version of the 'basic assertion'. A basic assertion is a straightforward statement describing feelings, opinions or beliefs or desires: 'I want you to give me back my football.' An example of an elaborated assertive statement would be: 'I feel frustrated when you borrow my football and don't give it back straight away because then I can't play football. I understand that you haven't got

Table 10.2   Learning about a win–win outcome

The teacher introduces the activity to the class by saying, 'We are now going to play a game. You are all going to try to win. If you win ten points you will get a prize.' (Note that the teacher has not mentioned the word 'competition'.) The children work in pairs. The teacher instructs them: 'I want you to sit opposite each other, each person placing their right elbow on the table with the palm of your right hand placed against the palm of the other person's hand. Each time that the back of your partner's hand touches the desk, you will win one point. When you have won ten points you will get a prize.'

The children begin, most of them immediately starting to 'arm wrestle' – one person pushing, the other resisting. Of course, the teacher never mentioned arm wrestling or resistance in the instructions. After one minute the teacher stops the children. 'Who has won any points?' A few children have one or two points – nobody has enough to win a prize. 'Hmm. That's interesting – not many people are winning lots of points, are they? It seems that in your pairs, if one person wins, the other loses.'

The teacher begins a discussion with the class about strategies for improving the winning scores of everybody. Eventually, pupils begin to realise that if neither of them resists, in fact they collaboratively move their arms in an arc so first one person's hand touches the desk and then the other person's, then both people win. This is a win–win solution! Before long, all the children are scoring plenty of points and claiming their well-earned prizes.

The session ends with a discussion about other situations where pupils might seek a win–win solution and how this might be achieved.

a football of your own but I need you to give it back to me when I ask you to.'

Although both the active listening skills and the assertive statements may seem quite sophisticated, even young children can learn to use simple forms effectively (Kirkland *et al.* 1982; Arora 1989; Childs 1993; Cowie and Sharp, in press). They depend not only on specific ways of speaking, but also on body language, tone of voice and eye contact.

Building upon communication and listening skills, children can be taught how to negotiate. A commonly used model (Kreidler 1990; Fisher and Ury 1992) is the six-stage negotiation process which leads to a win–win outcome. It is similar to the mediation process described earlier, but involves only the participants rather than a third party and has no written agreement and follow-up.

Conflict resolution can be taught directly. Children can be explicitly taught the skills mentioned above. As Walker (1989) writes: 'It is not possible to teach non violent behaviour but rather to teach such inter-personal skills as communication, co-operation and problem solving which will perhaps result in non violent behaviour.' In addition to direct teaching about conflict resolution, key issues can be reinforced indirectly if teachers choose lesson topics, stories, examples, assembly themes which reconfirm the cooperative ethos of the school and which reflect the values underlying

Table 10.3   The win–win negotiation process

1 *Identify 'wants' and 'needs'*: think about what you want and why you want it.
2 *Present and listen*: you say what your wants and needs are *and* you listen
   carefully to what the other person says they want and need. Be very specific.
3 *Brainstorm possible solutions*: think of all the possible ways you might solve
   the problem. Try to think of as many as you can and write them down if you
   can. Don't discuss whether you think they are good or bad.
4 *Choose a fair solution*: read through all the ideas on your list. Choose ideas
   which will make everyone feel like a winner.
5 *Make an action plan*: when you have agreed on one idea, plan how you will
   put it into action. Decide exactly who will do what and when.

creative conflict resolution. The way the classroom and the school as a
whole is managed can model positive conflict resolution and can indirectly
teach children how to handle difficult situations constructively. This may
require some staff to move away from more traditional disciplinary
methods when handling peer conflict and disagreements. Walker (1989)
points out that 'there is little value in "teaching" non violence for one or
two hours per week when the principles advocated are not put into practice
on a day to day basis'.

FROM THE CLASSROOM TO THE PLAYGROUND

By introducing creative conflict resolution into a school community,
schools are encouraging a collective responsibility for promoting cooperative behaviour and are taking positive steps to reduce tension and
frustration around the school. Teaching conflict resolution has implications
for all aspects of school life but it can have particular benefits for pupil-
structured social situations such as breaktime.

This chapter may have seemed distanced from the playground. This is
because conflict resolution must be introduced through the curriculum as
well as reflected in the organisation and management of the school. Essentially, conflict resolution is an approach which has implications for all
aspects of school life; it is not only a playground issue. However, pupil
behaviour – in particular, pupil conflict – can be very much a problem in
the playground. We would suggest that conflict resolution introduced
through the classroom and reinforced through the school ethos and staff
behaviour will have a marked effect on pupil behaviour in the playground
and on the way staff approach pupil conflict situations.

In making conflict resolution a whole-school concern, creative conflict
resolution skills should not be restricted to child–child or adult–child
relationships, but also to adult–adult matters. Indeed, the Council for
Europe Report on Violence and Conflict Resolution in Schools (Walker

1989) recommends that 'Teachers should themselves use the personal problem solving skills that they teach their children to deal with intra-staff problems'.

For conflict resolution to become a part of a school's behaviour management programme, staff themselves must be comfortable with conflict and feel confident to act as mediators as opposed to legislators in the first instance. By staff, we do not only refer to teaching staff. If this is to be carried through to the playground, then supervisors and dinner helpers need to be involved in training and preparation as well. Staff need to view conflict as a part of human relationships, neither good nor bad. They need to be able to allow pupils to find their own solutions, helping them to do this where necessary rather than imposing solutions upon them. As conflict often arises because of differences, staff must be willing to explore rather than ignore diversity. All staff also need to be committed to finding non-aggressive conflict resolution styles and appreciate the value of peaceful, collaborative processes.

REFERENCES

Arora, T. (1989) 'Bullying – action and intervention', *Pastoral Care in Education*, 7: 44–7.

Childs, K. (1993) 'A follow-up study of the long-term effects of assertiveness training for victims of bullying', Unpublished dissertation, University of Sheffield.

Cowie, H. and Sharp, S. (in press) 'Working directly with bullies and victims', in P. K. Smith and S. Sharp (eds) *School Bullying and How to Cope with It*, London: Routledge.

Department of Education and Science (DES) (1988) *Education Reform Act: 1988*, London: HMSO.

—— (Elton Report) (1989) *Discipline in Schools*, Report of the Committee of Enquiry chaired by Lord Elton, London: HMSO.

Fisher, R. and Ury, W. (1992) *Getting to Yes*, London: Hutchinson.

Glasser, W. (1984) *Control Theory*, New York: Harper & Row.

Kingston Friends Workshop Group (1987) *Ways and Means: An Approach to Problem Solving*, Friends House, Euston Road, London NW1 2BJ.

Kirkland, K. D., Thelen, M. H. and Miller, D. J. (1982) 'Group assertion training with adolescents', *Child and Family Behaviour Therapy*, 4: 1–12.

Kreidler, W. J. (1984) *Creative Conflict Resolution*, Glenview, IL: Good Year Books.

—— (1990) *Elementary Perspectives, 1: Teaching Concepts of Peace and Conflict*, Boston, MA: Education for Social Responsibility.

Johnson, D. W. and Johnson, R. T. (1991) *Teaching Children to be Peacemakers*, Edina, MN: Interaction Book Company.

Johnson, D. W., Maruyama, G., Johnson, R., Nelson, D. and Skon, L. (1981) 'Effects of cooperative, competitive, and individualistic goal structures on achievement: a meta-analysis', *Psychological Bulletin*, 89: 47–62.

Lange, A. and Jakubowski, P. (1976) *Responsible Assertive Behavior*, Champaign, IL: Research Press.

Leimdorfer, T. (1992) *Once Upon a Conflict*, Friends House, Euston Road, London NW1 2BJ.

McCaffrey, T. and Lyons, E. (1993) 'Teaching children to be good friends – developmental groupwork with vulnerable children', *Educational and Child Psychology*, 10: 3.

National Curriculum Council (1993) 'Spiritual and moral development: a discussion paper', York: National Curriculum Council.

Toch, H. (1972) *Violent Men*, London: Penguin.

Walker, J. (1989) *Violence and Conflict Resolution in Schools*, Quaker Council for European Affairs, 50 Square Ambiorix, 1040 Brussels, Belgium.

Whitney, I. and Smith, P. K. (1993) 'A survey of the nature and extent of bullying in junior/middle and secondary schools', *Educational Research*, 35: 3–25.

Chapter 11

Ways of involving children in decision making

Helen Cowie

There is a growing recognition that playtime can have a profound effect on the quality of school life. This book highlights some of the problems which surround current approaches to the organisation and management of playtime and, at the same time, documents some innovative ways for developing new approaches.

The perception that playtime might be problematic presents pupils with a challenging opportunity, and in this chapter I argue that young people have the potential to be actively involved in decisions relating to playtime and the playground and to live with the consequences, whether good or bad, of those decisions. First I consider the general issue of pupils' roles in decision-making processes; second, I give examples of ways in which pupils themselves in primary and secondary schools have taken responsibility for making changes in their own environment. I also discuss some of the barriers, perceived and real, which can make it difficult to achieve active participation on the part of pupils and genuine power-sharing on the part of teachers.

THE RIGHT OF YOUNG PEOPLE TO PARTICIPATE

There is widely reported official commitment to the aim of giving young people the opportunity to participate in decisions that affect their everyday lives. The Elton Report (DES 1989) on Discipline in Schools argued the case for the creation of a school context where quality of relationships and a sense of school community were held to be of value. In order to achieve this aim the Elton Report recommended that headteachers and teachers should recognise the importance of ascertaining pupils' views and should encourage active participation of pupils in shaping and reviewing the school's behaviour policy.

The Government's White Paper, *Choice and Diversity: a New Framework for Schools* (DfE 1992), stated that children should be encouraged to grow up 'as active citizens':

In a variety of ways and across a range of subject areas, young people should always be taught that, in addition to rights and expectations, they also have important duties and responsibilities to their community, they should be encouraged to be involved members of those communities, to grow up as active citizens. They should be taught the importance of developing a strong moral code that includes a concern for others, self-respect and self-discipline, as well as basic values such as honesty and truthfulness.

(DfE 1992)

There is no room for complacency, however, argues Newell (1993), chair of the council of the Children's Rights Development Unit. He suggests that while young people's democratic rights may be acknowledged in current legislation, much of educational practice ignores them. Children, in his view, are not given enough scope to make rules and guidelines and to take responsibility for their own school community. Democratic principles, he argues, are the ones most frequently broken in schools. Such anxieties were also expressed by Harber and Meighan (1989), who point out that in many supposedly democratic countries educational practices that enable the learners to take part in important decision-making processes and that actively promote power sharing are rare and may often meet with irrational opposition. Rhetoric is not enough, they argue, since the promotion of truly democratic educational practice takes time and involves letting go of some long-established traditions. Harber and Meighan point to the need for a working partnership between teachers and pupils and a sense of trust in the capacity for creative ability in young people. The problem is that many teachers do not trust their pupils to behave responsibly. For much of the time pupils do what they are told to do or find ways of not doing what they are told to do. Pupils are still very much accustomed to having the teacher in control of what they do in school. Lewis and Cowie (1993) interviewed teachers about their attitudes towards cooperative group work and found that one of the most difficult aspects of putting it into practice was the letting go of power. It is not easy to make the transition to a way of working in which young people can play an active part in making decisions about their own social environment.

PUPIL OWNERSHIP OF THEIR SCHOOL COMMUNITY

At this point we have to ask the question, to what extent is it realistic to expect pupils to have a sense of 'ownership' of their school community or to give them power to question, to challenge, to create? While many adults in authority over young people clearly consider that the answer is a resounding 'No!', there is some evidence to show that pupils respond well to the opportunity of taking responsibility, but that certain conditions are necessary before this can be achieved.

Salmon and Claire (1984) showed that young people could work collaboratively on issues of common concern in their classrooms provided that there was a willingness to establish common goals and mutual understanding among both teachers and pupils. This process took time and often ran counter to established practice. Adelman (1989) argued the case for democratic schooling but pointed out the need for teachers to be aware of the difficulties inherent in creating a balance between fostering a pupil's individuality alongside fostering a sense of social responsibility. In his view, there should also be a recognition that the *process* itself is vitally important in giving pupils a meaningful opportunity to reflect on what they do and to consider the impact of their actions on others.

This was confirmed by Cowie and Rudduck (1990), who showed that, by working collaboratively on a real task, pupils could be given the valuable experience of practical reasoning. For example, when pupils played an active part in choosing options in PE, they not only made their choices; they also talked about coming to a decision and the procedures involved. Initially, the reactions of pupils to those who did not get their choices was 'Tough!'. But when they were given the chance to challenge this fatalistic response, the pupils came to explore ways of ensuring that as many people as possible could have their choice of activity. In the end, multi-gym, which had originally been a minority choice and therefore out-voted, was in fact later selected as one of the options. In the process of their discussions, the pupils came to understand means in relation to ends, and gained in empathy for the feelings of others as they are affected by the outcomes of a decision-making procedure. They also learned to weigh up alternatives thoughtfully as a way of determining what was right and appropriate. There were useful outcomes from this exercise in practical problem solving since it enabled pupils to come to a deeper understanding of the principle that responsibility involves not simply getting what is best for oneself but should take into account the perspectives of others. Pupils are thus given the opportunity to take a moral stance and reflect on ethical issues as they emerge.

The ability to make decisions, however, is best learned through experience. It is surely also an essential part of education that young people learn how to come to a decision in a logical manner which shows awareness of the situation, sensitivity to other people and a realistic understanding of the resources which are available. The great advantage of giving pupils this experience is that it encourages them to take their own ideas, and those of their peers, seriously. Pupils who participate in a decision-making process of this kind are more likely to be committed to the procedures which ensue. Furthermore, if pupils develop a sense of control over their lives in their own school community, this is likely to result in a more positive self-image.

Two case studies illustrate ways in which young people can work very effectively to make changes to their school environment. The first, in a junior school, shows children using the strategy of the Quality Circle to improve playtime (Cowie and Sharp 1992). The second, in a secondary school, describes pupils working together to set up a peer counselling service to help the victims of bullying (Sharp *et al.* in press).

'MAKING SCHOOL A BETTER PLACE'

The Quality Circle (QC) idea comes from industry but its methods and techniques can easily be adapted to school settings. Essentially the QC consists of groups of people – of around five or six pupils each – who meet together regularly to identify common problems, evolve solutions and present these solutions to 'management' – in this case a panel of adults, such as the headteacher, school governors, parents. The members of the QC are introduced to appropriate skills and strategies for problem solving and effecting change: skills for generating ideas, observation and data collection, developing strategies for solutions, and communication, both within the circle and when presenting to management.

The QC is distinctive because it gives participants the opportunity to acquire a range of skills which facilitate a problem-solving approach to social life. The QC method actively discourages behaviour which is domineering or destructive or which discriminates against group members. As the group works together to research an issue and to generate ideas for finding solutions to the problem, there is an opportunity for satisfaction in experiencing at first hand the creativity of team work and for acknowledging that a solution can come from any member. Thus the techniques of the QC affirm democratic values by demonstrating how constructively people can work together when there is an atmosphere of trust and a willingness to acquire accurate information on the topic under investigation. Members of the QC are also made familiar with techniques for conflict resolution through debriefing and regular group evaluation sessions.

By using the techniques of the QC, members develop in their own ability to relate effectively to one another. In addition, they have opportunities to experience the process of playing a part in the management of change. Thus the QC method aims to give young people a sense of ownership of their own school community. This will stand them in good stead in their future roles and responsibilities as adults. For a step-by-step account of how to run QCs in the classroom, see Cowie and Sharp (1992).

In one junior school, children used the QC method to address the problem of improving their school environment. A broad aim identified by the children was 'to make school a better place'. Through initial brainstorming, the QC agreed that the playground and breaktime were posing difficulties for their peers. A survey confirmed this, so the group used the QC techniques to identify causes and to suggest possible solutions. There were immediate outcomes. The first was to do something practical about the layout of the games pitches in the playground. The first QC, with the help of their teacher, wrote to the manager of the local shopping centre, who replied with the offer of help from his staff in actually painting out various sports pitches as the children had requested. First he wanted designs and appropriate colourings. This resulted in intensive planning by the QC of possible layouts in the playground. They made drawings, wall displays and three-dimensional models. They designed ideal playgrounds as well as possible ones. A presentation to Assembly centred on three aspects of their planning:

Where we were.
Where we are.
Where we would like to be.

This helped the QC to clarify what the needs of the children in the school were and how accurate their suggested solutions to the problem had been. The QC was now in a position to make a confident reply to the manager.

Not only had the QC shown that they could turn dreams and ideas into practice; they had also learnt some very useful things about how decisions are made and about the processes which are involved in action. The pupils' evaluation of this QC was positive. When asked why they had liked taking part in a QC, these 9-year-olds replied:

'It helps children.'

'It is a good cause.'

'We learn about presentations.'

'We learn about the cost of things. We learn about money and effort.'

'It has been good because we were working on something real.'

The second line of enquiry was equally productive. This time, the focus was on how children play during lunchtimes and break. The QC set to work with great enthusiasm to teach younger children new games, including 'Grandmother's footsteps', 'Donkey', 'Cat behind the curtain' and 'What's the time, Mr Wolf?' The QC devoted its time to identifying games which would develop friendship and cooperation amongst younger children. They wrote booklets with step-by-step instructions and they took it in turns to demonstrate and teach the games during breaktime. There were immediate, observable improvements in the quality of playtime for the younger children. The members of the QC gained greatly in confidence as they discovered how satisfying it can be to share your knowledge and experience with another person. Again the evaluations were positive:

'It is fun.'

'It stops children fighting.'

'I have learned what it is like to be a teacher by showing younger children how to play.'

'TIME TO LISTEN': PEER COUNSELLING IN ACTION

The second case study concerns the establishment of a pupil-initiated peer counselling service designed to improve relationships at school and specifically to provide a safe place where bullied pupils can talk freely about their experiences and explore possible solutions. This has been found to have an immediate effect on the quality of life in the playground. The school staff had already found that, by including pupils in the development of a whole-school policy on bullying, victims were more likely to tell someone about bullying incidents (Sharp and Smith 1991). The staff were anxious to build on this increased reporting in a way which would continue to encourage the pupils to talk about their bullying experiences but without placing an unrealistic, and therefore unachievable, burden on school staff. Many pupils wanted to be actively involved in tackling the problem of bullying. It was an issue which they felt strongly about and they believed they were able to support their peers in practical ways. They also pointed out that pupils who were being bullied sometimes only wanted someone to listen to them – they did not necessarily involve teaching staff straight away. Some victims might prefer to talk through their own solutions before taking action. The playground was where it happened, and many pupils dreaded break and lunchtimes.

The role of the 'bully line' (named by the pupils themselves) was to offer a listening service for pupils in the school. The pupils negotiated clear ground rules to achieve their aim of providing a safe forum where pupils could talk freely and explore possible solutions. If necessary, they were eager to act as advocates for the bullied pupil by telling a member of staff what was happening to them, or perhaps by accompanying the bullied pupil whilst they themselves told a member of staff. They agreed not to intervene in a bullying situation or tackle the bullying pupils on behalf of another pupil. They also learned specific techniques to empower victims to see themselves and their situation in a more constructive way.

In one case, a peer counsellor helped a younger girl see that she need not be intimidated by a bully at breaktime. She used a specific problem-solving technique called 'force-field analysis' to structure her session. Mary came to the peer-counselling bully line with a problem. She was afraid to go out into the playground because of intimidation from Annie, an older girl. At that time, she saw no way out of her dilemma. Her confidence was waning and she was often on the verge of tears. Mary was encouraged to write her problem in the centre of a sheet of paper and to apply one of the techniques which the peer counsellors had learned on their training day – force-field analysis – in order to design a plan of action. Mary was asked to draw lines representing forces which might facilitate change and forces which might hinder it. She was encouraged to consider ways in which she could strengthen facilitating forces and ways of weakening those which were preventing her from attaining her goal – to be able to walk freely and without anxiety in the playground.

Figure 11.1 shows the problem as it was first presented. Mary and her peer counsellor discussed each factor in turn and adjusted the lines accordingly. Her first task was to be clear about her own right to be in the playground. The peer counsellor encouraged her to think more positively about herself and to begin the process of clarifying her own rights as a member of the school community. She was asked to explore her statement, 'I think that I might have offended her', and could find no time when she had deliberately set out to cause offence. This arrow was shortened. She was then asked whether she could enlist the help of her two friends in keeping her company whenever she went out into the playground. She also affirmed her statement that Annie was not liked – and was probably feared – because of her unpleasant behaviour to other pupils. This helped Mary to feel less isolated, and enabled her to see that there were a number of people who were sharing in the same problem. She was reminded that the school had a policy on bullying.

As this process of clarification went on, the arrows representing the helping forces became longer and those representing the hindering forces were shortened. Mary's new force-field analysis is shown in Figure 11.2. Mary had been enabled to see practical ways in which she could begin to use her existing network of friends to help her enjoy breaktime and to understand that the problem was something which could be challenged. In the process, she came to see that she was not the only person in the school who did not like this kind of bullying behaviour.

The team of pupils who act as peer counsellors have shown a strong sense of responsibility. The language adopted by them to describe the service is quite formal and is based on adult role concepts. They describe the pupils who use the service as 'clients' and refer to themselves as 'bully line counsellors'. The pupils who welcome the 'clients' and help with the administration of the service are 'receptionists'. The peer counsellors included pupils from most year groups, including year 7, and represented an even mix of boys and girls. The pupils work together in teams of three to four members.

During the training, great emphasis is placed on confidentiality. This confidentiality is set within certain parameters. Should a pupil be told that someone is being badly hurt or sexually abused, they immediately refer to the named member of staff. They have been provided with a script for such

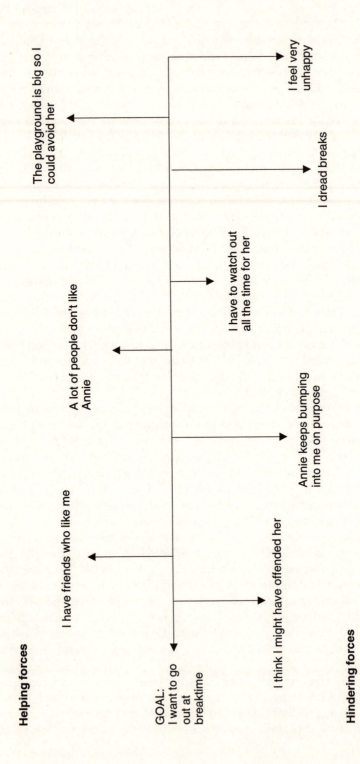

Helping forces

I have friends who like me

A lot of people don't like Annie

The playground is big so I could avoid her

GOAL:
I want to go out at breaktime

I think I might have offended her

Annie keeps bumping into me on purpose

I have to watch out all the time for her

I feel very unhappy

I dread breaks

Hindering forces

Figure 11.1 Mary's first force-field analysis

Helping forces

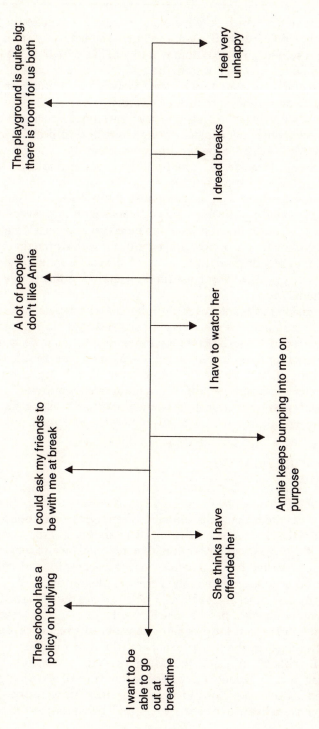

The playground is quite big; there is room for us both

I feel very unhappy

A lot of people don't like Annie

I dread breaks

I could ask my friends to be with me at break

I have to watch her

The schoool has a policy on bullying

Annie keeps bumping into me on purpose

She thinks I have offended her

I want to be able to go out at breaktime

Hindering forces

Figure 11.2 Mary's second force-field analysis

occasions. This script, which they have all practised, is as follows: 'I am sorry. I cannot help you with this, you need to tell a member of staff. Shall we go and find someone now? Whom would you like to tell?' If the pupil refuses to talk with a member of staff, the bully-line counsellor still seeks out the key member of staff to let them know what is going on. The counsellors have agreed never to promise secrecy.

One major advantage of the bully line from the school's point of view is that there is now a safety net in place during lunchtimes, especially for the year 7 pupils. Most usage of the service comes from the younger year 7 pupils, who have just transferred from primary school. Several have set up regular meetings with their chosen peer counsellor, and this work focuses on raising self-esteem as well as discussing the problems of bullying. Another benefit is the way in which the peer counsellors and receptionists have taken on responsibility and have remained reliable over time. Staff have become willing for the pupils to take more of a managerial role for the bully line. The pupils themselves have decided to set up a management committee where pupils will organise fund raising, advertising, role planning and administration.

One of the major disadvantages of the bully line is its dependence on too few staff for its running. The school is split site and consequently staffing resources are stretched. It is difficult for one member of staff to be available during four lunchtimes each week for any length of time. Strategies for easing this situation include the bully-line counsellors being given their own filing cabinet and office space. This should free them from the frustrations of waiting for a teacher to give them their counselling files and diary each day. For a description of this initiative, see Sharp *et al.* (in press).

THE PROCESS OF CHANGE

Teachers and their pupils, like everyone else, need to go through particular stages when they try out something new. It is important to recognise this, otherwise it is easy to become discouraged when trying to introduce new procedures into the classroom. If there is understanding and support in the early stages of trying out an innovation, then the transition to working in new ways will be easier. It is also helpful for the teachers to work collaboratively with other colleagues over the period of the transition – and even after. It is in any case more enjoyable to be able to share the ups and downs of an experience with other people. (See Figure 11.3.)

It may be helpful to view the process of transition as a sequence of stages in a cycle of change. In the first place, there is a need for orientation or preparation for change. In each of the case studies reported in this chapter the school had already accepted in principle the value of allowing pupils to be involved in decision-making processes. The teachers were open to the idea that there were likely to be changes in pupil behaviour as they made

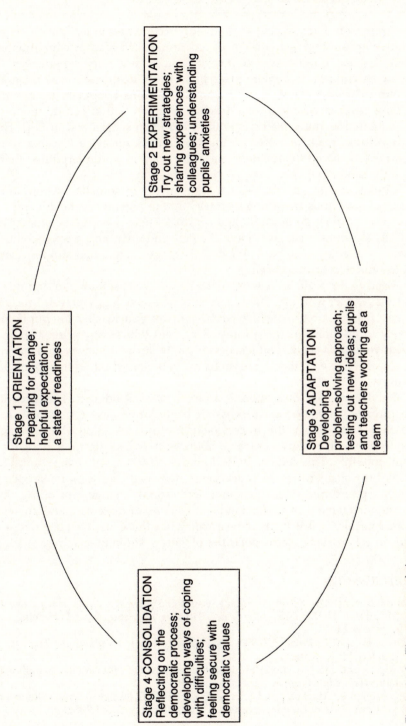

Stage 1 ORIENTATION
Preparing for change;
helpful expectation;
a state of readiness

Stage 2 EXPERIMENTATION
Try out new strategies;
sharing experiences with
colleagues; understanding
pupils' anxieties

Stage 3 ADAPTATION
Developing a
problem-solving approach;
testing out new ideas; pupils
and teachers working as a
team

Stage 4 CONSOLIDATION
Reflecting on the
democratic process;
developing ways of coping
with difficulties;
feeling secure with
democratic values

Figure 11.3   The process of change

the transition. Each teacher was already experienced in facilitating cooperative group work activities in the classroom. The teacher who initiated the QCs had trained as a counsellor and so was very experienced in allowing children to explore ideas in an open, democratic way in small groups. The teacher who was the main driving force behind the peer-counselling service was a drama teacher with an active commitment to experiential learning methods both in her main subject and in PSE. The ground was ready for each of these initiatives since the teachers were enthusiastic about the methods and the values which underpinned them and the school policy was supportive of this way of working.

The second stage involves a period of experimentation where both teacher and pupils are feeling their way. At this point it may be difficult for the teacher to let go of traditional controls. There may also be anxiety as pupils too show insecurity about the new and unfamiliar responsibilities which are being handed to them. This is the stage when support from colleagues can be most useful.

In stage three the 'survivors' of the process are beginning to find this a normal way of working. They experience satisfaction at achievements and pleasure in the progress which has been made. Both teacher and pupils are likely to be more tolerant of any difficulties which may arise. This is a creative time as pupils and teachers begin to devise new ways of working themselves. Even setbacks are problems to be solved rather than personal failures.

Finally, in stage four, there is a period of consolidation. The essential features of the democratic process are being formulated and refined. The teacher is reflecting on the process, being more precise about which strategy matches which activity, is more at home with procedures for making it all run smoothly. This stage may lead on to a new cycle of change, and it is useful to consider that the transition to democratic decision making contains opportunities for personal and social change, including the acknowledgement of understandable feelings of insecurity and anxiety. Paradoxically, this is likely to be a time when those involved begin to feel safe in acknowledging the polarities of values within themselves.

REFERENCES

Adelman, C. (1989) 'Setting the scene: issues and prospects', in C. Harber and R. Meighan (eds) *The Democratic School*, Ticknall, Education Now Publishing Co-operative Ltd.

Cowie, H. and Rudduck, J. (1990) *Cooperative Learning: Traditions and Transitions*, London: BP Education.

Cowie, H. and Sharp, S. (1992) 'Students themselves tackle the problem of bullying', *Pastoral Care in Education*, 10 (4): 31–7.

Department of Education and Science (DES) (1989) *Discipline in Schools*, Report of the Committee of Enquiry chaired by Lord Elton, London: HMSO.

Department for Education (DfE) (1992) *Choice and Diversity: A New Framework for Schools*, London: HMSO.

Harber, C. and Meighan, R. (1989) *The Democratic School*, Ticknall: Education Now Publishing Co-operative Ltd.

Lewis, J. and Cowie, H. (1993) 'CGW: Promises and limitations. A study of teacher's values', *British Psychological Society, Education Section Review*, 17 (2): 77–84.

Newell, P. (1993) 'Too young to be kept in chains', *Times Educational Supplement* 1 January 1993, p. 27.

Salmon, P. and Claire, H. (1984) *Classroom Collaboration*, London: Routledge.

Sharp, S., Sellars, A. and Cowie, H. (in press) 'Time to listen: setting up a peer counselling service to help tackle the problem of bullying in school', *Pastoral Care in Education*.

Sharp, S. and Smith, P. K. (1991) 'Bullying in school: the DfE Sheffield Bullying Project', *Early Child Development and Care*, 77: 47–55.

Chapter 12

Changing playground society
A whole-school approach

Carol Ross and Amanda Ryan

LAYERS AND LEVELS TO THE PLAYGROUND

Children spend approximately one-fifth of their school life in the playground. It is a time when they can interact freely with one another, gain social skills, and be active and inventive in their play. It is the most unstructured part of the school day and the place where children are most left to their own devices. For many children it is also a time of extreme stress and the experience of school which overrides all else.

Over the years, we have worked with many inner city schools that have expressed concern about their playgrounds and the sorts of experiences children are having in them. Much of what occurs in the playground may be felt to be out of line with (or even undermining) school policy. There is a powerful 'hidden curriculum' on the playground where issues of race, gender, class, sexuality, disability and culture can come together in 'raw power dynamics' and an ethic of 'might is right'.

Through our involvement in a wide range of initiatives, we became increasingly aware that there are many layers and levels involved in addressing playground issues. We have found, for example, that the playground touches everyone in the school community, each in a different way; that it often involves issues of bullying and/or racist and sexist behaviour; and that it involves issues of the use and management of play space.

With a commitment to creating playgrounds that offer positive learning experiences, support fair play, allow equal access, and address bullying and harassment there is a need to concentrate on a variety of areas of focus and involve all members of the school community (see Figure 12.1).

WHY A WHOLE-SCHOOL APPROACH?

A whole-school approach to the playground is based on the recognition that

1   each group (pupils, teachers, supervisors, parents, governors) has its own concerns and has a role to play;

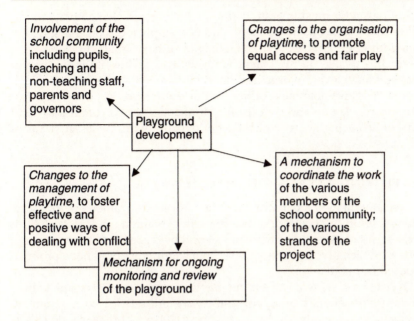

Figure 12.1   Playground development

2   a positive ethos regarding the playground depends upon shared values
    and clear procedures which address the concerns of all groups, and are
    consistent and understood by everyone.

Implicit in the second point is the role of 'ownership' in the process of
change. Where members of the school community have felt they have had
a voice in, and are part of this process, we have observed that cooperation,
motivation and momentum are much higher.

The second point also has to do with acknowledging the impact of the
social context in which the behaviour of individual pupils occurs. We have
come to believe firmly that playground dynamics should be viewed as a
social system within which children must operate as best they can. It is a
society which is based on unspoken rules, values and codes, all too often
rooted in an ethic of power and powerlessness.

Most children move between being involved in the victimisation (or its
collusion) of others and being victimised themselves in their attempts to
negotiate playground dynamics – with some children entrenched in
polarised roles of bullies or victims. This is not to deny the way that
children's lives outside school may predispose them (but have not necessarily done so) towards these roles. But we would stress that playground
society (like the wider society it is a reflection of) is greater than the

individuals who must operate within it. Attempts to change playground culture must take this into account and not simply focus on changing the behaviour of the children in it or on the physical environment alone.

Effective change to the playground involves giving unified, coherent messages at all levels of organisation. A system needs to be created which both models and maintains values of cooperation, positive ways of negotiating conflict, care and concern for all members of its community, and ways of achieving status which do not depend upon the lesser status of others.

DEVELOPING A PLAYGROUND POLICY

The development of a playground policy can set the framework for establishing the sort of playground society a school is aiming to achieve. It is, in fact, a series of agreed practices and should be regarded in terms of being a *process* which involves the whole school community (and not a product, imposed from outside).

Devising a system for governing playtime should aim to ensure that all children have equal play opportunities, are protected from harassment, and are safe. Issues such as the status and authority of playground supervisors, the time and space claimed by different activities and various groups of children, and the way incidents are handled also affect playground society and give messages about how and why people are valued, how problems are solved, and how racist and sexist behaviour are responded to.

There are three broad levels to developing a playground policy:

1   identifying the issues the policy must address;
2   agreeing on expectations and procedures (rules and enforcement);
3   monitoring outcomes and modifying practice accordingly.

In our experience, schools with the most effective policies have begun by analysing the playground situation at the first step. Through clarifying the way the playground is currently operating (the underlying values, rules and organisation), schools are able to identify their next step. Consultation and monitoring can pinpoint such concerns as the ramifications of the way space is used and the activities engaged in; identify 'trouble spots'; show who does and does not get access; and indicate the type and frequency of incidents that occur.

The case study that follows illustrates the way consultation and monitoring can highlight issues that need to be addressed in a playground policy. (This example is taken from one primary school, but the issues raised are representative of most schools we have worked with.) We also include extracts of their subsequent policy which formed the basis for establishing rules and management systems. Most importantly, this process served to involve everyone in the school community in changing playground society.

CASE STUDY OF A CONSULTATION PROCESS ON THE PLAYGROUND

Pupils

Children in this class were asked to investigate what was causing problems in the playground. The investigation took the form of class discussions about their experiences in the playground and their own monitoring of playtimes.

Themes of bullying, taunting and fighting in the various forms these take ran through much of their discussion. They talked about the ways in which football caused fights, and how it often resulted in girls being pushed off the play space when boys started a game. The children also talked about name calling as a major problem. The name calling they described was often explicitly racist and sexist. They described name calling as a non-physical form of bullying and as a 'trigger' for starting fights. Exclusion of a child from a group or a game was described as another way in which problems began. It emerged as a powerful aspect of playground dynamics.

The issues raised in the children's discussion became the basis for further investigation. They created questionnaires and interview schedules to find out how many other pupils had the same experience, and monitoring sheets for recording what happened at playtimes.

Teachers

In a staff meeting, teachers complained that dealing with playground incidents intruded into their lunchtime break, often carried over into the classroom and caused parents to complain. It was decided that for four weeks teachers would systematically record the amount of time they spend settling their class down after playtime.

The outcome of this monitoring more than backed up the teachers' complaints in revealing that, not only did playground incidents claim a great deal of classroom time but also, even once the class was calm, some children remained unsettled throughout the afternoon. In addition, conflict that arose between children in the classroom was often attributable to a playground incident. Furthermore, it was revealed that playtime-related incidents were the single largest reason for informal parental visits to the school.

Playground supervisors

An interview was conducted with the playground supervisors to discuss lunchtime play. As well as providing an opportunity to share their observations about children, these interviews raised central issues about the important role playground supervisors can play, not only in the playground but also within the whole school community.

They stated their primary concern as being to ensure the safety and comfort of the children and did not see themselves as educationists. (We observed this to be in conflict with the view that teachers expressed of the role of playground supervisor.) Younger and smaller children and many girls were felt to be vulnerable and marginalised. Football games 'taking over' the play space and causing conflict between the children was also identified as a major problem. The fact that children were excluded from a game or group was talked about as a covert form of bullying and highlighted as a source of major concern. Winter and very cold days created additional problems.

The status of supervisors within the school community was considered to be very low (with differences between full-time and part-time posts). Playground supervisors expressed a feeling that they were often cast in a negative role. As local people who were often able to liaise with parents or be more available than teachers and on an informal basis, supervisors could play a valuable role, but this was felt to be under-used. In addition the playground supervisors felt they could contribute information to the teachers about children's playground experiences and inform them about any difficulties, thereby reducing further possibilities for conflict. The supervisors identified the need for back-up from the school with clear rules and procedures for dealing with problems and incidents.

Parents

Parents of children from the school were interviewed. The points raised in the interviews related directly to the incidents that the children described and also to the concerns of the playground supervisors. They illustrated how difficult it can be as a parent to know how best to support your child when they are having difficulty at playtime. The following quotes have been extracted from the interviews:

'The little ones can be scared to come to school.'

'There are long lunch hours and nothing to do but football.'

'Incidents which start in the classroom explode in the playground.'

'My children don't want to come to school because of feeling bullied on the playground.'

'There is the sense that anything can happen on the playground.'

'The playground is the main school experience.'

'The playground is geared to the boys – girls are left out.'

'If children are excluded it can be terribly painful.'

'Racism is so ingrained on the playground.'

'Stronger kids rule – might is right.'

'I don't think kids tell parents much about what goes on in the play-ground.'

'Football causes most fights on the playground.'

'Do I say "don't fight" or "stand up for yourself"?'

'Children don't tell the helpers about bullying or name calling.'

'My boys cope by making themselves rougher and tougher.'

'I think it's important to have a safe place on the playground.'

'It takes a very long time for children to adjust to the big playground.'

'Some helpers know the children better than the teachers do.'

'The helpers don't seem to have the power to carry out rules – they don't have the status.'

'It's the main reason why I come to school.'

'I worry about safety.'

'I don't know what the rules are for the playground.'

AN EXTRACT FROM THE CASE-STUDY SCHOOL'S PLAYGROUND POLICY

1 We will ensure that all children have equal rights in terms of access to space and resources.
2 We will ensure that the playground is a safe environment for all children.
3 We will ensure that a broad range of play opportunities are available.
4 We will ensure that staff and pupils understand what constitutes bullying and harassment and that such behaviour will not be tolerated.
5 We will ensure that we will work with the appropriate outside agencies to combat bullying and harassment.
6 We will ensure that counselling and support are available for victims of bullying and harassment.

7 We will ensure that strategies exist for dealing with bullying and harassment behaviour.
8 We will ensure that all playground supervisors are treated with the same respect as teaching staff.

STRATEGIES FOR CHANGE

The sorts of action a school needs to take to promote change usually emerges clearly from the consultation and monitoring process. It mainly falls into the following categories:

- changing play space;
- reconsidering activities on offer;
- finding ways to ensure access to play opportunities to all pupils (such as timetable and notes);
- developing appropriate rules to govern different playground areas and activities;
- developing an agreed playground code of behaviour;
- identifying clear procedures for enforcement;
- developing negotiation skills to cope with conflict situations (for both pupils and staff);
- addressing bullying and harassment;
- finding ways to support individual children identified as particularly vulnerable;
- maximising the role of the playground supervisors and raising their status within the school;
- establishing communication networks between the various members of the school community;
- establishing mechanisms for reviewing practice.

Practical ideas for facilitating these changes are detailed in our book 'Can I Stay in Today, Miss?' Improving the School Playground, Stoke-on-Trent: Trentham, 1990.

COORDINATING PLAYGROUND DEVELOPMENT

Involving the whole school community necessitates the establishment of mechanisms to coordinate the various strands of playground development and the different groups involved. Schools we have worked with have managed this in various ways, including using the school council, forming a playground committee and producing a regular playground newsletter. The main purpose is to provide a forum in which playground issues can be discussed and action planning reviewed and updated. To be effective it needs to:

1 allow all members of the school community to voice their views;
2 establish clear channels of communication with those individuals who are responsible for decision making within the school.

This is well illustrated by the experience of one school we worked with. In this school (a mixed comprehensive) it was decided that the existing school council should be the mechanism by which playground development was coordinated. It set as its first task the agreement of a basic playground code. Almost immediately, problems arose concerning the role of the students on the council as to how they could adequately represent the views of their classmates. To resolve this, forms held half-termly meetings in which they could raise concerns they wanted to put on the school council agenda, and had feedback from their representatives. The second problem, which emerged at a later stage, concerned the relationship between the school council and those with the authority to make decisions. In order to establish procedures by which recommendations could be passed on, a governor was invited to join the school council, and the playground became a set agenda item at governors' meetings (see Figure 12.2).

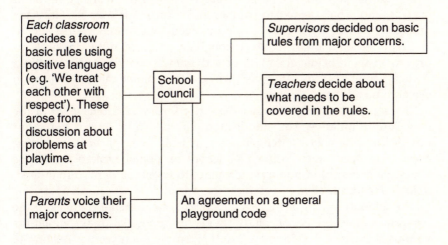

Figure 12.2   Role of the school council

DRAWING UP AN ACTION PLAN

Often in schools there are many different playground initiatives going on simultaneously. For example, there may be work going on with pupils about bullying, racism and sexism; an incident recording system may be established; staff meetings may be held about pupil behaviour; parents may be fund raising for a piece of equipment; a policy may be developing; there may be a new play structure; and there may be an environmental artist working in the school.

In our experience, it is not unusual to find many people involved in a variety of areas with no sense of how they interrelate and are working towards the same goal. Although to some extent various initiatives may be brought together through the coordinating mechanism, there needs to be a clear picture of how distinct areas of work are actually strands of a cohesive, whole-school playground initiative. Without this, a lot of hard work can be going on without a feeling that much progress is being made.

For example, in one school, fund raising for major environmental improvements was a three-year Parents' Association target. During this period, pupils were doing a term's project on 'rights and responsibilities', and playground supervisors attended a short course on conflict resolution. In the second year of fund raising, the Parents' Association began to question the school's commitment to playground improvement, and it became clear that there was no overall vision of how all the groups' contribution fitted together.

We suggest two things: first, that schools draw up an action plan to show what had happened so far, the various aspects of the work going on at present, and what needed to happen in the future. It was to clarify the different strands, who needs to be involved (when and where) and to outline a reasonable time scale. Through an action plan the physical improvements and management of social dynamics can be brought together. Action planning is most effective when it is incorporated into the Institution Development Plans.

The second suggestion is that there is a formal announcement of the playground initiative. This notification may take a variety of forms: for instance, an assembly, a letter to parents, a display of pupil work, a meeting about outcomes of monitoring. One school developed a role-play exercise about the playground into a performance to which parents were invited, followed by discussion.

The announcement of the school's intentions to make changes to the playground and the action plan provide an 'umbrella' under which the various strands of development can be identified and seen in relation to one another. In our experience, the importance of this cannot be overstated. It promotes a sense of whole school and fosters a sense of purpose and progression. Without it, initiatives can feel 'bitty', the aims unachievable and everyone may become demoralised. We include two examples of playground action plans, one from a primary school and one from a secondary school (see Figures 12.3 and 12.4).

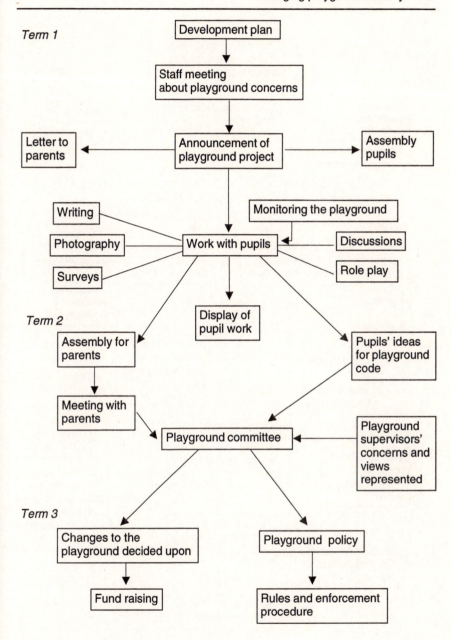

Figure 12.3   Action plan of a primary school

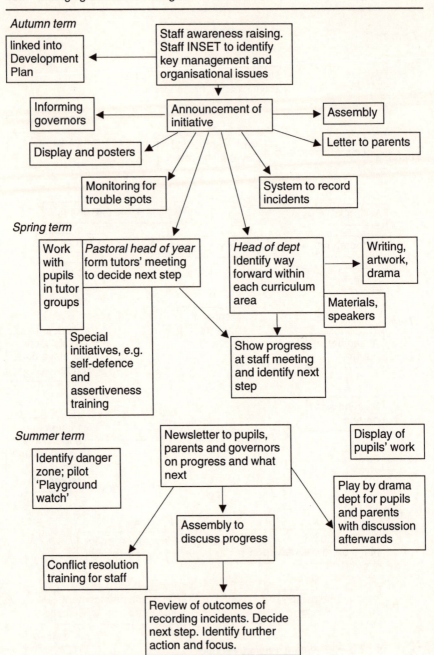

Figure 12.4   Action plan of a secondary school

MONITORING, REVIEWING AND UPDATING

In this chapter we have been talking about the need to recognise that there are layers and levels to promoting effective playground change. We have advocated a whole-school approach to developing a playground policy and stressed the importance of drawing up an action plan to identify specific targets. We have also suggested that playground improvement needs to be viewed as a process, rather than as a finished product. At the centre of this process are monitoring, reviewing and updating initiatives (see Figure 12.5).

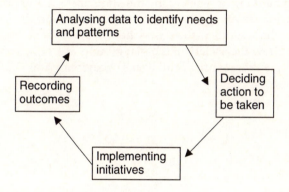

Figure 12.5   Process of monitoring, reviewing and updating action plan

MONITORING AS AN ONGOING PART OF PLAYGROUND DEVELOPMENT

Monitoring processes should be built into every stage of playground development and form an integral part of playground policy with each new initiative. The situation will change and new issues will arise that will need to be addressed. The following examples taken from two primary schools and a secondary school show this process in action.

One primary school's monitoring showed that only a small number of pupils were getting access to a new piece of equipment; it therefore instigated a rota to ensure that all children had access. After a period of time, when the children were well acquainted with this structure, playground supervisors felt that a new system was needed which recognised that fewer children wished to use it but for longer periods of time.

An 'incident book' was established in a secondary school, intended to back up the behaviour code. Monitoring of the book revealed that the same names were recurring. Concerns were raised that further action was necessary both in dealing with repeated offenders and in re-examining the playground in terms of what was causing conflict.

One primary school put a lot of effort into creating a safe climate so that children would tell staff if they were being bullied. When, after two terms, teachers reviewed the number of incidents being reported, they felt that the original initiative had been successful but that further development was now needed to support victims of bullying and to work with bullies.

What has become fundamental to our approach to playground development, through years of working with a wide range of schools, is that it is essential to maintain an overview. Whatever the area of focus (whether addressing bullying or redesigning the play space), it is important that it is not pursued in isolation. Playground development needs to be viewed in relation to the overall picture of school management, with an understanding of how the society of the playground operates, and a systematic approach to making sense of children's behaviour within it.

Chapter 13

Understanding and changing school breaktime behaviour
Themes and conclusions

Sonia Sharp and Peter Blatchford

In this chapter we review main themes to emerge from the contributions to the book, and put forward some conclusions.

UNDERSTANDING PLAYGROUND BEHAVIOUR

The value to adults of knowing more about playground behaviour

If asked about their pupils' playground activities, teachers may well show interest, but other demands in school quite understandably tend to dominate. The added pressures brought about by the introduction of the National Curriculum and the accompanying assessment arrangements have made it even more difficult to focus attention on what happens during recreational breaks. So the arguments in favour of adults looking seriously at playground behaviour need to be strong. There is space here to mention only a few.

One argument could be allied to recent changes in education. As we discussed in the first chapter and as seen in different ways throughout this book, the playground and the school grounds can be a surprisingly rich setting for teaching and the curriculum. With origins that predate the National Curriculum, Susan Humphries and Susan Rowe (Chapter 7) show how the school grounds can do more than just enliven school work: they can be used as the mainstay of a complete approach to the curriculum and to teaching young children.

But perhaps the main reason why playground behaviour should be of interest to adults – and this is a main theme of the book – is that adults can learn much from it about children. Many of the contributors have made the same point: when allowed to play and interact freely, children reveal much about themselves and their social world – more, or at least different things, than are revealed in the more closely supervised world of the classroom. So by looking more attentively at playground life we can better understand something essential about children.

The school grounds, therefore, are an important setting for the study of children. In the chapters in the first part of this book we have seen a number of areas of interest: developments in games and play behaviour, group interaction, social skills, and aspects of social relations such as friendships, power and status, fighting and teasing, bullying and harassment.

Researchers seem to be learning some things about pupils' behaviour in these and other areas, but there still seems much to be learnt. For example, we need more information on the formation of friendship groups and factors affecting entry into games. Another interesting area is the continuities and discontinuities over time in the structure and content of games. Is the structure stable while the content is more susceptible to change? Teachers within schools would be well placed to provide the information for such an enquiry.

A careful study of playground behaviour can also reveal much about important developments in children's behaviour. Peter Smith (Chapter 2) shows how one can see developments with age; for example, in features of group formation, and use of rules in games, and what this can tell us about underlying social and cognitive processes.

Studying children at breaktime can also tell adults much about the existence of a separate children's 'culture'. Adults, if they approach children in an open-minded and responsive way, can be repayed by gaining privileged access to another social world; indeed, the notion of an anthropologist finding out about an indigenous culture is a particularly apt one when considering research on playground life. As with all human cultures there is much to be learnt about rules and norms, and social patterns.

Another theme arising out of research on playground activities is that adults can be surprised by it. Even in the case of primary-aged children, games can seem violent, and some rhymes and language can be scurrilous, scatological and surprisingly worldly. Iona Opie has revealed in press coverage of her new book (1993) that much of the material she collected on playground rhymes was censored by her publishers, who would not allow anything stronger than rhymes with 'knickers' in them.

A related theme is that it is easy for adults to misunderstand what goes in the playground. Our assumptions about what is happening can be incorrect. Many of the contributions to this book show that a superficial look can underestimate pupils, and that beneath the surface one can detect a good deal of structure and sophistication in social interaction. Hasty conclusions – for example, about the dominance of low-level aggression between pupils – need to be treated with caution, unless they result from close observation.

The pitfalls of misunderstanding playground behaviour are present for researchers and for playground supervisors. Michael Boulton (Chapter 3) has shown one instance of this – in the way adults and pupils do not always agree about when behaviour is playful and when it is aggressive. It seems that the pupils are usually right. Another example of misunderstanding can be in the case of pupil friendships, where adult perception of frequent making and breaking of relationships may not do justice to the child's experience.

So the main point here is that the playground and the school grounds are a valuable setting within which adults can learn much about children. But studying playground behaviour is by no means straightforward – it requires imagination and forethought. Adults have to work hard to make sure that they adequately capture what goes on. As Peter Blatchford (Chapter 1) argues, it is difficult to research playground life: pupils worry what you are doing there, and may not behave in their usual way. One has to consider carefully how to present oneself and how best to collect information.

But the problems can run even deeper. As Elinor Kelly, Bill Lucas and Carol Ross and Amanda Ryan point out, it is difficult to gain access to the world of the playground because there is a powerful hidden curriculum, out of line with the school culture, and perhaps undermining it.

The value of breaktime for pupils

If adults can learn much about children, what are children themselves learning? What is its value to pupils?

There is much one could say on this – as much as, for example, debates about the value of play in child development. A few themes come through in this book. The first is that children can learn valuable social skills that are integral to adult life. The Opies argued that the function of playground games is essentially social; for example, because relationships can be established within the set procedures of a game. Peter Smith, in this book, concludes that it is difficult to show that play has cognitive benefits, and that the unique opportunities provided by play are in the social domain – in practising skills and cementing relationships. In a similar way to the Opies, Smith shows how games can 'scaffold' interactions amongst similar-age peers, so that each participant has a role within a shared structure, and that this can enhance prediction of, and effectiveness in, social behaviour. Michael Boulton and Peter Blatchford also point out the social value to pupils of school breaktimes.

There is also a wider sense in which playground activities are social; commentators have pointed to the way in which playground activities reflect the wider culture. From this point of view, one function of outside play is the coming to terms with aspects of this wider culture, and with power relations within it.

One of the original purposes of school breaks was the opportunity it gave youngsters to run around and take physical exercise. Given reports about the poor diet and exercise routines of many children of school age, one might restate the purely physical benefits of breaktime. Although the 'letting-off steam' function of playtime is a questionable application of outdated psychological theories, there is an obvious sense in which children – after sitting and concentrating for some time – could benefit from running around outside. As Peter Smith says, there is some support for the connection between 'confinement' in school and the need for physical exercise, but more attention could be paid to the implications of playground time for physical exercise.

Some worries about the value of breaktime for children hinge on the view that, although breaktime may potentially be of value, in fact activities are largely either low-level or unacceptable, as in the case of bullying and harassment. An allied view is that there has been a decline in traditional games and in the quality of outside activities. These are discussed by Peter Blatchford (Chapter 1), who suggests caution in any broad generalisations about the quality of outside play. To return to a theme discussed above, it is all too easy to assume that differences in play and games (perhaps in comparison to memories of one's own childhood) can be equated with a decline in quality. One must beware of underestimating children.

A final value to children of outside activities is also easily underestimated. Perhaps the dominant impression one gets from observing playgrounds and from talking to pupils about breaktime is the sense of enjoyment and fun that they experience then. Its free-ranging nature appeals to them. Worries about the problems experienced by some children should not detract from the fact that most pupils like it (see Blatchford, Chapter 1), and they do not find equivalent experiences within the school and classroom.

The problems of breaktime for pupils

Peter Blatchford (Chapter 1) highlights the dominance of what he called 'romantic' and 'problem' views of playground behaviour. These are unlikely to be mutually exclusive, in the sense that breaktime can be both a positive and negative experience for pupils. It is possible to overstate the difficulties pupils face, but one must appreciate the darker face of playground activities. Some children may have particular problems: they may feel friendless, excluded and rejected, and they may be teased or bullied.

But apart from these difficulties of individual pupils there seem also to be systematic group differences. The main difference, examined by all the contributors to Part I of the book, is that between boys and girls. These authors reinforce, from their reviews of research, what is often said within schools: the differences show how power, dominance and conflict can operate in the playground. Typically, girls are disadvantaged, in terms of the space and control of dominant activities. But they also show big differences in play and other behaviour, that seem to reflect deep attitudes that divide the sexes. Whether or not these have roots in socialisation or are innate, they indicate that changing playground behaviour will not be easy.

Elinor Kelly (Chapter 4) shows ways in which playground behaviour should be seen in the context of the school: its 'ethos', its response to conflict and its hierarchy. She shows how harassment, related to gender and ethnic origin, is different from bullying, in that it is 'normal' and legitimises mistreatment. For that reason it is more easily tolerated and more resistant to change. Elinor Kelly shows that the social lessons being learnt in the playground may need to be questioned; unless schools directly address some behaviours then – by default – injustice and inequality may prevail.

The adult's role in the playground

Another theme of chapters in this book concerns the role of adults in the playground. As Peter Blatchford remarks (Chapter 1) there has been little research on adult–pupil interaction in the playground. There seems to be a good degree of uncertainty about how adults should behave and what their appropriate role might be. And one senses that many who supervise in the playground – teachers as well as lunchtime supervisors – feel rather uncomfortable, though perhaps for different reasons. Teachers are uncertain whether to be teachers, facilitators or just supervisors. There is a tension between their normal proactive role in the classroom and the non-interventionist role they may feel is more appropriate for the playground. In contrast, lunchtime supervisors are only assigned a supervisory role, and this can place strains on their credibility in the eyes of some children and parents.

CHANGING BEHAVIOUR IN SCHOOL GROUNDS

A 'holistic' approach

From the chapters in Part II of this book one can see that school grounds and lunchtime arrangements have tremendous potential for development. Some of the main areas are:

- improving supervision;
- streamlining the dinner system;
- enhancing opportunities for play/activities;
- improving the environment;
- involving pupils in decision making.

A main point to be made is that the most successful approaches are likely to treat these different areas as interlinking aspects, rather than as separate initiatives, begun in isolation. It is important, when considering change to the school grounds and activities there, to take the time to consider all the different facets and not to be seduced by a quick initiative in only one area. It is very easy, for example, when faced with the desire to reduce squabbles amongst pupils and 'improve the playground', to assume, understandably, that what is required is something for pupils to do. It is an obvious step to then purchase new and inevitably expensive playground equipment. This is a single and public act and it is relatively easy to organise fund raising around it, and to convince school governors that this is money well spent.

Another approach, growing in popularity, is the training of lunchtime supervisors. This is an important development, as we discuss in this volume (see Chapter 9 by Fell, and Chapter 8 by Sharp). It is now becoming recognised that there is a misalignment between the large amount of time supervisors spend in charge of pupils and their low pay and lack of training. But, if carried out in isolation, such an initiative does carry with it the danger of an over-concentration on one thing – an emphasis on the control of pupils in the school grounds. This is the road towards containment of pupil activity, rather than the recognition of playground activities as potentially positive. The logical end point of this road, when control does not work, is the containment and possible demise of breaktime itself.

So this kind of piecemeal approach is – if not doomed to failure – then guaranteed only partial success. On many occasions the editors of this book have heard staff in schools say that the benefits of a school ground initiative has been short-lived, and that it would have been better to have examined all the different facets more thoroughly and worked out a strategy more deliberately. Obviously, funds will be limited and one has to start somewhere, but many of the authors in the book stress that this should be in the context of a fundamental review of aims and purposes, based on attention to staff and pupil needs. Perhaps the word that best encapsulates the point here is the need for a 'holistic' approach to the different areas represented in the second half of this book. Yet, as Bill Lucas says, the parts covered in this book are not usually assembled into a coherent whole. And Carol Ross and Amanda Ryan make the point that several initiatives may be taking place at the same time in a school with little sense of how each strand fits together.

Involving all in schools

The expression 'whole-school approach' has probably been over-used to the point of banality, but it does serve to state a truth commonly recognised by those working on changes to breaktimes and school grounds. The heart of this is the need to involve all in a meaningful dialogue about change. The word 'meaningful' is important in this context because it is very easy to make gestures towards an involvement that in reality masks little real dialogue. So, as we discuss shortly, and has been expressed in different ways throughout this book, particularly by Carol Ross and Amanda Ryan, this must involve all those in school – teachers, supervisors, pupils – and, if possible, parents and the community.

Because of the imbalance of power in schools, the participation of pupils carries the greatest risk of superficial involvement. Yet Helen Cowie (Chapter 11) and Sharp, Cooper and Cowie (Chapter 10) both show the exciting and fundamental benefits that can arrive from initiatives that empower pupils, such as conflict resolution, Quality Circles and peer counselling. Such techniques can offer alternative solutions to pupils unable to break from the 'fight or flight' and the 'might is right' ethos of the playground.

Another point about change arises in several chapters: initiatives relating to the school grounds need not be marginal to the classroom. They can have beneficial effects on social relationships within school. If pupils and supervisors are clearer and happier about breaktime, then teachers in the classroom can expect to benefit.

The process of change

It needs to be said that change in the school context is unlikely to be smooth or easy. In an interesting paper, Ouston *et al.* (1991) describe the difficulties that six London secondary schools faced in bringing about overall improvements. Some schools were more successful in bringing about change than others, and all found the process painful and disruptive. Much depended on the will for change, and the acceptance that something needed to be done. Active staffing policies and a clear and coherent educational philosophy were vital. Perhaps most importantly, change involves risk, and the most successful schools seemed to have accepted the need to be bold.

Changes may also not be straightforward. It cannot be assumed, for example, that setting up a forum within which pupils – girls and boys, and pupils from different ethnic groups – have an opportunity to air their views, will necessarliy make them more tolerant of one another.

The processes involved in overall school change are likely to be the same as changes to school grounds and breaktimes. The difference, perhaps, is that it is easier to introduce rather superficial changes; for example, to the look of the playground. But the conclusion of school improvement research is also applicable to school grounds and breaktime changes: it depends on a well-managed and fundamental review.

The scale of development will depend on the resources and energies of the school staff and its community. Change can be small-scale and gradual and cost little, but can still have an impact on the ethos of the school beyond the classroom. Whatever the scale, such change requires commitment to action from the majority of the school community and in particular from the senior staff.

Any institutional change, whether to the school grounds or the curriculum, in order to be effective can be seen to pass through three critical stages:

planning, consultation, implementation. The implementation stage must also include a scheme for evaluation and feedback. In relation to school grounds and lunchtime systems in particular, this process can be seen as a cycle. It is helpful, once an overall aim and plan has been established, to break it down into small chunks, each piece being subject to its own mini-cycle of planning, consultation, implementation and evaluation. Minor adjustments may be needed until feedback confirms that our aims in making the change have been met. Carol Ross and Amanda Ryan (Chapter 12) provide a valuable account of their experiences of how schools can change.

The role of senior staff in this process includes maintaining a clear sense of direction. It is easy to lose a sense of the overall aims when change occurs in small steps. Once the school community begins to lose its global perspective, it is difficult to maintain motivation or to recognise achievement.

Identifying what we want to achieve

As we have seen, there are assumptions about pupil behaviour in school grounds which are not necessarily based on hard fact. When making changes, we are usually driven by the conviction that we can 'make things better'. To be able to know whether or not this is true, we need to establish an accurate picture of the current situation within the school grounds and management system. This can be done on three levels.

First, research on behaviour in school grounds, as described in Part I of this book, can challenge some of the misconceptions we hold about playtime and school grounds generally and guide us in our decision making. At the time of writing, more than one tragic consequence of violence in the playground has made headline news. Many individuals and groups are beginning to question whether or not the playground culture of today is more violent than ever before. Without research, we will not be able to answer this question.

There is a temptation for us to patronise children's play behaviour, whether it is the chase or play fight of the primary yard or the 'messing around' of young adolescents. We need to recognise the value of pupil-organised social and play activities and make sure that our motives for initiating change are not based on adult mythologies which unnecessarily trivialise the meaning of lunchbreak and breaktimes for pupils.

Second, we can consider lessons learnt from practice in other schools which have made changes to their school grounds or lunchtime systems. Information collected by organisations such as Learning Through Landscapes (see Bill Lucas, Chapter 5) can provide an overview of the range of strategies available and the consequences of implementing them. Making contact with professional organisations which have access to a broad range of information about grounds and management styles can open up perspectives in the planning stages. Landscape architects, as pointed out by Lyndal Sheat and Anne Beer (Chapter 6), can facilitate the design process underpinning environmental change. Educational psychologists, behavioural support teams and local advisory services may offer advice on management and supervision systems for lunch and breaktimes or play activity schemes. Information supplied from broader research can be expanded by drawing on knowledgeable bodies outside the school, either locally or nationally.

Finally, but importantly, research can be carried out to identify the individual needs of the school as perceived by supervisors, teachers, families and pupils. Once we are fully aware of the nature and extent of factors negatively affecting our lunch and breaktime systems, we can establish clear purposes for our efforts and therefore plan more effectively.

Participation of pupils in the school-based investigatory stage is essential, as they are the main users of the grounds. Who better to identify what needs changing and what does not? With guidance, pupils are effective and keen researchers. As pointed out by Helen Cowie (Chapter 11) and others in this book, when provided with a real problem to solve pupils have much to offer and can carry out meaningful research on behalf of the school. Some of the techniques described by Lyndal Sheat and Anne Beer can assist with this process.

Lunchtime supervisors, as Gil Fell (Chapter 9) graphically portrays, experience lunchtimes every day, and can provide valuable insights into problem areas and pressure points around the school grounds and in the dinner system. By involving them in the improvement process from its outset, they are shown that they are valued members of staff and that their knowledge and understanding of the lunchtime system is recognised. This reinforces their role as managers of the lunchtime situation and reconfirms their responsibilities in relation to lunchtime, not only to themselves but also to teachers, families and pupils. By engaging in a participative approach, schools can indirectly address some of the underlying difficulties faced by supervisors outlined by Gil Fell and Sonia Sharp.

Involving the wider community

For some members of the community, the school grounds are the only aspect of school life they see. From their observations of pupils at lunch-break and playtimes and the ways in which staff interact with them, they draw conclusions about the effectiveness of the school and the way in which it is organised and managed. Consulting with families and people in the community can help promote the image of the school and tap into local expertise and resources.

At the implementation stage, relationships between the school and its local community can be reaffirmed through the achievement of common aims and goals. These relationships themselves will improve the play-ground ethos and ensure that everyone – adult and pupil – holds a common sense of purpose in relation to the lunch and breaktime periods. The aim is to promote them from the second-rate spaces between lessons in order to acknowledge them as important aspects of the school day.

Appropriate training for supervisors, teachers and pupils can assist with the implementation of planned changes. This training may be connected with improving supervision or enhancing behaviour management skills (see Sonia Sharp, Chapter 8, and Gil Fell, Chapter 9). It may also involve helping pupils to carry out research or to resolve conflicts themselves, or it may simply be aimed at expanding their repertoire of possible activities for self-organised time. Conservation, planting and growing, building, decor-ating, keep-fit and so on all have a place in the school grounds and all involve the development of specific skills. Training can take place within the curriculum, thus building bridges between the classroom and the school grounds in relation to lunch and breaktime periods.

Evaluation

Evaluation needs to run alongside implementation. The effects of rearrang-ing the dinner-queue system or installing seats may have benefits but equally may have drawbacks. At the end of the day we have to be able to say how we know whether or not our efforts have been worthwhile. There is a temptation in these busy times to skip over the evaluation stage and base our assumptions that 'things have got better' on unsubstantiated impressions. The problem with everyday observations of pupil or staff behaviour, especially in the school grounds, is that they only reveal tiny snapshots of points in time. To piece together a complete picture of what is actually happening, we have to be more rigorous in our search for evidence. Again, the role of pupils and supervisors in the evaluation process should be emphasised.

The effectiveness of evaluation depends on how the information gained through it is used. Evaluation is of little value unless it is used either to confirm that our initial aims have been met or to reformulate strategy if they have not. The lessons learnt through evaluation can therefore be fed back into the change cycle outlined above. Evaluation processes can be used to identify how different strategies have affected pupil behaviour or man-agement systems, to explore barriers to change and to identify helping processes. The information gathered can also help to inform the broader area of general research. If schools themselves are engaged in good research practice, their conclusions can in turn be used to supplement and guide the kinds of studies described in the second half of this book.

Making changes – where next?

Change has become a feature of educational lifestyle. Having scrutinised the curriculum, the management of the classroom, the organisation of the school as a whole, it is perhaps only natural for the school grounds to become involved in the drive towards change.

The need for school improvement may seem self-evident, but we must nevertheless make sure that our purposes in seeking such change are grounded in real need. We should examine the strategies on offer to ensure that they are entirely appropriate for meeting our aims. We need to check that, once implemented, they are effective. We will be assisted in doing this by continuing research in relation to lunchbreaks and breaktimes. Within such research there is a clear role for both academic investigation and practitioner analysis. Individual schools can learn lessons from the broader views developed through academic studies, both in the United Kingdom, and abroad. They can also apply research techniques from academic studies to their own context to enhance the rigour of their own evaluation procedures. In turn, academic research can be guided by the practice of individual schools: it can try to answer the questions arising from developments in school grounds which require a wider perspective than can be achieved within an individual school.

Locally and nationally, there are groups and organisations which can help schools improve their school grounds and lunchtime systems. Teacher training courses could include the issue of playground management and design within their syllabus, incorporating methods of achieving pupil participation in the development process. Effective supervision skills can also be taught.

Nationally and internationally, there is a need for an organisation which provides an overview of the different strands which affect playgrounds and lunchbreaks. This body could act as a coordinator of information, research and practice and, as such, could not only provide clear direction for future developments but also act as a knowledge base and resource for existing work in these areas.

There also needs to be a shift of focus in the way that playground issues are viewed. There is still a heavy emphasis on the primary phase, which helps support the myth that somehow breaktimes and lunchbreaks are not important enough at the secondary stage. There is a need to pursue research and development in the secondary sector in a way which matches the vigour invested in the primary schools.

On a practical level, LEAs usually employ people with a range of expertise in relation to health and safety, buildings and design. They are not always based within the Education Department, but are perhaps part of Building and Planning Services or the Parks Department. This kind of expertise can be immensely helpful to schools which are planning to make

196 Changing behaviour during school breaktimes

structural or design changes to their grounds. Local authorities vary in their interpretation of building and safety regulations. Perhaps, if they are not able to provide a direct advisory service for schools, a small booklet which details key information would be helpful.

Training schemes for supervisors can also by supported by the LEA. Although under Local Management of Schools (LMS) the training budget for supervisors is held by schools themselves, there may still be staff within the LEA who can help to deliver effective training. Whether employed directly by the schools or not, there are some regulations pertaining to the employment of supervisors (such as supervisor–pupil ratios) which are usually sent to schools. This can be supplemented with health and safety information and names of useful contacts for schools which wish to improve supervision. Clusters of schools could work together to provide training schemes which could go beyond a one-off course and provide an ongoing programme of learning opportunities for supervisors. Appropriate professional development events could be open to supervisors, and perhaps there is an opening here for a course for headteachers and school managers which would explore effective ways of working with supervisors to achieve an effective play environment.

One likely area of development for the future is the continued consideration of the school grounds in relation to the curriculum and teaching. This will be partly, one suspects, a reaction to the demands of the National Curriculum and the search for ever-new ways to find applications and settings for the coverage of attainment targets. But there are signs that school grounds are being considered in a more proactive way as their status and potential comes under review.

Another likely area of development stems from the greater involvement of pupils. The school grounds and breaktime represent a ready-made opportunity for the greater involvement of pupils in decision making within the school. If we are to take training for citizenship seriously, then where better to start than the one part of the school day when and where pupils are the experts? The involvement of pupils can be threatening – inevitably, in an institution which is essentially asymmetrical in terms of power. But it is essential in a democracy that pupils learn the skills of participation and the compromises and hard work involved in achieving political objectives. Children's councils, Quality Circles and other developments described in this book give some instances of how pupils can have a real voice in the governance of the school.

We may also need to reconstruct our notion of breaktime. We have perhaps become stuck in a traditional concept of breaks and lunchtimes. We impose a fairly standard structure upon them – at 10.30 a.m. or thereabouts, all the pupils leave their lessons and spend, on average, twenty minutes engaged in social activities as well as attending to toileting, refreshments and so on. A similar experience is repeated a lunchtime and perhaps at some point in the afternoon. Breaktimes are important, and the authors in no way advocate that they should be abolished – but do we need to be more imaginative in the way they are organised? What are the alternatives to the traditional breaktime? By rethinking breaktime as a concept, we may also find we need to reshape our notions of supervision and environment.

In 1989, one of us considered these issues and also deliberated about the effect of the Continental day (Blatchford 1989). In secondary schools, in particular, this is now becoming a more common feature of the school timetable. However, this has also led to discussion about child care extending beyond the school day. There are now a growing number of initiatives which offer 'after-school clubs' for pupils across the age range to fill the gap between the end of the school day and the end of the adult working day. What are the implications of these kinds of initiatives for schools, children and their families?

AN END NOTE

It is evident that, over the last few years, there has been a growth of interest and work in relation to school grounds, their management systems and pupil behaviour beyond the classroom. As an area for concern, it is beginning to be taken seriously and is the focus of attention from a number of different sources, as demonstrated by the range of contributions to this book. We hope that interest in this area continues to grow so that the drive to improve knowledge about breaktimes and school grounds gathers momentum and becomes more cohesive, drawing from all the different areas of expertise which are connected with it.

However, to finish, we return to perhaps the main point to be made in this book: the need to consider the child's point of view. This is what links the two parts of the book. We need to ask what changes will mean to children in the playground, and to ensure that changes are not made just for adults' convenience. We have to understand pupils' reactions, and their use of the grounds after change, to know what changes might work and later to see if they have worked and have been understood in the ways expected.

REFERENCES

Blatchford, P. (1989) *Playtime in the Primary School: Problems and Improvements*, Windsor: NFER-Nelson.

Opie, I. (1993) *The People in the Playground*, Oxford: Oxford University Press.

Ouston, J., Maughan, B. and Rutter, M. (1991) 'Can schools change? Practice in six London secondary schools', *School Effectiveness and School Improvement*, 2 (1): 3–13.

Name index

Aboud, F. 43
Adams, E. 81, 82
Adelman, C. 161
Ahmad, Y. 42
Aldis, O. 54
Archer, J. 41
Arnstein, S.R. 93, 94
Arora, T. 155
Atwood, M. 42, 66

Baldassari, C. 91, 92
Barnett, Y. 24, 32
Beer, A. 77–8, 90, 96, 97, 104, 193
Besag, V. 65
Bjorkqvist, K. 42
Blatchford, P.: (1989) 1, 2, 7, 23, 24, 30, 51, 63, 197; (1993) 6, 18; (this volume) 13, 83, 187, 188, 189; *et al.* (1990) 4, 19, 23, 24, 51
Boulton, M.J.: (1988) 51; (1992) 23, 24; (1991) 54; (1992) 65; (1993a) 59; (1993b) 52, 56; (this volume) 14, 25, 40, 83, 186, 187; and Smith (1993a) 42, 43; and Smith (1993b) 45; and Underwood (1992) 6, 51; Smith and (1990) 54, 55, 56–7
Bromley, D.B. 27
Brown, F. 99
Burns, A. 26, 32

Child, E. 43
Childhood City Newsletter (1980, 1981, 1982/3) 93
Childs, K. 155
Claire, H. 161
Cohen, E. 64, 67, 72
Cohn, T. 18
Coie, J.D. 46

Commission for Racial Equality (1988) 67
Connor, K. 59, 60
Cooper, F. 78, 191
Coulbourn, D. 25
Cowie, H.: (this volume) 78, 191, 193; and Rudduck (1990) 161; Lewis and (1993) 160

Dale, R.R. 31
Davidoff, P. 91
Davies, B. 26, 27, 32
Department of Education and Science (1988) (Education Reform Act) 146
Department of Education and Science (1989) (Elton Report) 5, 18, 19, 51, 119, 126, 147, 159
Department for Education (DfE) (1992) 159–60
Donaldson, M. 38
Dunn, S. 24

Eifermann, R. 36, 38, 39–40, 43
Elliott, M. 18, 19
Environmental Education (1990) 82
Evans, J. 23–5, 27–8, 30, 32

Fell, G. 19, 78, 129, 190, 193–4
Fiander, J. 23
Finkelstein, N.W. 42
Finnan, C. 24
Fisher, R. 155
Francis, W.D. 43
Fry, D. 54, 58

Gardiner, V. 127
Garvey, C. 39
Gergen, M. 58

193, 194; and Smith (1991) 164; and
  Smith (1993) 6; *et al.* (in press) 162,
  168; Cowie and (1992) 7, 162; Cowie
  and (in press) 155
Sheat, L. 77–8, 90, 96, 97, 104, 193
Shefatyah, L. 44
Sluckin, A. 39, 44; (1979) 36, 41; (1981)
  17–19, 25–8, 32, 36, 41, 45, 57
Smilansky, S. 44
Smith, D. 30
Smith, P.K.: (1977) 36; (1986) 40; (1988)
  44; (this volume) 13–14, 83, 186, 187,
  188; and Boulton (1990) 54, 55, 56–7;
  and Hagan (1980) 46; and Lewis
  (1985) 54; and Thompson (1991) 19;
  et al. (in press) 45; Ahmad and (in
  press) 42; Boulton and (1993a) 42,
  43; Boulton and (1993b) 45;
  Humphreys and (1984) 39, 44, 53;
  Humphreys and (1987) 25, 32, 50,
  51, 54; Pellegrini and (in press) 46;
  Sharp and (1991) 164; Sharp and
  (1993) 6; Whitney and (1993) 6, 18,
  30, 51, 65, 150
Stea, D. 88
Stephenson, P. 30

Stephenson, R. 99
Strathclyde Regional Council (1990) 67
Sunderland, M. 127
Sutton-Smith, B. 19, 20, 22, 43
Symons, G. 99

Tamplin, A.M. 28
Tattum, D. 6, 18, 65
Thomas, G. 84
Thompson, D.A. 19
Titman, W. 84, 86, 89
Tizard, B. 2, 4, 25
Toch, H. 150
Troyna, B. 26, 32, 64, 67, 72

Ullah, A.I. 25–6
Ullian, D.Z. 41
Underwood, K. 6, 51
Ury, W. 155

Walker, J. 155, 156
Webb, F.D. 21
Whitney, I. 6, 18, 30, 51, 65, 150
Wilkinson, J. 127
Wolverhampton Safer Cities Project
  (1991) 65

Subject index

active learning 81
adult: misunderstanding playground
    behaviour 59–61, 186–7; perceptions
    of aggression 25, 32, 49–50, 59–61;
    role 19, 24, 29, 189
after-school clubs 197
age: changes and what they show
    36–9; changes in types of activities
    39–40; developments 14, 186
aggression: adult perceptions of 14, 25,
    32, 49–50, 59–61; boys' 42; causes of
    135; fighting 51–2; girls' 42; pupil
    observations 32; teachers' views 3
Australia, playground supervision 30

ball games 20–3, 44, 70
behaviour see playground behaviour
breaktime: benefits of 46–7; bullying
    see bullying; conflicts,
    understanding 147–8; dining room
    142–3; evaluation of changes to 194;
    functions 8; involving the wider
    community in changes to 193–4;
    lining up 142; making changes –
    where next? 195–7; problems for
    pupils 3, 188–9; process of changes
    to 191–3; time spent in 2; value for
    pupils 187–8; wet play 141;
    whole-school approach to 143–4
bullies 45, 71, 173
bullying: denial of 71; gender
    differences 31, 42; harassment and
    14–15, 64–6; incidence 18, 30–1, 172,
    188; peer counselling (bully line)
    164–8; playground consultation 175;
    punishment 71; research on 6, 16,
    18, 33; schemes to combat 19; social
    context 26; victims 6, 45, 66, 173; see

also violence

catching games 17, 20
change: process of 168–70, 191–2;
    strategies for 178
chasing games 17, 20, 21, 23
cheating 56
chess 43
clapping games 20, 23, 40
community involvement 7, 193–4
confinement, effects of 45, 188
conflict: attitudes towards 148–50;
    management skills 150; myths of
    149–50; process of creative
    resolution 151–3; relevance to
    playground 156–7; resolution 78,
    191; teaching resolution skills in
    schools 153–6; understanding 147–8
conkers 21
constructive play 44
Continental day 8, 197
controversial children 45
Coombes County Infant and Nursery
    School 77–8; approach to school
    ground developments 107–10;
    description of school ground
    developments 110–17
cooperative games 28
councils, children's 6–7, 29, 196
cultural differences 42–4, 53
culture, children's 17, 24, 32, 33, 186
cussing 64, 67

daring games 17, 20, 23
decision making: involving pupils 93,
    159–60, 191, 196; process of change
    168–70; pupil ownership 160–2
desultory behaviour 3, 18